I0130849

Media Consumption and Everyday Life in Asia

Media Consumption and Everyday Life in Asia considers the emerging consequences of media consumption in people's everyday life at a time when the political, socio-economic, and cultural forces by which the media operate are rapidly globalizing in Asia. The book argues for the centrality of the media to Asian transformations in the era of globalization, and explores the way the profusion of the media today is reworking people's identities at individual, national, regional, and global levels.

Media Consumption and Everyday Life in Asia provides a critical understanding of the place of the media in different nations and regions of Asia and marks an important stage in media studies. The book will appeal to scholars and students in media and communications studies, cultural studies and Asian studies.

Youna Kim is Associate Professor of Global Communications at the American University of Paris. She was formerly at the London School of Economics and Political Science where she taught after completing her PhD at Goldsmiths College, University of London in 2003. She is the author of *Women, Television and Everyday Life in Korea: Journeys of Hope* (Routledge, 2005).

Routledge Advances in Internationalizing Media Studies

**1. Media Consumption and
Everyday Life in Asia**
Edited by Youna Kim

Media Consumption and Everyday Life in Asia

Edited by Youna Kim

Routledge
Taylor & Francis Group
New York   London

First published 2008
by Routledge
270 Madison Ave, New York, NY 10016

Simultaneously published in the UK
by Routledge
2 Park Square, Milton Park, Abingdon, Oxon OX14 4RN

Routledge is an imprint of the Taylor & Francis Group, an informa business

Transferred to Digital Printing 2009

© 2008 Taylor & Francis

Typeset in Sabon by IBT Global.

All rights reserved. No part of this book may be reprinted or reproduced or utilised in any form or by any electronic, mechanical, or other means, now known or hereafter invented, including photocopying and recording, or in any information storage or retrieval system, without permission in writing from the publishers.

Trademark Notice: Product or corporate names may be trademarks or registered trademarks, and are used only for identification and explanation without intent to infringe.

Library of Congress Cataloging-in-Publication Data

Media consumption and everyday life in Asia / edited by Youna Kim.
    p. cm. — (Routledge advances in internationalizing media studies ; 1)
    Includes bibliographical references and index.
    ISBN 978-0-415-96245-2
    1. Mass media—Asia—Audiences.   2. Mass media and culture—Asia.   I. Kim, Youna.
    P96.A832A786 2009
    302.23095—dc22
    2008007498

ISBN10: 0-415-96245-5 (hbk)
ISBN10: 0-415-87838-1 (pbk)
ISBN10: 0-203-89248-8 (ebk)

ISBN13: 978-0-415-96245-2 (hbk)
ISBN13: 978-0-415-87838-8 (pbk)
ISBN13: 978-0-203-89248-0 (ebk)

To OH, SOOAN
and
OH, JEILL

Contents

PART II
The Rise of Asian Media: Regional Consumption

PART III
Everyday Life in Transition: Contesting Identity

Acknowledgments

I wish to thank my colleague Roger Silverstone (1945–2006) at the London School of Economics and Political Science, for encouraging me to embark on this project and for sharing experiences whenever we sat together at lunch in the LSE Senior Dining Room.

Special thanks to Anthony Giddens for his valuable advice and friendship, as always. I am also grateful to Chris Berry, Nick Couldry, James Curran, Sonia Livingstone, Robin Mansell, Terhi Rantanen and Daya Thussu for their constant support back in London and especially at a time of transition.

In Paris now, my new colleagues, Kathleen Chevalier, Waddick Doyle, Yudhishthir Raj Isar, Celeste Schenck and Julie Thomas, have been warm and inviting. The publisher Routledge and Erica Wetter have been a great pleasure to work with. Thanks to my dedicated PA and friend Diane Willian for helping me wherever I am.

I am deeply appreciative of the contributors in this book for collaborating so willingly and delightfully. Thank you all.

Youna Kim
Paris, January 2008

Introduction
The Media and Asian Transformations

Youna Kim

The media are central to everyday life—ubiquitous, yet inconspicuous and deeply ingrained in what we take for granted as an essential component of contemporary experience. We live in an increasingly mediated world. What grasp do we have of the relationship between the consumption of the media and the shaping of individual lives and identities? This book explores people's everyday experience of the media in Asian countries in confrontation with huge social change and transition and the need to understand this phenomenon as it intersects with the media. It argues for the centrality of the media to Asian transformations in the era of globalization. The profusion of the media today, with new imaginations, new choices and contradictions, generates a critical condition for reflexivity engaging everyday people to have a resource for the learning of self, culture and society in a new light. Media culture is creating new connections, new desires and threats, and the identities of people are being reworked at individual, national, regional and global levels. The multiple manifestations of such transformations are under discussion in this volume. Within historically specific social conditions and contexts of the everyday, the chapters seek to provide a diversity of experiences and understandings of the place of the media in different Asian locations. This book considers the emerging consequences of media consumption in people's everyday life at a time when the political, socio-economic and cultural forces by which the media operate are rapidly globalizing in Asia.

MEDIA GLOBALIZATION IN ASIA

The proliferation of satellite and cable television and online networks, enabled by sophisticated digital technologies and the deregulation and liberalization of broadcasting and telecommunications in the 1990s, has created a new global media landscape, a complex terrain of multi-vocal, multimedia and multi-directional flows offering enormous challenges and opportunities (Thussu 2007). Such media flows have been accelerated by a shift from a state-centric and national view of the media to an imperative defined by commercially driven globalization, consumer interest and transnational

markets. The earlier model adopted in much of Asia was of a dominant public broadcaster that was seen as integral to the development of nation states,
modernizations and conceptions of national identity. Since the 1990s the
new borderless media have penetrated the emerging markets of Asia, capturing the imaginations of people who were accustomed to the traditional
domestic media under government control (Thomas 2005). There has been
a growing chorus of voices in many Asian governments including Malaysia,
Singapore, India and Indonesia responding to the anxieties brought by this
process of media globalization, by projecting an Asian cultural identity, a
common "Asianness" and "our space" being eroded by a permanent flow
of the media, capital, people, technologies and ideas (Ang 2001). Today the
growth in satellite platforms, transnational television channels and online
communication communities in Asia is said to be the most rapid worldwide.
Though the process of media globalization takes place not in a uniform but
in a differential pace and scale from nation to nation, its interrelated trends
have marked not only a quantitative change but also a subtle "qualitative
shift" (Flew 2007: 55) in the dynamics of socio-political and cultural relations within and between nation states, societies and individuals.

Two significant forms of global media flows can be noted across Asia:
first, the dominant flows largely emanating from the West with the United
States at their core; and second, the transnational Asian media emerging
as new regional players alongside the rise of affluent middle classes, both
of which constitute the primary agents of cultural globalization in the
region. Asia, including the world's two largest markets of China and India,
has become a priority area for the US-led corporations, a test site for the
global media of both online and offline advertising and the hybridity of the
global with the local (Thomas 2006). Since the 1990s Chinese viewers have
become more selective in the programs they watch, using satellite dishes
and the Internet (Dong and Shi 2007), and some Chinese can receive the
border-crossing cultures of democracy and capitalism from Hong Kong and
Taiwan without the need for satellite dishes (Fung in this volume). While
viewers in Asia tend to privilege national programming over its imported
counterpart and rarely turn to Western programs when local alternatives
are available (Chadha and Kavoori 2000), the pervasiveness of the Western
media is a key characteristic of globalizing Asia. Leaders of this phenomenon include Hollywood, MTV, Disney, CNN and Google Internet, all
combining to create a current condition parallel to "banal globalism" (Urry
2000) in metropolitan affluent parts of Asia.

US exports of film and TV programs to Asia reached $1,835 million
(Thussu 2007: 17). In Japan, China and South Korea, the Hollywood film
market share is 62 percent, 45 percent and 41 percent, respectively, but in
countries with a limited audio-visual domestic industry the dependence
on Hollywood is even more striking. The high cost of local production
and the increasing dependence on advertising revenue from domestic and
global marketers have provided an impetus for the growth of transnational

television via satellite and cable networks, legal or illegal (Thomas 2005). HBO claimed penetrations of 80 percent with the substantial popularity of the show *Sex and the City* among young women in Taiwan (Huang in this volume). MTV localizes in many countries including China under various political and economic constraints, not by seeking to circumvent the state authorities but by maximizing manoeuvrability through collaborations with the authorities and advertisers and by tuning into the specific cultural and political configurations encountered (Fung 2006). As a result of the localized, culturally contextualized and hybridized media products, the media landscape in India has come to be marked by discourses joining the global and the national, the modern and the traditional, the scientific and the religious (Juluri in this volume). Transnational television has become a key player in amalgamating commodity cultures with local audiences (Butcher 2003), legitimizing the cultural logic and becoming the new missionaries of global capitalism (Herman and McChesney 1997).

While the privatised and deregulated broadcasting, satellite and cable networks are prominent examples of the changes in media globalization, the increasing role of information and communication technologies and online spaces is also central to everyday life in contemporary Asia. Most Internet users live in Asia (330 million), followed by Europe (243 million) and the United States (185 million) (OECD 2006). South Korea is leading the world in broadband penetration, with over one third of its population having access to broadband and participating in online communities called Cyworld (Schonfeld 2006; Hjorth in this volume). In Laos, although only 50,000 among its population of five million use the Internet, the online site is central to debating ideas about post-revolutionary Laos unavailable in the conventional news media (Mayes 2007). The digital globalization has ensured that media content is transnationally shared and discussed in online spaces, resulting in unpredictable patterns of identification and learning of the self among the Chinese (Hu in this volume). Mobile phone ownership is over 90 percent in Singapore, Hong Kong, Bangkok and Kuala Lumpur (Synovate 2006). In Muslim Southeast Asia, such as Malaysia and Indonesia, traditional media sit alongside the plenitude of regional and Western cultural products available through television, radio, cinema, billboards, online sites, mobile phone extras and games aimed specifically at Muslim youth, transforming cultural values and religious faith (Nilan in this volume).

Against globalization as a mediated "Western" cultural force, Asian media have emerged as new players for transnational consumption, changing the dynamics of the media landscape in the region. The growing visibility of the trans-Asian cultural traffic "moving in/out" (Erni and Chua 2005) is constitutive of the restructuring process of uneven cultural globalization (Iwabuchi 2004), and the significance of each wave is an example of the decentralizing multiplicity of global media flows (Kim 2007). The flow of global media products is multiplied with the increasing contra-flow and the plurality of regional media players emerging to service an ever growing geo-cultural market (Thussu 2007). While the characterization of the global media as Western or US-centric remains largely valid, capital and cultural products from peripheral countries crisscross and realign in the region defined by common cultural, linguistic and historical connections (Chan 2005). Arguably, the term "peripheral" is less relevant in Asia today as it applies to the media globalization (Keane 2006: 838). Prior views that emphasize a one-way flow from the West to the peripheral rest are now being reassessed in light of the increasing volume and velocity of the transnational and multi-directional media flows that emanate from Southern urban creative cities, "media capitals" of resources, reputation and talent (Curtin 2003: 205). Many of the creative hubs are at the heart of the transformation of regional media cultures (Chalaby 2005), a phenomenon that is manifested in East Asia (Chua in this volume), Southeast Asia (Nilan, Siriyuvasak in this volume) and South Asia (Athique, Raju in this volume).

A key feature of the rise of transnational media flows is the active role of the nation states in the region; the state-assisted responses to global competition (Keane 2006), the alliance of the national government and private corporations in the globalization of the culture industry (Kim 2007), and the government's cultural policy focusing on the creation of "cool" national brands or "brand nationalism" (Iwabuchi 2007). Nationalism has been central to the globalization of media cultural products; therefore, to question how global such media are is to ask how nationalistic they are (Chan 2005). The Japanese government's J-pop policy, the South Korean government's K-pop promotion, as well as Taiwanese-pop and Hong Kong, have identified the importance of culture industries in shifting the local economy from labor-intensive manufacturing towards high-value-added services and export of national brand cultures including the media, tourism and fashion. The brand of "Bollywood" has been invoked by the Indian government and the film industry, who recognize the economic incentives of forging symbolic and emotional ties with its relatively affluent diaspora and articulating a new form of "cultural nationalism," a cultural unifier for people of Indian origin around the world (Punathambekar 2005) and among the South Asian diaspora (Kaur and Sinha 2005). These audiences can no longer be treated merely as markets catalyzing the globalization of Bollywood, but rather must be seen as an integral part of the cultural imaginary of Bollywoodization (Desai 2004), embodying the multiple histories and directions of cultural flow to enable a transversal and flexible experience inside and outside the geo-linguistic domain (Govil 2007).

Although globalization is generally viewed as Westernization, Islamist religious faith has come to be a new regional phenomenon in Muslim Southeast Asia as an alternative modernity for those uncomfortable with Western capitalist modernity. The cultural project of Islamization is assisted by the role of Muslim youth media in Malaysia and Indonesia (Nilan in this volume). In the South Asian region, such as Pakistan, Bangladesh and Sri Lanka, Bollywood, with its associated cultural paraphernalia, including songs, posters and websites, has strong visual and aural presence in everyday life; however, few studies have focused on the significance of consumption in this region (Athique, Raju in this volume). In Burma, Laos and Cambodia, Thai media such as drama are consumed from satellite signals, as well as dubbed and distributed in a pirated form of VCD; thereby the transnational media are providing a main window on the outside world and creating an ambivalent site of interaction with mediated modernity (Jirattikorn 2007). Consumption of the Vietnamese "cute," unthreatening cultural exotics laden with attractive, sensitive, authentic Vietnamese subtexts, has become a facet of everyday life in Japan without fear (Carruthers 2004). Asian-pop cultural products, including a wide range of media artefacts from television drama, music, film, websites and online games, to comic books, magazines and fashion, have emerged as a common choice for urban middle-class youth across Asia (Siriyuvasak and Shin 2007).

Media globalization has occurred with the rise of affluent Asia and mundane consumer culture (Sen and Stivens 1998; Watson 2005; Yuwa 2007). The media and technological change is socially constructed and does not emerge itself without the involvement of the users who have to accept it as relevant in everyday life. Along with neo-Confucianism and "Asian values" debates, Asian cultural distinctiveness has been emerging around the desires and cultural consumption patterns of a rising urban middle class rather than the state-sponsored official culture (Chua 2004). A dramatic growth in globalized consumerism has been identified among a youth segment called "lifestyle consumers" and the "new rich" in East Asia (Chua 2000: 13). In Muslim Southeast Asia, despite a different history and economic development, roughly similar demographic, social and economic trends—urbanization, dependency on media technology, extended periods of education, later marriage, and the rapid expansion of the middle class—are apparently ripe for distinctively Islamic cultural products and massive growth in middle-class consumerism (Nilan in this volume). But the language, perceptions and styles of middle-classness may vary, thus the middle class is not simply an empirical formation (Rajagopal 2004). Class background has been a key category by which media industries such as Bollywood anticipate, construct and imagine audiences (Srinivas 2005) or "non-resident audiences" as belonging not only in a spatial but also a symbolic sense (Athique in this volume). Typically, they are imagined to be younger generations under age thirty, "urban-middle, rural-rich" classes (Thomas 2005: 217), linked to global economic and cultural circuits as a result of employment or overseas education, and seen to be culturally cosmopolitan and technologically literate. Media consumption or "cool culture consumption" (Wang 2005) has become another element of social distinction, a search for a different future by a young generation and the negotiation of the hegemony of official culture at the level of everyday life (Siriyuvasak 2004).

These significant changes in media globalization and the rise of Asian economies are affecting the scale and the manner in which people consume the media today. The emerging socio-cultural consequences deserve to be analyzed and explored fully in an increasingly global media environment. What place have the media come to occupy in people's everyday lives and experiences? What are the consequences? This book explores the dynamics of everyday life in the confrontation with media globalization, and the implications of media consumption for an understanding of socio-cultural change in the lives of people across and within Asia's diverse societies. It is the diversity of experiences across and within Asia, not a singular and unitary region, which the book attempts to explore. *Asia* is a conceptual category of vast differences—economic, political, cultural and historic. What is meant by *Asia* does not always garner consensus (Holden and Scrase 2006: 11). Its heterogeneity does not produce one Asia (Berry et al. 2003: 5) but many Asias (Erni and Chua 2005: 12), acknowledging unique social spaces and contexts. Each contextual analysis in this book conveys the diversity of Asia's spaces today at a time of globalization when a future for Asia is being imagined, and this imagining is not just a sign of a newly found self-confidence but also of anxiety (Ang 2001) in an increasingly mediated everyday life.

MEDIA CONSUMPTION AND EVERYDAY LIFE

The significance of everyday life, its particular character and distinctiveness, provides a context for understanding the dynamics of media consumption and the complexities of socio-cultural change in contemporary Asian societies. The media are embedded in the multiple discourses of everyday life (Silverstone 1994). It is in the everyday that people work through the functional and cultural dimensions of the media through the various ways in which they engage with and incorporate the media into the familiar, ordinary and more or less secure routines of their everyday life, while constructing relationships and meanings within it. The unique character and significance of television is best understood within the everyday social context in which engagement and meaning take place (Kim 2005). New media technologies such as the Internet are embedded in and continuous with other social spaces, happening not just within a virtual world that is somehow disconnected from the everyday, but within mundane social structures and relations that they may transform but cannot escape (Miller and Slater 2000).

Four dimensions, at least, can be highlighted concerning the significance of everyday life and its relationship to media consumption. First, everyday life is the domain in which the economic and material as well as cultural and symbolic resources that permit meaningful engagement with the surrounding world are or are not made available. It is in the ordinariness of the everyday that the different portions of power and resources, their presence or absence, are most keenly felt—the significance of such difference and inequality largely determined by social structure. Everyday life is thus a site of struggle. The trivial and petty side of life, the humble and disappointing aspects of social praxis, the suffering and the "misery of everyday life" (Lefebvre 1971: 35) are a battleground, in which a dialectical relationship between the dominating and the dominated is displayed in tension. This tension is inevitable in the struggle to manage the unwanted influence of domination, to find meaning and order as well as pleasure in everyday life.

Second, however, it is also in the domain of everyday life that the individual and collective capacities of people to create their own life world are realized and achieved through everyday practices, albeit with different power and resources. It is in everyday life that genuine "creations" are achieved, those creations that people produce as part of the process of becoming human; the human life world that is not defined simply by historical, ideological and political super-structures, by totality or society as a whole, but by this intermediate and mediating level of everyday life or the "power of everyday life" (Lefebvre 1971: 37). Everyday life is both structured and structuring, making and remaking meaning, while acknowledging its dynamics and possibilities for transformation. Everyday life becomes the site for, and the product of, the working out of significance (Silverstone 1994: 164).

The media are among sources of the creations, the working out of significance in everyday practices. They give shape to the social and cultural environments of everyday life and provide a framework for making sense of the world; herein lies the possibility that a multitude of meanings can emerge and circulate. The circulation and movement of meaning, or mediation (Martin-Barbero 1993), involves a constant yet dialectical transformation of meaning with consequences, whether intended or unintended, significant or insignificant. The significance of media consumption practices can be understood as a creative, dynamic and transformative process, often involving active and intended engagement. The capacity to make sense of the world, create everyday life, and sustain as well as challenge its meaning have become dependent on the mediation that is increasingly present in the daily exigencies of people and integrated into ongoing ways of living and being.

Third, it is within the sphere of everyday life that people create and sustain their own experiences, both lived and mediated, in many different and specific ways. The media are central to contemporary everyday experience—as a mediating, not determining, process through which people constitute and reconstitute experiences in their distinctiveness within a shared, yet contested and highly differentiated social space governed by different power, resources and constraints. This often invisible and taken-for-granted category of experience should be made visible and confronted to understand how subjects are constituted as different, how they operate differently, how they contest the workings of given ideological systems; in other words, to politically rework the "project of making experience visible" (Scott 1992). The purpose of this project is to manifest this easily ignored hidden world that has been suppressed, and to open new possibilities of the challenges of the experiences and activities in the ordinariness of the world.

Finally, it is within the sphere of everyday life that ordinary and taken-for-granted experiences and activities emerge as a significant and defining characteristic of what takes place in society as a whole, its social transformations. The society and its structure or macro-processes of structuration are reproduced within the micro-operation of everyday interaction between individual subjects (Giddens 1984). What takes place in the everyday life of people within society is a crucial determinant of what makes the society as a whole, which leads to an understanding of what lies behind cultural change, the cause and consequence of this progressive, or possibly regressive, mediation of everyday life (Silverstone 2005). To understand a contested process of cultural change and a fundamental characterization of the nature of such change, it is necessary to look at and understand what people are doing in their everyday lives and in their relationships to the media—where and how meanings are created and contested, structures are accepted and challenged, and the possibility of change emerges in that tension. The everyday is a site for significant action, and media consumption is at the heart of the "politics of everyday life" (de Certeau 1984: 31), with its poaching, tireless, invisible, quiet but potentially transformative activity. Though media consumption may not lead to dramatic social or political change in the short term, and though the importance of the transformations generated by the media in the long term are problematically obscured by the attention to short-term immediate effects (Martin-Barbero 2003), people's mundane changes, imagination and critical reflection, triggered by the media and expressed in the practices of everyday life, can be the basis of social constitution or political subjects (Kim, Iwabuchi in this volume). Social transformations become possible through reflexivity, the capacity for rethinking, rearticulating and revising the givens of prevailing dimensions of social construction, a capacity that emerges through the dynamics of everyday practices and the realization of their otherwise denied potential in an increasingly mediated world.

EVERYDAY REFLEXIVITY

The media are central to everyday reflexivity—the capacity to monitor action and its contexts to keep in touch with the grounds of everyday life, self-confront uncertainties and understand the relationships between cause and effect yet never quite control the complex dynamics of everyday life. Reflexivity is an everyday practice. It is intrinsic to human activity, since human beings routinely keep in touch with the grounds of what they do, what they think, and what they feel as a circular feedback mechanism. But there is a different and significant process in contemporary everyday life, which has changed the very nature of reflexivity by providing conditions for increased capacities for reflexivity "in the light of new information or knowledge" (Giddens 1991: 20). This reflexivity involves the routine incorporation of new information or knowledge into environments of action that are thereby reconstituted or reorganized. Everyday people have the ability to reflect on the social conditions of their existence and to change them accordingly, going beyond traditional markers and the givens of social order (Beck et al. 1994).

The question, however, is, to what extent and in what ways? Whose reflexivity? This reflexivity is experienced differently by different social subjects in different social locations, defining those societies as distinctive. Reflexivity needs to be understood not as a universal capacity of subjects or a "generalized experience that cuts across social divides" (Beck 1998), but in specific life world contexts where it arises unevenly and often ambiguously with competing reflexivities. There is a need to recognize situated reflexivity, specifying the different experiences of reflexivity situated within different social spaces. The degrees of reflexivity and its particular character and content may differ in Asia—stronger and weaker, emotional and rational, positive and negative in its implications—since it is mediated by a remarkably high level of education in a Confucian society (Kim 2005: 195–202), it operates at a more collective, rather than individual, level than in the West (Nilan in this volume), and it can be influenced by the lack of the reflexive forms of media representations in a relatively rigid society (Hu in this volume).

Increased flows of the media can be seen as an important resource for the triggering and operating of everyday reflexivity. The media are not the only contributors to the process of reflexivity, but the degree of the media's contribution depends on what other sources of reflexivity might or might not be available and who can access and utilize them as meaningful resources. When other sources such as psychotherapy and self-help expertise are not readily available in the actual circumstances of day-to-day life, individuals can appropriate transnational television programming and online discussion and writing generated by viewers for an implicit therapeutic function and self-analysis in light of issues of gender, social institutions and existential anxiety to better deal with the culture of everyday life they live in (Hu in this volume). It simply cannot be assumed any more that information or knowledge from books is the best or main route to everyday reflexivity in today's primarily visual, electronic media-dominated cultures (Couldry 2000: 42). It is not just media's ubiquity in everyday life, but its unique and plausibly powerful capacity to affect the meaning-making of everyday life experience, its capacity to trigger a heightened reflexive awareness of the world, which is arguably a key cultural dynamic and challenge.

Television above all, accessible and understood by lay people, has become not just the site where such reflexivity takes place, it actually provides the specific terms and forms of everyday talk and practice in the light of incoming knowledge. Often, when local media productions largely fail to respond to the changing socio-economic status and desire of women in a transitional society, it is global television that is instead appropriated for making contact with the diverse formations of culture and for talking about the everyday issues of gender and sexuality (Huang in this volume). It is via the increased exposure to Others and to reflexive capacities that the working class make sense of life conditions that differ from their own and come to realize a lack of social mobility for themselves and to critically question the taken-for-granted social order (Kim in this volume). Significantly, what is emerging here is the problematization of society itself, the increasing awareness of its structural rigidity and discontents as well as the interrogatory attitude towards the surrounding world. Ordinary people may not destabilize the whole system, but the border-crossing television prompts them to critically reflect on the legitimacy of their own social system, including class ideology, and to break through the hegemonic control of the society at the level of the everyday (Fung in this volume). Engagement with the media constitutes a heightened awareness vis-à-vis gender, sexuality, class, social mobility and so on—not only the familiar form of "national differences" but also many "different forms of cultural difference" (Pieterse 2004: 41).

Such changes in awareness, knowledge and the questioning attitude towards the world may not always lead to social transformation in the short term, but new possibilities may arise from this heightened capacity for critical reflection and questioning that serve as the basis for agency, that is, the socially constituted and differentially produced capacity of human beings to engage in action. Reflexivity could make a difference when the forms of talk and thought are translated into action, individual or collective (Chan 2005). The consequences of action prompted by post-text encounter or engagement with the transnational media are not limited only to micro-social settings but can trigger broader transformations in the perceptions of postcolonial politics, ethnic relations and social discrimination, thus redefining and revising social practices in the light of ongoing self-reflexive discoveries (Iwabuchi in this volume). This evolving reflexive project is not just a direct cause-and-effect in the speed of social and cultural change but an increasingly insistent and intense process of mediation.

With the increased capacity for the reflexive project, it is also necessary to recognize the partial nature of reflexivity in relation to the relative openness of the social world and the different restraints on agency in contemporary Asian societies. Despite high levels of reflexivity and possibilities potentially available for change, agency is not "becoming freed, unleashed or released from structure and its constraints" (Beck and Beck-Gernsheim 1995); rather, agency is regulated by structure, operating within broader systems of constraint. The process of reflexivity is a dialectical one with inevitable tension. The social and cultural fields are not totally restrictive but dialectically positioned; the complexity neither closes the avenue for change for the working class and the middle class, nor leaves it wide open for any kind of empowerment (Siriyuvasak in this volume). Sexual empowerment, sexual freedom of women in particular, is in continual tension with real-life social constraints, the pressures that the imperative of society places on individuals, and the socio-economic disempowerment of women who lack the resources to claim a social space for sexuality (Huang in this volume).

While recognizing a transformative potential of reflexivity, it is also necessary to question the perceived cause-and-effect between "reflexivity and de-traditionalization" (Giddens 1994) and its claim for a decline in the relevance of tradition as a fait accompli. A closer examination of the media's role in re-imagining tradition reveals that new meanings arise in relation to issues of tradition, religion and the nation in the realm of global media consumption wherein tradition colludes with the agents of globalization (Juluri in this volume). There emerges a process of re-traditionalization in which tradition is re-invented and re-interpreted through the rejuvenation of traditional forms of life and foundational morality acceptable to the moral capacity of the contemporary self. Often, younger generations in Asia have a set of competing values and reflexivities—simultaneously modern and traditional—the strong desire to choose individualized lifestyles, but at the same time, the respect for elders and the importance of family ties that might clash with their lifestyle choice and individual freedom (Kim, Nilan, Juluri, Huang in this volume). Reflexive modernities coexist with reflexive traditions; they are not mutually exclusive but intertwined and they compete at various times during the life of an individual. Reflexivity is a multi-stepped, ambivalent and dialectical process through which tension, conflict and contestation arise with complicated implications for the construction of identity—for determining how to act and who to be.

CONTESTING IDENTITY

The media involve the complex processes of social change and transition—from the conduct of everyday life, to the reflexive understanding of a global world, to the construction of a new identity and a constant tension in its expression within the everyday. Identity is in the process of being redefined and reconstituted through the everyday reflexivity, and the media are central to the ongoing identity project. Identity can be seen as a "reflexively organized symbolic project" (Thompson 1995: 210) in which individuals appropriate their own resources in order to construct a meaningful, provisionally stable identity in an otherwise uncertain world. The formation of identity can be imagined as a particular organization of social, physical and material forces, with a marginal power in the real world (Siriyuvasak 2004). But it is a space of power, nonetheless, that contains not only victims but also actors producing their own meanings (Hall 1991: 34). Those meanings emerge from very specific historical formations as discursive practices and must be negotiated. The sites of negotiation, contestation and tension are manifested in multiple and highly complex ways under the conditions of media globalization.

The media globalization in Asia needs to be recognized as a proliferating, indispensable, yet highly complex and contradictory resource for the construction of identity within the lived experience of everyday life. For instance, young people are attempting to adapt their identities; sometimes traditional aspects of identity offer resistance, sometimes compliance and at other times the young are left open to ambiguity between the global and the local particular identities (Butcher 2003; Kim 2005). The proliferation of mediated social interaction and the reflexive identity project enable possibilities for the construction of multiple identities that can be creative and emancipatory but also contradictory and conflictual in their consequences. Tensions arise in the dynamics between freely chosen identity and social validation and acceptance. Identity may appear to be a repertoire of choices to be made, or a mobile, free-floating, personal project; however, identity is also a "social, other-related, mutual recognition" (Kellner 1992: 141). One's identity is dependent upon recognition from others, combined with self-validation of this recognition. There is still a traditional structure of interaction with socially defined roles, moralities and obligations among which one is expected to choose and appropriate in order to gain identity in a complex process of mutual recognition.

Traditional identity markers, especially the bodily attributes of age, gender and sexuality, are fundamental in a hierarchically fixed Asia and contesting in tension with the openness of global processes. Media cultural practices in the region have seen emerging forms of modernization and individualism that do not fit a Western or Anglo-American model. While individualism is certainly becoming more and more a part of the way young generations think about themselves and the world, they are not invited to stand out as individuals or "do their own thing" but are expected to remain in traditional, family and relational networks. The sense of oneself as a freely choosing individual has not been paramount in cultural traditions and the creation of collective religious identity stands antithetical to Western ideas of individualism (Nilan in this volume). The process of individualization, the self-determined biography through work (Beck 1994: 13) and the life politics of self-actualization (Giddens 1991: 214) remain largely incomplete and unresolved, becoming a source of ambivalence in the educated woman's identity formation where gendered socio-economic conditions interplay with rapid processes of modernization. Female individualization as an alternative, emancipatory life politics is limited for reasons that are structural to the gendered labor market, posing the question, whose individualization? (Kim 2005: 169–77). Increasing contact with representations of individualized lifestyles has enormously inspired modern women to resist hegemony around the regime of sexuality, while making them struggle to create both self-fulfilling and manageable lives of mutual recognition (Huang in this volume). In many Asian societies, singles most often live in their parents' homes well into their twenties or thirties until they (are forced to) get married. When this everyday life of surveillance is marked by long working hours and high broadband connectivity, mobile technologies and Internet use can create a new form of sociality, feminization of virtual life empowerment (Hjorth in this volume). Youth have to comply with the family rules, as well as negotiate with family through transnational cultural spaces where the imagination of freedom can be transformed into a collective imaginary to subvert the official power and regulations (Siriyuvasak in this volume).

Where the spaces of everyday life are highly regulated and administered within re-invented tradition aimed at eliciting conformity from the populations, global media culture can be transformed in the local as an imaginary terrain of freedom where individuality and differences rule in the body politics of Asian nations (Chua 2000: 16). Contestation of meaning has always been played out between authoritarian regimes and cultural warriors (Erni and Chua 2005: 14). Cultural spaces become the very arena in which identity is contested, with multiple reasons and motives enmeshed in neglected historical experiences and "long-standing battles for recognition and struggles for power" (Martin-Barbero 2002) that are contained in a highly diverse configuration of the consequences of media globalization.

While this media globalization has raised profound concerns about cultural homogenization in Asia, there are also distinctive trends towards fragmentation at multiple levels—regional, national, local—fostering resistance and individuals' critical engagement with the media to suit their cultural priorities. The transnational flow of the media in the region has led to the emerging questions of a pan–East Asian identity (Chua in this volume), a trans-Asian identity (Darling-Wolf 2004), a regional trans-Muslim identity (Nilan in this volume), an Asianization process (Siriyuvasak in this volume), whether and how the current dense flow of the media fosters transnational dialogues (Iwabuchi in this volume) and the structure of feeling as a part of the social imaginary for an increasingly regionalized Asian modernity (Erni and Chua 2005), or a "parallel modernity" that is an alternative to the pervasive influence of a secular West (Athique in this volume). Cultural proximity is articulated through "here and now" in Asian urban contexts—close and distant, similar and different, fantasizing and realistic—these intertwined perceptions arouse a sense of relatedness, a "we Asian" feeling (Iwabuchi 2004). Despite varied national origins, electronic spaces and online communities of fans define themselves as "Asian," and this virtual Asian-ness serves as a common identity between the online participants living in cultural environments as different as Thailand, Indonesia, China and so on (Darling-Wolf 2004). Music and film have become more regionally transnational, accelerated by pirated forms of circulation, representing not merely objects of consumption but also a site of performance as fans attend star appearances and appropriate the aesthetics (Siriyuvasak and Shin 2007; Athique, Raju in this volume). Regional cultural forms invite youth in Muslim Southeast Asia to construct themselves as members of a community of believers that overrides any other individual, ethnic, linguistic, geographical, national identity (Nilan in this volume).

The construction of a regional identity has emerged as a consumerist practice, and the pan-Asian identity is possibly constituted in the consumer community and consumerist modernity (Chua in this volume). The media are situated within a broader process of consumption and modernity wherein the middle class deploy a new sphere of consumer culture to create local cultural distinction and imagine connections to transnational publics, as shown in a class-salient society like Nepal (Liechty 2003). In Southeast Asia, it is the cultures of urban spaces that are most immediately and directly influenced by globalization in terms of consumption patterns, media and new forms of material culture among the new middle classes (Clammer 2003). There is an emergence of an Asian generation of middle-class youth across urban cities, for whom the identification with Asianness is not about essential Asianism but about "pop Asianism" (Siriyuvasak and Shin 2007). The transnational construction of Asia as a unitary imagined community is further reinstated and reified by the nation, despite significant cultural differences within the region (Ang 2001). The nation's speaking position in the struggle for national identity amidst Western media flows is not explicitly associated with a particular national position, but as an "Asian" in order to disrupt the Western influence of modernization and raise the status of Asian civilization, now that the borders of the nation are becoming increasingly vulnerable to Western hegemony of globalization.

Globalization produces nationalisms that take on a binary construction of East versus West, constructing both national and transnational forms of nationalism that not only reject Western hegemony but seek to promote the ascendancy of the East and to be differently modern (Ong 1999). Media globalization is thought to weaken the nation, but nations are still centrally important (Curran and Park 2000). While the current transnational processes and connections may appear to negate the continuing significance of national borders, boundaries and national identities, nationalisms have been re-ignited to realign and reconfigure the nation. The media are central to the construction and re-construction of national identity, standing for the nation as a means by which the nation can represent itself to its subjects. Even a Western-borrowed reality TV, *Malaysian Idol*, exemplifies the media's centrality to the formation of national identity and the need for a unifying symbol in multicultural postcolonial Malaysia (Lim in this volume). The search for, and the recognition of, the idol as a national subject are operating to build symbolic bonds that work to hold the nation together as a singular body and community, by creating a cinematic experience of fears, anxieties, aspirations and pleasures through this very popular Western-borrowed genre. Whilst national identity is re-learned and re-imagined amidst the threatening presence of the mediated space of the West, democracy has become a consumerist practice in capitalistic-communist China in the voting process of *Super Girls,* the Chinese version of *American Idol* (Chan 2007).

Nationalism re-articulates and reinforces itself, paradoxically, in an intensification of globalization. The phenomenon of "pop nationalism" arises from the way that viewers make sense of national and global discourses on music channels like MTV (Juluri in this volume). It is manifested in the experience of localized MTV and animation film where people rediscover and express a feeling of being a national subject, the very essence of national identity in terms of familial, relational or religious values. Religion can return as religious nationalism in contemporary manifestations of globalization, powered by the very mechanisms of markets and the media that had earlier been assumed to assure the extinction of religious traditions and the ascent of modernization (Rajagopal 2004). The global has come to be experienced, imagined and acted upon with meaning in the everyday lives of people in an unpredictable and contradictory manner that belies a simplistic assumption of cultural homogenization. Global media culture and its consumer communities in the local are confronted with larger non-consumer communities reinforcing nationalist discourses with the complicity of local media productions and the state (Chua in this volume). While Indian Bollywood might be seen as a non-threatening alternative to US Hollywood in Southeast Asia, it has frequently been regarded as a source of cultural imperialism acting upon other South Asian states (Athique in this volume). Re-invented symbols and images of national identity become key mechanisms for mediating between the global and the local. Any impact of the global on the local can be filtered by a nationalization process to resist global capitalism, but at the same time, any local appropriation of the global can challenge and contest the hegemony of the national control (Fung, Raju in this volume).

What constitutes the global is a result of the interplay of diverging human activities and discursive contestations over the meaning and significance of globalization (Chan 2005). Globalization is not the unalterable horizon of events, whatever it is, presenting itself as both ideal type and real historical process (Rajagopal 2004). The global needs to be understood as local negotiations of historically shifting relations of production and consumption, in which social and psychic contestations are the very core of how people constitute their own relationship to the media and create new and ambivalent articulations of bodies, pleasure, desire and identity (Desai et al. 2005).

Negotiations are centered not on fixing and securing meaning, but on articulating and mobilizing semiotic regimes of power with social practices in the service of sectional interests. The micro-politics of sexual identity situated in place leads to an understanding not to see the global and the local as two arenas utterly separate and opposed, but to consider the mechanisms and meanings of the localization of transnationally mobile understandings of sexuality (Berry et al. 2003). Evoking ambivalence and contestation, it coexists with diverse forms of resistance and power struggle.

The politics of identity is perhaps most concerned with socially marginalized groups, including women and homosexuals, in a rapidly globalizing Asia. Sexuality provides an interesting lens through which to examine the tremendous changes happening now (Shahani 2008), marking an important locus at which competing reflexivities intersect and clash as the most contestable feature of difference in the level of intimacy (Kim in this volume). Sexuality is a historically constructed multiple identity whose relations to other social formations are constantly shifting in conflict. Globalizing is synonymous not with homogenizing but with contesting dramatically in the realm of sexuality in Asia, where women have become increasingly active participants in higher education, employment, and media consumption that exposes them to a pluralization of life politics; however, actual changes to gender roles, sexuality and body politics have come slower. Increasing contact with global television such as *Sex and the City* and the rare cultural space it creates for young Taiwanese women to have "sex talk" are seen to be constant negotiation of generation-specific experience, conflict and struggle in the process of individualization (Huang in this volume). Although young women's viewing experience is routinely regulated by their positioning within the everyday power structure, male and parental surveillance and policing, their continual viewing and contestation is an act of resistance to traditional sexual subjectivity. Thai girls are no longer shy about expressing their sexual desire through imaginary idols of popular music, but they rarely manifest their sexuality in a public arena (Siriyuvasak and Shin 2007). Seemingly modern women, whether lesbian or heterosexual, have not been empowered to practice their desire for sexual autonomy. Sexual empowerment is in tension with the normalizing regime of female sexual unspeakability in public and private spaces.

MULTIPLE MOBILITIES

Multiple mobilities and tensions are expressed in the context of a significantly mobile Asia, between public and private spaces, between online and offline communications. Emerging mobile technologies have given rise to new contingencies for subjectivity, alternative ways of presenting gender, emotion, sociality as well as a performative space to negotiate online and offline identity. Mobile phones in the Philippines have affected the rise of new subjects, allowing socially marginalized groups to exercise a daily presence in everyday culture and extend networks of intimacy (Pertierra 2002). Ordinary people express democratic voices through ICT blogs, mobilizing a potential of democratization of everyday life with contentiously different forms, levels and interpretations (Tacchi 2005; Baber 2005; Skoric 2007). Whilst the meaning of "cute" in the West is associated with child's play, in the Asian region cute is appropriated to domesticate, feminize and make warm the coldness of new technologies (Hjorth in this volume). With the rise in female consumers of new technological spaces such as the Internet, mobile phones and camera phones, a new possibility arises from a "prosumer" agency, a transformative capacity from the role of consumers to producers in the feminization of mobile spaces translating localized notions of intimacy.

The feminization of masculinity is a contesting transformation in gender and sexuality of Asia, with the emergence of young men employing feminine aesthetics and new masculine identities (Iida 2005). Despite nationalist fear and tension over the boundary-crossing practice that challenges the hitherto clearly defined gendered order, the young men distance themselves from conventional masculinity by standing in the position of the feminine, where they can engage ambiguously in the construction of alternative gender identities. The Internet has created the spaces for the emergences of Asian gay and lesbian communities and the proliferation of new modes of eroticized subjectivity (Shahani 2008). Transgender cultures, cultures of non-normative gender identification, arise out of the embedded histories of often long-established local transgender identities and practices in Asia, creating a space for transgender voices to be expressed and heard (Martin and Ho 2006).

The media are seen to be enabling mobilities at multiple levels, by the symbolic, virtual and imaginary travels through space or actual physical movement between different places. There is an increasing awareness of the possibility of movement, with an increasing tendency towards the "inner mobility" (Beck 2000: 77) of an individual's own life. The media have transformed the ways in which people imagine themselves and their lives, playing a significant role as a catalyst for the emergence of contemporary international migration towards the West and within Asia (Fujita in this volume; Jirattikorn 2007). The movement of people across national or cultural boundaries has been followed by new flows of the media, which have grown both in quality and quantity in the late twentieth and early twenty-first century (Thussu 2007). Media globalization is reshaping international migration patterns with distinctive features that differentiate them from earlier migration categories of the working class, victim, slave, trade and imperial. It intersects with new kinds of migration and greater mobility by the highly educated, professionals, guest workers, cultural migrants and tourists and a large-scale migration of students overwhelmingly from Asia (UN 2005; World Bank 2006; IIE 2007).

There is a significant intersection between the large-scale movement of people and media globalization in Asia where real-life situations are felt to be particularly constrained and mobility in a variety of capacities and forms becomes more important. This phenomenon has expanded to the everyday lives of middle-class young people who are increasingly becoming mobile transnationals, de-territorialized in their physical, virtual and imaginary existence through regular travels, networks and communications across territorial boundaries. Young people's daily experience of the transnational flows of the media impacts upon their migratory project and conceptions of the West not always as distant exotics but as possible lives. The linking of media and transnational mobility is a relatively new and under-explored field of investigation, but the importance of the media as a pull variable has been recognized (King and Wood 2001).

Longing for Western modernity does not adequately explain the reasons to migrate to Western cities for many Japanese youth (Fujita in this volume). A significant push factor is the rise of youth unemployment since the 1990s and the increasing number of singles, twenty-five to thirty-five years old, who find it difficult to have full-time work and independent lifestyles. It is common for women to quit their "office lady" jobs and move to a Western destination (Kelsky 2001). In South Korea, the unmet promises of education, the increasing awareness of inequalities and the lack of social mobility in the homeland have propelled a new surge of movement to the West (Abelmann 2003). More and more Chinese seek opportunities in Western higher education that may allow them to access international jobs outside the Chinese labor system (Turner 2006). Migration from India accounts for the largest group of international students, followed by China, South Korea, and Japan (IIE 2007). A pulling effect of the media can play a role in this process of migration. Young people's mediated symbolic encounter with the West generates "imaginations of alternative lifestyles and work" (Fujita in this volume; Kim 2005). People seem to imagine routinely the possibility that they will live and work in places other than where they were born, and their plans are affected by a mass-mediated imaginary that frequently transcends national space (Appadurai 1996). This mobility is seen as an extension of the previous immersion and the ongoing reflexivity of people in consuming images transmitted from a Western destination, while constructing imagined selves and translating the imagination of possible lives into facets of reality.

THE BOOK IN OUTLINE

How significant are the media to Asian transformations? This book is divided into three thematically linked sections, each demonstrating the centrality of the media to Asian transformations in the era of globalization. Globalization is a multi-dimensional, complex process of profound transformations in all spheres. Part I of the book is concerned with global-ization as a mediated cultural force and with its relationship to everyday experience. It considers what the globalization might mean to the different groups and cultures in its variations and its differences. Chapters in this sec-tion explore, specifically, how ordinary men and women, the young and the old, the working class and the middle class, actually live in global culture through the consumption of everyday media and how they reflect on the meaning of the global in everyday life.

Chapter 1 (Youna Kim) details the specific ways in which the cultural experience of globalization impinges upon, and becomes integrated into, the changing lives of young Korean women of different classes. It argues that global TV helps to create an important condition for the practice of reflexivity, by opening up a rare space where Korean women can make sense of their life conditions in highly critical ways and can imagine new possibilities of freedom—social mobility and individualization—within the multiple constraints of their social context. Chapter 2 (Pamela Nilan) explores the place of the media in the shaping of young people's lives and identities in Muslim Southeast Asia in a time of intense globalization. It shows that young Muslims are invited to exercise reflexive subjectivity in a collective rather than individual fashion and that many aspects of tradition remain strong. Chapter 3 (Vamsee Juluri) further shows how tradition is re-imagined in global media consumption, using case stud-ies from MTV to Hanuman animation in India. Tradition is re-invented through the ways in which people negotiate the meanings of media texts in terms of family, religion and the nation. Chapter 4 (Joanne B. Y. Lim) further demonstrates how the nation and national identity is re-invented through a popular cultural text in postcolonial Malaysia. Focusing on the nationwide popularity of a Western-borrowed reality TV program, *Malaysian Idol,* it addresses the contours of Malaysian nationalist inten-sifications amidst the perceived threat of Western culture. Chapter 5 (Anthony Y. H. Fung) explores how the Chinese, who live under the socialist system, make sense of the border-crossing Hong Kong TV, glo-balized cultural products of the capitalist system. The Chinese criticize the capitalist system and its class logic, but also come to self-evaluate the limits of their own national system through the global influence. Reveal-ing the critical reflexivity at work, this chapter argues that the meaning of the global is never complete.

Against globalization as a mediated "Western" cultural force, Asian media have emerged as new players for transnational consumption, chang-ing the dynamics of the media landscape in the region. Part II of the vol-ume draws attention to the rise of the transnational Asian media and the implications of regional consumption at socio-cultural and political levels. Chapters in this section explore the culturally specific meanings and sig-nificance in various locations, and how this emerging trend is impacting the construction of new "possible" identities.

Chapter 6 (Chua Beng Huat) argues that the regionalization of East Asian pop culture stands in the way of complete hegemony of the globalization of US media culture. Focusing on three historical flows of the media—Chinese language media, Japanese media culture, and most recently, Korean popular culture—it addresses the multiple levels of identifiable community that are constructed from this increasing regional consumption and give rise to the possibility of the transnational "East Asian" identity formation. Chapter 7 (Kelly Hu) explains why Japanese media culture, TV drama in particular, is appealing to Chinese people as a rare source of everyday reflexivity. Chinese fans discover narrative reflexivity in the drama and carry out implicit therapy on themselves through online discussions and writing on the positioning of the self and existential anxiety in transitional society. Chapter 8 (Koichi Iwabuchi) explores the social and political impact of Korean popular culture in Japan; how Japan's postcolonial ambivalent desire has resurfaced, as the Korean Wave is excessively celebrated and disavowed in the public discourse; how Korean television is received by ordinary Japanese women and acts on them to prompt post-text encounters with Korea, causing change in their perceptions of postcolonial politics and relations. Chapter 9 (Adrian M. Athique) and Chapter 10 (Zakir Hossain Raju) consider Bollywood movies that have emerged as major contenders to Hollywood, especially with a huge following in South Asia and Southeast Asia. From a transnational culture perspective, they examine the heightened visibility of Bollywood phenomena, signalling the construction of a de-territorialized imagined community and a hybrid identity, as well as the struggle for its impact and signification.

To reflect the nature of social transformations intersected with media consumption, Part III of the book further approaches the media's profound significance in and for everyday life through an understanding of the interplay between lived relations and mediated processes. Chapters in this section explore the culturally specific ways in which every experience of the media becomes integrated into the fabric of everyday life and how the media impact upon the changing lives and identities of people—with new openings and possibilities, tensions and contradictions of transition occurring in the everyday world. This final part also considers how the increasingly diverse and intrusive media environments, including information and communication technologies, transform everyday life by creating alternative networks of identity.

Chapter 11 (Ubonrat Siriyuvasak) reflects on the question of trans-Asian identity formation generating reflexivity, freedom and pleasure within the constraints of socio-economic structure and lived relations. Chapter 12 (Yachien Huang) demonstrates that mediated experience often leads to an unresolved identity—an ambivalence of close identification and distancing, contestation and resistance—and how the young Taiwanese women's sexuality talk around *Sex and the City* manifests a dialectics of freedom and constraint in everyday life. Chapter 13 (Larissa Hjorth) draws attention to a new and striking phenomenon in the emergence of Cyworld, an Internet-based community, and explores the culturally nuanced ways that this new type of virtual world is operating side by side with the offline one among young Koreans. Chapter 14 (Yuiko Fujita) observes a large number of young Japanese migrating to the West in recent years, arguing that not only economic and political factors but also cultural factors act as the main forces to induce the contemporary migration. Especially, the media play a significant role, as the Japanese youth increasingly imagine and reflect on alternative lifestyles and identities through the long-term consumption of global popular culture. The media are central to the construction of imagined worlds, reflexive selves, multiple mobilities—physical, virtual or imaginary—and the transformations of everyday life.

REFERENCES

Abelmann, N. (2003) *The Melodrama of Mobility: Women, Talk and Class in Contemporary South Korea,* Honolulu: University of Hawaii Press.

Ang, I. (2001) "Desperately Guarding Borders: Media Globalization, Cultural Imperialism and the Rise of Asia," in Y. Souchou (ed) *House of Glass: Culture, Modernity and the State in Southeast Asia,* Singapore: Institute of Southeast Asian Studies.

Appadurai, A. (1996) *Modernity at Large: Cultural Dimensions of Globalization,* Minneapolis: University of Minnesota Press.

Baber, Z. (2005) *CyberAsia: The Internet and Society in Asia,* Leiden: Brill Academic Publishers.

Beck, U. (1994) "The Reinvention of Politics: Towards a Theory of Reflexive Modernization," in U. Beck et al. (eds) *Reflexive Modernization: Politics, Tradition and Aesthetics in the Modern Social Order,* Cambridge: Polity.

———. (1998) *World Risk Society,* Cambridge: Polity.

———. (2000) *What is Globalization?* Cambridge: Polity.

Beck, U. and Beck-Gernsheim, E. (1995) *Normal Chaos of Love,* Cambridge: Polity.

Beck, U., Giddens, A. and Lash, S., eds. (1994) *Reflexive Modernization: Politics, Tradition and Aesthetics in the Modern Social Order,* Cambridge: Polity.

Berry, C., Martin, F. and Yue, A. (2003) *Mobile Cultures: New Media in Queer Asia,* Durham: Duke University Press.

Butcher, M. (2003) *Transnational Television, Cultural Identity and Change: When STAR Came to India,* New Delhi: Sage.

Carruthers, A. (2004) "Cute Logics of the Multicultural and the Consumption of the Vietnamese Exotic in Japan," *Positions,* 12(2): 401–29.

Chadha, K. and Kavoori, A. (2000) "Media Imperialism Revisited: Some Findings from the Asian Case," *Media, Culture & Society,* 22(4): 415–32.

Chalaby, J. (2005) "From Internationalization to Transnationalization," *Global Media and Communication,* 1(1): 28–32.

Chan, J. M. (2005) "Global Media and the Dialectics of the Global," *Global Media and Communication,* 1(1): 24–28.

Chan, S. W. (2007) "From Bad Girls to Super Girls: Femininity, Individuality and Democracy," paper presented in the AAS China & Inner Asia session, Boston.

Chua, B. H. (2000) *Consumption in Asia: Lifestyles and Identities,* London: Routledge.

———. (2004) "Conceptualizing an East Asian Popular Culture," *Inter-Asia Cultural Studies,* 5(2): 200–21.

Clammer, J. (2003) "Globalization, Class, Consumption and Civil Society in Southeast Asian Cities," *Urban Studies*, 40(2): 403–19.

Couldry, N. (2000) *Inside Culture: Reimagining the Method of Cultural Studies*, London: Sage.

Curran, J. and Park, M. (2000) *De-Westernizing Media Studies*, London: Routledge.

Curtin, M. (2003) "Media Capital: Towards the Study of Spatial Flows," *International Journal of Cultural Studies*, 6(2): 202–28.

Darling-Wolf, F. (2004) "Virtually Multicultural: Trans-Asian Identity and Gender in an International Fan Community of a Japanese Star," *New Media & Society*, 6(4): 507–28.

De Certeau, M. (1984) *The Practice of Everyday Life*, Berkeley: University of California Press.

Desai, J. (2004) *Beyond Bollywood: The Cultural Politics of South Asian Diasporic Film*, New York: Routledge.

Desai, J., Dudrah, R. and Rai, A. (2005) "Bollywood Audiences Editorial," *South Asian Popular Culture*, 3(2): 79–82.

Dong, S. and Shi, A. (2007) "Chinese News in Transition: Facing the Challenge of Global Competition," in D. Thussu (ed) *Media on the Move: Global Flow and Contra-flow*, London: Routledge.

Erni, J. and Chua, S. K. (2005) *Asian Media Studies*, Malden: Blackwell.

Flew, T. (2007) *Understanding Global Media*, London: Palgrave.

Fung, A. (2006) "Think Globally, Act Locally: China's Rendezvous with MTV," *Global Media and Communication*, 2(1): 71–88.

Giddens, A. (1984) *The Constitution of Society: Outline of the Theory of Structuration*, Cambridge: Polity.

———. (1991) *Modernity and Self-Identity: Self and Society in the Late Modern Age*, Cambridge: Polity.

———. (1994) "Living in a Post-traditional Society," in U. Beck et al. (eds) *Reflexive Modernization: Politics, Tradition and Aesthetics in the Modern Social Order*, Cambridge: Polity.

Govil, N. (2007) "Bollywood and the Frictions of Global Mobility," in D. Thussu (ed) *Media on the Move: Global Flow and Contra-flow*, London: Routledge.

Hall, S. (1991) "The Local and the Global: Globalization and Ethnicity," in A. King (ed) *Culture, Globalization and the World-System*, London: Palgrave.

Herman, E. and McChesney, R. (1997) *The Global Media: The New Missionaries of Global Capitalism*, London: Cassell.

Holden, T. and Scrase, T. (2006) *Medi@sia*, London: Routledge.

Iida, Y. (2005) "Beyond the Feminization of Masculinity: Transforming Patriarchy with the Feminine in Contemporary Japanese Youth Culture," *Inter-Asia Cultural Studies*, 6(1): 56–74.

IIE (2007) *Open Doors Report on International Educational Exchange*. http://www.iie.org

Iwabuchi, K. (2004) *Feeling Asian Modernities: Transnational Consumption of Japanese TV Dramas*, Hong Kong: University of Hong Kong Press.

———. (2007) "Contra-flows or the Cultural Logic of Uneven Globalization? Japanese Media in the Global Agora," in D. Thussu (2007) *Media on the Move: Global Flow and Contra-flow*, London: Routledge.

Jirattikorn, Amporn. (2007) *Transnational Broadcasting: The Consumption of Thai Soap Opera among Shan Communities in Burma*, part of PhD thesis in Anthropology, University of Texas at Austin.

Kaur, R. and Sinha, A. (2005) *Bollyworld: Popular Indian Cinema Through a Transnational Lens*, New Delhi: Sage.

Keane, M. (2006) "Once Were Peripheral: Creating Media Capacity in East Asia," *Media, Culture & Society*, 28(6): 835–55.

Kellner, D. (1992) "Popular Culture and the Construction of Postmodern Identities," in S. Lash et al. (eds) *Modernity and Identity,* Oxford: Blackwell.

Kelsky, K. (2001) *Women on the Verge: Japanese Women, Western Dreams,* Durham: Duke University Press.

Kim, Y. (2005) *Women, Television and Everyday Life in Korea: Journeys of Hope,* London: Routledge.

——. (2007) "The Rising East Asian Wave: Korean Media Go Global," in D. Thussu (ed) *Media on the Move: Global Flow and Contra-flow,* London: Routledge.

King, R. and Wood, N. (2001) *Media and Migration,* London: Routledge.

Lefebvre, H. (1971) *Everyday Life in the Modern World,* London: Penguin.

Liechty, M. (2003) *Suitably Modern: Making Middle-Class Culture in a New Consumer Society,* Princeton: Princeton University Press.

Martin, F. and Ho, J. (2006) "Editorial Introduction: Trans/Asia, Trans/Gender," *Inter-Asia Cultural Studies,* 7(2): 185–87.

Martin-Barbero, J. (1993) *Communication, Culture and Hegemony: From the Media to Mediations,* London: Sage.

——. (2002) "Identities: Traditions and New Communities," *Media, Culture & Society,* 24 (5): 621–41.

——. (2003) "Cultural Change: The Perception of the Media and the Mediation of its Images," *Television & New Media,* 4(1): 85–106.

Mayes, W. (2007) *Urban Elites and Social Change in Laos,* part of PhD thesis in Anthropology, Australian National University.

Miller, D. and Slater, D. (2000) *The Internet: An Ethnographic Approach,* Oxford: Berg.

OECD (2006) *Broadband Statistics.* http://www.oecd.org/sti/ict/broadband

Ong, A. (1999) *Flexible Citizenship: The Cultural Logics of Transnationality,* Durham: Duke University Press.

Pertierra, R. (2002) *Txt-ing Selves: Cellphones and Philippine Modernity,* Manila: De La Salle University Press.

Pieterse, J. N. (2004) *Globalization and Culture: Global Melange,* Lanham: Rowman & Littlefield.

Punathambekar, A. (2005) "Bollywood in the Indian-American Diaspora: Mediating a Transitive Logic of Cultural Citizenship," *International Journal of Cultural Studies,* 8(2): 151–73.

Rajagopal, A. (2004) "Comparative Studies in South Asian Culture and Society," *Anthropological Quarterly,* 77(1): 127–44.

Schonfeld, E. (2006) "Cyworld Ready to Attack MySpace," *Business 2.0,* 27 July.

Scott, J. (1992) "Experience," in J. Butler and J. Scott (eds) *Feminists Theorize the Political,* New York: Routledge.

Sen, K. and Stivens, M. (1998) *Gender and Power in Affluent Asia,* London: Routledge.

Shahani, P. (2008) *Gay Bombay: Globalization, Love and (Be)longing in Contemporary India,* New Delhi: Sage.

Silverstone, R. (1994) *Television and Everyday Life,* London: Routledge.

——. (2005) "Mediation," in C. Calhoun et al. (eds) *The Handbook of Sociology,* London: Sage.

Siriyuvasak, U. (2004) "Popular Culture and Youth Consumption: Modernity, Identity and Social Transformation," in K. Iwabuchi (ed) *Feeling Asian Modernities: Transnational Consumption of Japanese TV Dramas,* Hong Kong: University of Hong Kong Press.

Siriyuvasak, U. and Shin, H. (2007) "Asianizing K-pop: Production, Consumption and Identification Patterns among Thai Youth," *Inter-Asia Cultural Studies,* 8(1): 109–36.

Skoric, M. (2007) "Is Culture Destiny in Asia? A Story of a Tiger and a Lion," *Asian Journal of Communication*, 17(4): 396–415.

Srinivas, L. (2005) "Imaging the Audience," *South Asian Popular Culture*, 3(2): 101–16.

Synovate (2006) *Survey about Young Asians*. http://www.synovate.com

Tacchi, J. (2005) "Supporting the Democratic Voice through Community Media Centres in South Asia," *3CMedia*. http://www.cbonline.org.au

Thomas, A. O. (2005) *Imagi-nations and Borderless Television: Media Culture and Politics Across Asia,* New Delhi: Sage.

——. (2006) *Transnational Media and Contoured Markets: Redefining Asian Television and Advertising,* New Delhi: Sage.

Thompson, J. (1995) *The Media and Modernity: A Social Theory of the Media,* Cambridge: Polity.

Thussu, D. (2007) *Media on the Move: Global Flow and Contra-flow,* London: Routledge.

Turner, Y. (2006) "Swinging Open or Slamming Shut? The Implications of China's Open-Door Policy for Women, Educational Choice and Work," *Education and Work,* 19(1): 47–65.

UN (2005) *Migration in an Interconnected World: New Directions for Action,* Geneva: UN Publications.

Urry, J. (2000) *Sociology beyond Societies: Mobilities for the Twenty-first Century,* London: Routledge.

Wang, J. (2005) "Youth Culture, Music, and Cell Phone Branding in China," *Global Media and Communication,* 1(2): 185–201.

Watson, J. (2005) *Golden Arches East: McDonald's in East Asia,* 2nd ed, Stanford: Stanford University Press.

World Bank (2006) *Global Economic Prospects 2006: Economic Implications of Remittances and Migration,* Washington: World Bank Publications.

Yuwa, H. W. (2007) *Succeeding Like Success: The Affluent Consumers of Asia,* MasterCard World Publications.

Part I

Media Consumption in Globalization

1 Experiencing Globalization
Global TV, Reflexivity and the Lives of Young Korean Women

Youna Kim

Globalization isn't only about what is "out there," remote and far away from the individual. It is an "in here" phenomenon too, influencing intimate and personal aspects of our lives.

(Giddens 1999: 12)

Globalization can be understood as a multi-dimensional, complex process of profound transformations in all spheres—technological, economic, political, social, cultural, intimate and personal. It has been variously conceived as time-space compression (referring to the way that instantaneous electronic communication erodes the constraints of distance and time on social organization and interaction); accelerating interconnectedness (understood as the intensification of worldwide social relations and consciousness of world society); action at a distance (whereby the actions of social agents in one locale can come to have significant consequences for "distant others"). Globalization thus suggests the expanding scale, speeding up and deepening impact of interregional flows and patterns of social interaction (Held and McGrew 2003). It has been influenced above all by developments in systems of communication (Giddens 1999: 10); there is no globalization without communications media. Contemporary individuals, subject to an extraordinary diversity of information and communication, can be influenced by images, concepts and lifestyles from well beyond their immediate locales. Globalization affects the basic identities of individuals who now live with a partial and precarious integration of the multiple dimensions of cultural referents (Castells 1997). And it is said, "its existence alters the very texture of our lives, rich and poor alike" (Giddens 1999: 11).

Specifically, in what ways does the existence of globalization alter the very texture of our lives? Much of the current debates about globalization operate at a level of abstraction but rarely offer an empirically grounded, detailed understanding of the phenomenon reaching into the heart of the intimate and personal sphere. Discussions of globalization gain by being grounded in the detail of particular cultures and by considering the particular complexities of global encountering in specific social, historical, and everyday experience (Robins 2000). Yet the domain of experience has generally received less attention in globalization analysis; particularly, experiences concerning women remain shadowlands of practice. The concern of mainstream globalization discourse tends to be with "out there" macro-processes, rather than with what is happening "'in here," in the intimate and personal aspects of our lives. A deeper understanding of "in here" processes is essential if we are to adequately appreciate the diverse and differential impact of globalization across distinct categories of people and localities and avoid "the risk of being so over-schematic as to hide all the differences that matter" (Morley 1992: 272). I thus begin by calling for a greater need to address globalization as everyday experience—lived and mediated—and to empirically ground it in the specificity of experience.

What happens to our sense of our own lives when globalization confronts our everyday experience? How deeply do we feel this? What are these main transformations, and what is the role of the global media in this transformative process? In this chapter I seek to explore these questions by bringing an everyday experience perspective to the discourse of globalization. My case study is based on ethnographic research in Seoul, Korea, amongst young women in their early twenties, of working-class and middle-class backgrounds. I am particularly concerned with the depths to which global media culture—television primarily—influences the way young women make sense of their lives and experiences. The media are the most visible cultural expressions of globalization and can not be left out of any examination of contemporary everyday experience, since the media "mediate" that experience as cultural tools and integrated resources (Martin-Barbero 1993). My intention therefore is to empirically engage with "globalization as a mediated cultural force and its relationship to experience" (Silverstone 1999: 108). The experience of the media will be approached as a "situated, mundane, practical activity" (Thompson 1995: 38–39) that individuals carry out as a part of their everyday lives. The aim of this chapter is to detail the specific ways that the cultural experience of globalization impinges upon, and becomes integrated into, the changing lives of young women in contemporary Korea.

The analysis offered in this chapter argues for the significance of reflexivity in the cultural experience of globalization. Global television, in particular, helps to create an important condition for the practice of reflexivity, by opening up a rare space in which Korean women can make sense of their life conditions in highly critical ways and can imagine new possibilities of freedom within the multiple constraints of their social context. This Korean study therefore suggests that what makes a difference in the lives of young women today is the deepening of reflexivity with the power of imagination in their journey across the globalization landscape. Similarly, a Chinese study (Lull 1991) suggested that the increasingly globalized diffusion of television programming during the late 1980s sparked critical reflexivity among Chinese people as it became the main reference point that the people used to compare and evaluate their own lives. They began to realize that their personal freedoms were few, and this shift in their thinking was fundamentally influenced by global television. The point here is that people have a reflexive and critical engagement with the new global television culture, which involves learning to deal with their life conditions with new information.

Reflexivity has, since the mid-1980s, been a crucial issue for social researchers in Western academic debates—notably, in critical ethnography (Clifford and Marcus 1986) and feminist epistemology (Skeggs 1995)— emphasizing the necessity of reflecting on the conditions (for example, power relations) under which knowledge is produced. But what about the reflexivity of ordinary people? What about women in a culture (for example, Korea, China) where repression is supposed to be pervasive? What is it about the globally connected media world that provides openings for everyday people to make sense of their lives in critical ways? Here, I set out to consider reflexivity as the major mechanism of grasping a relationship between globalization, as a mediated cultural force, and experience, since I argue that it is precisely reflexivity that is at work in the everyday experience of global media culture.

Reflexivity is increasingly understood, in recent social theory, to be central to the constitution of subjects under conditions of global modernity. Contemporary subjects are figured in terms of tendencies towards self-reflection, "self-analysis, self-confrontation" (Beck 1994: 5) and the "reflexive monitoring of action and its contexts" (Giddens 1990: 36) to keep in touch with the grounds of everyday life. This kind of reflexivity comes from an occasionally evident awareness of subjects' own experience of and position in society, with respect to the overwhelming power of dominant institutions and discourses; and such a capacity is already becoming "operative in the critique or the discourses of non-intellectual lay public groups at an informal and pre-political level" (Beck 1992: 7). It can operate more intensively "not in a situation of greater and greater certainty, but in one of methodological doubt" (Giddens 1991: 84), in the ambivalence of modernity, as a way of dealing with rapid social change and defining how to act.

Since reflexivity is intrinsic to all human life in all cultures, the difference resides not in the reflexive monitoring of action as such, but in a "specific form and degree of reflexivity" in a particular context in which it is achieved (Giddens 1990: 36). The difference also consists in the "scale of knowledge and information" made available in a global modern condition under which reflexivity takes place. Especially, the extraordinary range of knowledge and information that today's globalization makes available constitutes a unique phenomenon, whose importance for understanding present life situations can undermine traditional arrangements and transform traditional forms of social practices. Possibly, "social practices are constantly examined and reformed in the light of incoming information about those very practices, thus constitutively altering their character" (Giddens 1990: 38). The quantity and quality of reflexivity may be changing, as different kinds of understandings with the use of incoming non-local information (for example, through the media) can affect the reflexive monitoring of action in a culture-specific way.

Significantly, reflexivity is said to require resources to operate successfully, and the media are stressed as a nucleus of reflexivity (Beck 1992). Yet such a view, while stressing the central importance of the media, is surprisingly reticent about analyzing it. The depths and significance of reflexivity as socio-cultural phenomena in relation to the global media have not been fully addressed with an empirically grounded account (though, see Thompson 1995: 207–34). Nor have the dynamics of gender or gendered experience been incorporated as thoroughly as merited into this discussion in a specific culture. It seems important to note that, unlike Euro-American societies, in which women might draw on expert psychological knowledge in their understanding of the self, such models and sources are not widely available or used among Korean women. Unlike self-guided books and magazines that demand monetary obligations, the domestic presence of television is relatively free and available anytime, thus allowing all women, including the poor working class, to enjoy some of the benefits of self-reflexive use. Different meanings and understandings produced by the range of knowledge and information in global television provide them with tools for self-understanding. The following study will show how reflexivity actually operates in the cultural experience of global television and how it influences intimate and personal aspects of Korean women's lives.

CONTEXT AND METHOD

Globalization has entered Korean social life since the 1980s in the context of economic restructuring policies of neo-liberalism, and the nation has undergone rapid cultural changes. A relatively affluent, media-driven consumerist society emerged in the late 1980s as local culture industries began to accommodate the explosion of global mass-mediated forms. Television stands as the dominant representation of global culture—including Hollywood movies, travel shows, dramas and CNN—with the development of satellite DTH services (SkyLife) and 119 cable services reaching about 80 percent of the total 15 million households. Although the ratings of national programming (for example, dramas, news) are far higher than those of its imported counterparts, a closer look reveals that imported movies have the "third" highest ratings and are actively pursued by young women in their early twenties and teens (KBI 1999). Bound up with global media culture, since the mid-1990s affluent young women have displayed a consuming passion for foreign travel, a thoroughly modern and ordinary practice today.

As a consequence, new concerns have arisen about the lived effects of increasingly trans-cultural interaction and its changing role in the lives of young women. While statistically marriage is still the norm (73 percent), average marriage age has been pushed upward and the divorce rate has rapidly risen from 5.8 percent in 1980, to 11 percent in 1990, and 42 percent today (KWDI 2004). Greater equality of the sexes is claimed, although women's attitudes towards sexuality remain ambivalent between traditional moralities and modern desires. Family systems are under threat as women stand up for self-fulfillment at work and in education. Women's enrollment rates in high school (ages seventeen to nineteen) have reached 95 percent, with 63 percent of the women entering higher education (KWDI 2004). A majority of university graduates refuse to go back to traditional female roles but desire an individualized life through work. In short, Korean women are living through a major period of historical transition in the midst of trans-cultural dialogue. Although there is no definite answer as to whether and how actual changes in the lives of women relate to global media influence, any attempt to make sense of this phenomenon needs to engage with the ethnography of cultural globalization to understand how the proliferation of cultural globalization is experienced and what it means to women's everyday lives.

This study is part of a larger ethnographic project on Korean women's experiences of television in its national and global context. In order to understand how television intersects with the everyday lives of Korean women of different generations and classes, I conducted fieldwork to include a varied sample of women in their fifties, thirties, and twenties, of working-class and middle-class backgrounds: six different socio-economic categories, with seven women in each category. The present paper draws on the accounts of the women in their twenties (seven working-class and seven middle-class, aged twenty to twenty-two) as this younger age group demonstrated an active use of global television, compared to the older groups. This study is not intended to generalize but to give a sense of the transformation in Korean women's lives, intersected with cultural experience of globalization.

To identify women's class without provoking any discomfort and humiliation by asking their occupation, income and educational level directly, I instead solicited the expertise of real estate agencies and located two contrasting apartment-complexes in Seoul. Their information revealed the property size, price, geographical location and cultural environment, as well as indicating the residents' occupation, income and general level of education. On the notice board of each apartment-complex, I placed an advertisement offering a session of free English lessons to women in their twenties in exchange for participation in the study. Interviews were conducted in the women's homes, the natural habitat within which television viewing takes place. All these young women lived at the home of their parents, under fairly strict surveillance, as Korean parents generally do not allow their "single" children to live independently. Interviews were tape recorded and each interview lasted between 1.5 and 2 hours. On average, seven follow-up interviews ensured a consistent flow of data, while enabling the translation and interpretation of data. Interviews usually began with a question about the women's favorite television programs: "What television programs do you like most, and why?" The overall process of the interviews was, however, unstructured and open-ended; the women were not asked the same questions but rather were allowed to talk and develop their own particular interests and views on the subject.

It usually happened that in talking about viewing their favorite programs the women digressed surprisingly toward reflexive articulation of their personal lives—for example, their life conditions, private complaints and discontents. These digressions took place when there was a strong point of difference between characters' situations and their own. It then took the form of "storytelling": Women related the incidents, commented on the stories, and then moved from television to discussing their own lives and experiences and expressing their own aspirations and frustrations. The unstructured and open-ended interviews on the subject of television generated a corpus of data, some of which was not directly related to television itself but to the women's own lives. These Korean women were not asked to describe their personal life history, but this was often revealed in the context of their discussion of television. As the following analysis demonstrates, reflexivity is an integral process of TV talk and the women's reflection upon their self and their world is the major element of the experience of global television.

YOUNG WORKING-CLASS WOMEN: YEARNING FOR SOCIAL MOBILITY

The young working-class women in this study, aged twenty to twenty-two and single, live with their parents in the Jungwoo (pseudonym) apartment-complex. This old estate is located near a traditional market interlinked with a maze of narrow alleys and traditional residential areas of individual homes, and served by clusters of small shops and street vendors selling vegetables and fruits. Their mothers engage in some type of small-scale sales occupations and fathers in street cleaning, part-time manual work in a construction field, or are unemployed. These young women perceive social interactions outside the home—such as going to work, having friends and socializing on a regular basis—as more significant than staying in and watching television. Korean television, drama in particular, is fiercely criticized for its predominant representation of women within the limited sphere of home and for its failure to meet young women's desires to explore a wider world outside domesticity. This, however, does not mean that young working-class women do not value television. They nevertheless like to watch television whenever staying in the home and have a playful relationship with television. It is commonly said: "TV is my best friend." "TV is my teacher." Why? This has something to do with the young women's interest in the symbolic world of the West. In what follows, I discuss the ways in which they reflexively interact with the expansive world of the West on television and how the meaning gained from this is in sharp contrast to their discontent with the reality of everyday life:

> TV is my best friend. When I look around me, I don't find special people who can inspire me personally. Everything is just dull, common, all the same. (Kyung-joo, 22, sales clerk)

> I want something new and different in my life. That's the most interesting thing about watching foreign movies, travel shows. How can I experience the outside world, if not from television? (Yeon-jung, 22, 2-year vocational college student)

> When you read books you can imagine, only in words, the whole different world, but that's not satisfying for me. When you watch television you feel like you can really experience it through the visuals. (Soo-mi, 20, waitress)

Young working-class women tend to view their everyday life as "dull, common, all the same" or "uninspiring" and yearn for something "new and different." The living conditions and environment of the working class lead to relative deprivation and do not seem to offer meaningful stimuli. Such unpromising conditions draw attention to television programs about the West—particularly, Western movies and world travel shows. Through television, the socially and materially disadvantaged women, who have limited opportunities for travel and mobility in real life, get suddenly "plugged in" (Meyrowitz 1985: 223) and can "go" where they could not travel. Television provides a unique condition of "mobile privatization" (Williams 1983: 188), which enables the young women to distance themselves from the immediate locale of day-to-day life, and to imagine new lifestyles and possibilities beyond the constraints of the working-class reality. But what precisely are the yearned-for elements in the Korean women's imagination of the West?

> During my high school days I wanted to watch *Weekend Movies* (dubbed Western movies after 10:00 p.m.), but my mom told me to go to sleep or study. I came out stealthily late at night, sat in the dark and watched those movies. I tuned the TV volume as low as possible. Just the screen, sometimes no sound. Whenever I was restricted by my parents from watching those movies, I wanted to grow quickly to freely do anything. (Kyung-moon, 22, nurse trainee)

> I have been told in my life, "Don't do this, don't do that." I don't feel like I am living *my life*. I don't know if I will ever have *my life*. That's what I envy most about Western people (on TV). They look so free.

> They can do whatever they want to do. (Jung-hyun, 22, 2-year vocational college student; italics, her emphasis)

These young women are particularly attracted to Western movies on television—mainly American—and started watching them in middle school days (ages fourteen to sixteen). "Just the screen, sometimes no sound." This quotation, above, indicates a great desire to view Western movies in a constrained, small and dense space of the working-class home. Western movies are the center of gravity for the imagination, the "living, social mediation" (Martin-Barbero 1993: 166). The symbolic presence of the Other, *the West* in the Korean gaze, has become a critical condition for reflexivity to operate fully. The appeal of watching Western programs lies much in the opportunity to get a sense of how people live differently in other parts of the world, a sense that can give them a reference point to reflect on the conditions of their own lives. None of these working-class women have actually traveled to Western countries, but all freely talk about their imagination of the West and "freedom" (for example, "living *my life*"), which is in marked contrast to, thus a yearning element in, their constrained lives. More specifically, it points to "freedom of social mobility," class mobility, for the upwardly mobile transformation is a highly desirable and class-specific interest. The following accounts demonstrate their yearning for the freedom of social mobility that is decisively mediated by education, work and marriage:

> As I see the Western world [referring to the movie *Good Will Hunting*], a toilet cleaner can go to university. They seem open. In Western countries, it seems possible to have a good job even with a high school diploma, but in Korea a high school diploma is a piece of rubbish. It's useless because almost everybody has it. (Na-ri, 22, sales clerk)

> [In Western culture] a lawyer can choose to be a cook if she wants. But in our Korean culture, you are expected to work only in that field . . . After working for a long time you may want to go to university, but may be criticized, "Are you crazy? Why suddenly study at your age?" (Suh-jin, 21, waitress)

> This Cinderella movie [*Pretty Woman*] may come true in Western countries, but in our country nobody would approve of that kind of marriage (between a working-class woman and an upper-class man). But in America it seems like it's only yourself who makes all the decisions about your life. Western people are so free. (Soo-mi, 20, waitress)

These expressions can be seen to reflect the problematization of Korean society and the increasing awareness of its structural rigidities and strictures, and the limited possibilities for transformation that are a consequence. The women's mediated experience of the West gives rise to new dynamics in which lived experience and the moral fixities of society are compared, contrasted and evaluated against a Western cultural reservoir of alternative visions. Precisely, reflexivity arises out of specific material conditions and constraints of social context. The women's yearning for the freedom of social mobility is a "self-reflexive escape" (Schroder 1988: 74) that brings along enough of their working-class identities and real-life concerns—missing out on higher education, promising work and socially upward marriage. All of these working-class women had obtained a high school diploma, yet this was for them "a piece of rubbish," as one woman said frustratingly, given the extremely high level of mass education in Korea. The women's employment futures (as, for example, waitresses, sales clerks) are far less secure; hence, dependence through marriage is a way of achieving material security and social mobility. The sense of loss and consequent yearning to imagine a new mobility across a cultural space seem to be an integral part of working-class experience. This self-reflexive escape, intertwined with the experience of powerlessness, frustration and desire, is a space for hope. For these working-class women, watching Western movies is not simply an escape into dreaming: It is a space "of desperate dreaming, of hope for transformation" (Walkerdine 1986: 196). This desperate hope for transformation is detailed in the desire of women to get out and get away and to "forget" about working-class existence:

> After one sudden accident, she [in *Desperately Seeking Susan*] completely loses her memory. She goes completely blank! It would be so good to be able to forget the whole past, the whole present, and start a new life all over again! I consider this accident as an opportunity for change in life. (Jung-hyun, 22, 2-year vocational college student)

> Even though this movie [*Pretty Woman*] did not show her marriage, I can imagine she will marry and live happily. She will become a totally new person and lead a new life. She is given a new opportunity. In our country, that would be absolutely impossible. (Soo-mi, 20, waitress)

The boundary between inside and outside is temporarily dissolved in the women's close involvement with the film. As one woman puts it: "I constantly imagined, what if I were in that situation, what if I did that? I imagined as if I were her." To imagine is to leave something behind—the ordinariness and normal constraints of working-class life—to engage in an activity of "as-if culture" (Silverstone 1999: 59–64) that is meaningful. This allows them to be imaginatively "disembedded" (Giddens 1990: 53) from the conditions of local life and to explore a world of new opportunities and change. Thus, the process of self-invention is continuously shifting and revised, as these examples show:

> I used to think change might be an extremely difficult thing to do, so I didn't dare to try. I thought change might be almost impossible [in

Korea]. After watching this movie [*Desperately Seeking Susan*], I came to think change might not be that difficult. Once one change happens, this can lead to another change, and another. Only the first step seems difficult. (Jung-hyun, 22, 2-year vocational college student)

Whenever I encounter free [Western] images on TV, I feel stimulated. I want to change like that! I don't want to restrict my life by old [Korean] thoughts. (Kyung-joo, 22, sales clerk)

With the growing mediated experience of the West and with a high degree of imagination, young women struggle to be less constrained and fixed by an unchanging order. The self of young women can be seen as a "reflexively organized symbolic project" (Thompson 1995: 233) that is integrated from a diversity of mediated experiences within and against the constraints of actual life circumstances. Although the young women continue to live a local life, their willing and playful interaction with a wider symbolic world may alter their sense of everyday life. Their horizons of understanding may well extend beyond the immediate locale of day-to-day living, for the globalized diffusion of television triggers and deepens the practice of reflexivity, continuously providing new openings and new imaginations for the reflexive formation of their lives.

YOUNG MIDDLE-CLASS WOMEN: YEARNING FOR INDIVIDUALIZATION

English is a must for employment [in Korea]. I withdrew from the university for one year and went to Australia for an English course. To brush up English now, I keep the TV on and listen to CNN, drama, movies. Who would find CNN interesting? But it's good for a listening practice. I don't find American drama interesting, but it's best for learning spoken English. (Eun-soo, 22, university student)

The completion of an English course abroad is a boost on the employment resume. So many students travel to America, Canada, Europe. In this globalizing society it may sound strange if you haven't been abroad. You have to travel abroad to join the conversation. (Yoon-kyung, 22, university student)

To be a tourist is one of the characteristics of modern experience, travel is a marker of class status in modern society (Urry 1991: 4). This is certainly true for young middle-class women in this study, university students aged twenty to twenty-two and single, all of whom have been to Western countries. These young women live at home with their parents in an affluent apartment-complex, Shinwon (pseudonym). This recently built estate consists of twenty fifteen-floor buildings and lies at the heart of modern amenities, including a large department store, private educational institutes and many Western food retailers. In the middle-class families fathers are predominant economic providers, engaging in professional and white-collar occupations, and mothers do not work outside the home. Unlike their stay-at-home mothers, these educated young women pursue a free, independent, individualized way of life through participation in work. Thus, other than for pleasure, the main motive for their foreign travel lies in learning the English language, as this is a compulsory requirement in any employment recruitment targeting university graduates. Transnational culture today tends to be tied to the job market; it is more or less "occupational culture" (Hannerz 1990: 243). The compulsory requirement of English in the contemporary job market means that English, as a language of global modernity and a means of making a living, has become a crucial precondition for the women's attainment of work and quest for economic independence. As a consequence, these young women go on learning and speaking English, whether they like it or hate it. English has emerged as a new form of cultural capital in globalizing modern Korea. Learning English and involving themselves with wider Western culture through travel and global television is a distinctive characteristic of the lives of young middle-class women. Their openness towards new cultural experiences is increasingly self-reflexive:

> I watch lots of foreign movies [on TV]. Good movies make me think about myself, my life. Am I also living like that? How should I live? I want to live like that! (Sung-won, 22, university student)

> Travelling to other [Western] countries is always exciting. While walking down the street, popping into a store, eating a meal outside, queuing in a line, I turn around and observe people. It's interesting to see if they are different from us, and how they are different. (Hyo-jung, 21, university student)

The young middle-class women can be said to be cosmopolitan, in terms of "a willingness to engage with the Other, an intellectual and aesthetic stance of openness toward divergent cultural experiences" (Hannerz 1990: 239). They are sensation-seekers and collectors of experiences, perceiving the world as "a food for sensibility, a matrix of possible experiences" (Bauman 1998: 94). In anticipation of new and different experiences, they expect to treat the world as a series of spectacles to which they pay attention. Such tourist gazing is sustained and reinforced by non-tourist practices, such as television consumption. Through the implosive power of global television, mundane cosmopolitanism is becoming part of ordinary experience. For these young women, cosmopolitan experience is not just about a recognition of the familiar, but much more about an imagination of the new and different. Among large and different repertoires of Western images, they incorporate desirable features into the invention of meaningful ways of living: "Am I also living like that? I want to live like that!" The mediated experience invites the "intrusion of distant events into everyday consciousness" (Giddens 1991: 27) that invokes envy and yearning.

The young women's cosmopolitan experience is characterized more by an inquisitive search for "differences" rather than universalities. Thus, their imaginative voyage into the new territories of a global mélange proceeds with interesting discoveries of differences that sharply contrast with culture back home. What, then, are the differences that matter to these young Korean women? What is the most yearned-for feature of difference? It is often expressed: "I most envy their free lifestyle." "I like their passion for I, myself." What is common to this yearning is a "learning of the self" that is reflexively interpreted and understood by a contrast between imagined (Western) freedom and practical (Korean) restrictions. The following long extract illustrates what they mean by Western free lifestyles, and its details reveal some of the constraints on being free in Korean society:

> In *Friends* [an American comedy drama], they often get together in the coffee shop and chat sitting comfortably on the sofa. None of them seem to worry about life or work. Everyday life is just ha-ha-ho-ho happy and simple. They don't seem to have a nice job, yet life is jolly. The long blond works in the coffee shop as a waitress. The tall stupid woman sings stupid songs. Did they go to university? Probably they did, they don't look smart though. In Korean society, if we are a university graduate and work in a coffee shop, people will think of us as a total loser. Not to mention parents' fury, "Have I sent you to university to see you work in a coffee shop?" None of their parents seem to compel, "Quit fooling around, get married and settle down!" In their culture it seems OK to fool around and enjoy a life. Because nobody interferes in their life. I like such free social atmosphere. (Joo-hyun, 22, university student)

This manifests television's great capacity for evoking reflexivity in an endless chain of referentiality, intersected with the microcosm of everyday life. In the context of new cultural experiences, Korean ways of life and traditional norms are interrogated and criticized. Young middle-class women commonly criticize Korean gender models and appropriate forms of behavior that are predicated on rigidly defined matrimonial roles, middle-class family expectations and direct parental control: "Quit fooling around, get married and settle down!" On the other hand, they derive new interpretations of life from the Western images of free lifestyles: "It seems OK to fool around and enjoy a life." They are subject to new senses of possibility, new desires and new openings in the imaginary realm of freedom. Significantly, their yearning for Western freedom is crystallizing around the meaning of "individualization" that is fundamentally incompatible with traditional family values and is therefore repressed by social and cultural forces, often beyond individual control:

> I like Western people's free individualistic life. They are making their own life, while we are making life for others. (Eun-soo, 22, university student)

> I hate the [Korean] car commercial. It's so stupid—"My husband wanted to remodel the kitchen for me, but I wanted to get him a new car instead. For my husband's confidence." Then, the husband drives a car and the wife happily leans on his shoulder. I hate that commercial. I would earn money *on my own,* change the kitchen *on my own,* and drive *my own car!* (Bo-ra, 21, university student; italics, her emphasis)

Yearning for the sense of personal freedom and independent quality of life, these educated young women desire to take total charge of their own lives and constitute themselves as an "actor, designer, juggler and stage director of their own biography and identity" (Beck 1994: 13). By imagining different ways of living and being through the reflexive experience of television, they struggle to invent a more self-responsible, self-determined, "emancipatory life politics" (Giddens 1991: 214), a politics of self-actualization, which is no longer obligatory and embedded in traditional gendered roles. It is a struggle to break free from the fixities of social rules, norms and expectations to discover a new self: "How should I live?" "What do I want in life?" This search for a new identity is played out in the midst of trans-cultural experience, in heightened awareness of thoughts and feelings. The intensified self-reflexivity signals a deliberately hopeful movement, a transformative quest for individualization.

CONTESTING WESTERN SEXUALITY: "WHAT IS LOVE?"

But it is fallacious to suppose that all elements of Western cultures are instantly taken in as fuel for the aspiring imagination. While young women certainly envy and incorporate some Western values into the reflexive formation of their lives, they contest and resist others. They do not relate to all but selectively, according to the "relevance structure" (Thompson 1995: 229) that determines a set of priorities in social life contexts. For these Korean women of both working-class and middle-class backgrounds, the most contestable feature of difference lies precisely in the level of intimacy—relative openness of Western sexual morality—around which sharp boundaries between "them" and "us" are defined. This is explicit in the ways that middle-class women critically contest Western sexual morality, experienced and imagined through travel and television:

> When it comes to sex, they are totally different people. The striking difference between them and us is sexual morality. (Moon-sun, 22)

> Sexually, they are too free. For example, in *Dawson's Creek,* a male student and a female teacher have a scandal that implies a sexual relationship. I also can't understand *Friends.* How can they be still friends after sleeping together? They have sex with anybody if they like. In *Ally McBeal,* even the old judge sleeps with a married woman ... While watching TV, I wonder, do Western audiences not criticize it? If our Korean TV had produced such content, they would have received a spate of protest calls from audiences. (Eun-soo, 22)

> In Western society, even strangers have a sexual relationship on their first encounter [on TV]. Even though they don't know each other well, after having sex, they call it love. "I love you." No matter how great that sex is, that doesn't look like love to me, that's just sex. I am curious, what is love to them? (Sung-won, 22)

> We want more than just sex. Does free sex make women happy? Are Western women happy? (Yoon-kyung, 22)

"What is love?" "Are Western women happy?" Young middle-class women engage in a process of interrogating intimate and personal aspects of Western lives. Reflexivity here penetrates into the most intimate dynamics of the self and its deepest emotions. They question, reflect and criticize the most pronounced difference, Western sexual freedom, according to the moral framework and affectivity of local cultural conditions. Although Western homogenizing forces introduce and reinforce certain standardizing values in virtually every corner of the world, these influences do not enter uniformly because they always interact with diverse local conditions (Lull 1995: 147) and are subject to culturally specific systems of meaning. These young women appear to suggest that the Western meaning of love, albeit ambiguous, does not correspond to the Korean women's dominant social character and "structure of feeling" (Williams 1961: 64–80), their affective elements of consciousness and relationships in emotional and social involvement—for instance, placing more emphasis on the emotional quality of love than on physical sensations: "We want more than just sex." In contrast, this emotional quality of love, or an affective practice of intimacy and long-term bonding, is found by them to be curiously absent from Western cultural forms, which they see as oriented more toward immediate sensual pleasure. The situations of distant Others are brought to the Korean women not only as cognitive but also as moral and emotional concerns to be explored. In a condition of globalization, more moral and emotional demands are implicitly made on ordinary people than ever before (Tomlinson 1999: 177). In this case, a high degree of moral agency operates with an effect of criticizing Western sexuality, love and intimacy, primarily within the affective realm of consciousness. These middle-class women remain embedded in the dominant structure of feeling, while integrating new possibilities of Western individualization, yet simultaneously rejecting Western sexual freedom. In a similar vein, Western sexual morality encounters the voices of resistance from working-class women:

> They seem to sleep with anybody [on TV]. It seems promiscuous to me. They always say, "I love you," and go to sleep together. (Suh-jin, 21)

> While watching Western programs I notice, they easily talk to a stranger, laugh together, easily make a sexual relationship. In Korea, it takes a long time to have any relationship . . . I don't see the image of home, family inside [Western] TV. That's odd to me. Western people behave as if they did not have a family. They have a noisy, jolly time with lovers, but rarely with their family. (Jung-hyun, 22)

> Sexually, Western people involve too fast without considering what will happen to their children. It looks like there are many divorced women, single mothers, broken homes in Western countries. I think these may be the by-products of free sex . . . We are opposed to [Western] free sex, no matter how much we are dying to change, rebel to the old [Korean] stuff. (Yeon-jung, 22)

The Korean women's "talking back" (Hannerz 1997: 13) in their critical imagination of Western sexuality produces a "heterogeneous dialogue" (Appadurai 1990: 307) against the homogenizing forces of Western cultural discourse. The most popular and frequently discussed Western programs among these young women include Hollywood romance movies, world travel shows, current affair news and American dramas such as *Friends, Ally McBeal* and *Dawson's Creek*. Explicit sexual conduct and unchecked passion, as well as a frequent display of divorce, are perceived as distinctly Western features and conventionalized rules of human relationships. The working-class women demonstrate reflexive distancing from Western sexual freedom in moral condemnation. Reflexivity here moves between closeness and distance: It suspends a close involvement and withdraws to a "superior distance" (Schroder 1988: 76), expressing doubt, critique and repudiation.

The Korean women's repudiation of Western sexual freedom is influenced by the prevailing local moral rules they live by. Traditional sexual values appear to be more deeply entrenched than any other values concerning women's lives. Chastity, for example, is still perceived as something divine, or as a sexual asset for women's successful entry into the marriage and family system. The repudiation of Western sexual freedom is also linked to the women's emotional desire to sustain a sense of security. This is revealed through their affective investments, in which a host of questions are raised as to the consequences of sexual freedom on the family and the inherent tensions contained within: "Then what happens to children, if Western people are sexually too liberal?" There is much speculation and scrutiny concerning the unstable status of family life, which implies that the family retains its importance especially in working-class existence. Although these working-class women yearn for the freedom of social mobility, a stabilizing affective quality internalized within the traditional structure of family continues to have an enduring significance. The women's experience of the mediated cultural force of globalization is open to questioning, intuiting and reflecting in a complex dual force of, and a dialectical negotiation between, change and continuity.

CONCLUSION

This chapter has shown how young Korean women make sense of their lives through the cultural experience of globalization, and has argued for "reflexivity at work": The practice of reflexivity is a defining characteristic of the cultural experience of globalization, and television culture has become a critical condition for reflexivity. The young women engage in a process of self-analysis and self-discovery through continuous interaction with the global world of television. They demonstrate the capacity to reflect critically on the actual circumstances of their lives and activities. The practice of reflexivity involves learning to deal with life conditions in a new light, thereby attempting to expand the sense of self-fulfillment. By opening themselves up to reflexive learning about diverse forms of life, these women ensure that the cultural experience of globalization, television in particular, increasingly nourishes and enriches the process of self-invention. It opens up a rare space in which Korean women can make sense of their life conditions in highly critical ways and can imagine new possibilities of freedom within the multiple constraints of their social context.

It could be suggested that what makes a difference in the lives of young women today is the deepening of reflexivity with the power of imagination in their journey across the globalization landscape. Young women in this study demonstrate the capacity to use an indefinite range of imagination. They take images from available symbolic global materials, and reflexively reorganize them to construct or conjure up a preferred image of reality. Traditional social practices are questioned, examined, altered and undermined through the reflexive exploration of the boundaries between the women themselves and the Other, *the West*. The young women's yearning for freedom—social mobility and individualization—is an inevitable consequence of both the growing awareness of discontent in the exigencies of

Korean reality and the increasingly imaginative experience of the symbolic Western world.

The working-class women's structural positioning usually closes down access to economic security and improvement in social status, whereas symbolic and cultural ways to escape the working class are open to them in their deliberately playful and imaginative journey outwards to the global. For the middle-class women, the Western idea of individualization continues to fuel yearning, imagination and reflexivity in their increasingly cosmopolitan experience through travel and television consumption. But the Korean women's imagination of freedom is bounded by the pervasive main concept governed by local rules—sexual morality. Not every Western image of freedom is randomly taken in as fuel for the imagination; rather, a particular imagined world is socially constructed, in which Western sexuality is ruled out. This means that young women's lives are made and remade through the dialectical negotiation between locally imposed rules and globally defined fields of possibility.

Against a cultural imperialist impulse (see, for example, Tomlinson 1991), I would argue that, in experiencing the mediated cultural force of globalization, young Korean women struggle to reshape their lives towards a deliberately encouraging movement of freedom, gathering their own "resources for a journey of hope" (Williams 1983: 268). Enjoying global media culture for these young women is a self-reflexive and imaginative social practice for hope, not a simple escape from an unsatisfying reality to a mere fantasy world. It is "no longer opium for the masses whose real work is elsewhere, no longer elite pastime thus not relevant to the lives of ordinary people" (Appadurai 1996: 31). Television has emerged as an important resource for reflexivity in globalizing Korean society, which stimulates ordinary women to reflect upon their own lives for a journey of hope.

* This has previously been published in the *International Journal of Cultural Studies,* 8(4), 2005, and appears here with the permission of the publisher, with a slight revision.

REFERENCES

Appadurai, A. (1990) "Disjuncture and Difference in the Global Cultural Economy," in M. Featherstone (ed) *Global Culture: Nationalism, Globalization and Modernity,* London: Sage.

———. (1996) *Modernity at Large: Cultural Dimensions of Globalization,* Minneapolis: University of Minnesota Press.

Bauman, Z. (1998) *Globalization: The Human Consequences,* New York: Columbia University Press.

Beck, U. (1992) *Risk Society: Towards a New Modernity,* London: Sage.

———. (1994) "The Reinvention of Politics: Towards a Theory of Reflexive Modernization," in U. Beck, A. Giddens, and S. Lash (eds) *Reflexive Modernization: Politics, Tradition and Aesthetics in the Modern Social Order,* Cambridge: Polity.

Castells, M. (1997) *The Power of Identity,* Oxford: Blackwell.

Clifford, J. and Marcus, G. (1986) *Writing Culture: The Poetics and Politics of Ethnography,* Berkeley: University of California Press.

Giddens, A. (1990) *The Consequences of Modernity,* Stanford: Stanford University Press.

——. (1991) *Modernity and Self-Identity: Self and Society in the Late Modern Age,* Cambridge: Polity.

——. (1999) *Runaway World: How Globalization is Reshaping Our Lives,* London: Profile Books.

Hannerz, U. (1990) "Cosmopolitans and Locals in World Culture," in M. Featherstone (ed) *Global Culture: Nationalism, Globalization and Modernity,* London: Sage.

——. (1997) "Notes on the Global Ecumene," in Sreberny-Mohammadi et al. (eds) *Media in Global Context,* London: Arnold.

Held, D. and McGrew, A. (2003) *The Global Transformations,* Cambridge: Polity.

KBI (1999) *Television Reception Research,* Seoul: Korean Broadcasting Institute.

KWDI (2004) *Statistical Yearbook on Women,* Seoul: Korean Women's Development Institute.

Lull, J. (1991) *China Turned On: Television, Reform and Resistance,* London: Routledge.

——. (1995) *Media, Communication, Culture: A Global Approach,* Cambridge: Polity.

Martin-Barbero, J. (1993) *Communication, Culture and Hegemony: From the Media to Mediations,* London: Sage.

Meyrowitz, J. (1985) *No Sense of Place: The Impact of Electronic Media on Social Behavior,* New York: Oxford University Press.

Morley, D. (1992) *Television, Audiences and Cultural Studies,* London: Routledge.

Robins, K. (2000) "Introduction: Turkish (Television) Culture is Ordinary," *European Journal of Cultural Studies,* 3(3): 291–95.

Schroder, K. C. (1988) "The Pleasure of *Dynasty*: The Weekly Reconstruction of Self-Confidence," in P. Drummond and R. Paterson (eds) *Television and Its Audience: International Research Perspectives,* London: BFI.

Silverstone, R. (1999) *Why Study the Media?* London: Sage.

Skeggs, B. (1995) *Feminist Cultural Theory: Process and Production,* Manchester: Manchester University Press.

Thompson, J. (1995) *The Media and Modernity: A Social Theory of the Media,* Cambridge: Polity.

Tomlinson, J. (1991) *Cultural Imperialism,* London: Pinter.

——. (1999) *Globalization and Culture,* Cambridge: Polity.

Urry, J. (1991) *The Tourist Gaze: Leisure and Travel in Contemporary Societies,* London: Sage.

Walkerdine, V. (1986) "Video Replay: Families, Films and Fantasy," in V. Burgin (ed) *Formations of Fantasy,* London: Methuen.

Williams, R. (1961) *The Long Revolution,* London: Penguin.

——. (1983) *Towards 2000,* London: Hogarth Press.

2 Muslim Media and Youth in Globalizing Southeast Asia

Pamela Nilan

This chapter addresses young people engaging with media texts in Muslim Southeast Asia. It focuses specifically on Indonesia and Malaysia in the Southeast Asian region since these two countries combined have the highest Muslim population outside the Middle East. The specific examples of youth media engagement below are taken from data collected during current and recent research projects. The purpose of their inclusion as examples is to support the wider arguments in the chapter.

Theoretically, the discussion below addresses the limiting nature of Western theories of media engagement that focus on the construction of *individual* subjectivity and/or identity. It questions the paradigm of youthful reflexivity framed around the concept of the isolated, choosing and selecting individual so emphasized in Western youth studies of reflexive practice in late modernity. Reflexive engagement of youth in Southeast Asia with media does not appear to be silent and internal—but lived and talked out endlessly with siblings, cousins and friends as collective practice in face-to-face, cell phone-to-cell phone, and virtual modes of communication. In the discussion below, reflexivity in engagement with media does not imply an isolated, self-surveillant young person.

Although much of Southeast Asia has practiced the Muslim faith for a very long time (Hassan 2002: 23), globalized Islamist culture is a new regional phenomenon. In the 1970s and 1980s, cultural Islam in Southeast Asia was viewed by regional adherents as an alternative modernity for those uncomfortable with Western, capitalist modernity (Brenner 2005). The Malaysian and Indonesian *dakwah* movements of the 1970s and 1980s took a literal, evangelizing approach to Islam as the best religion for the whole world. As with Muslim clothing then (and now), so Muslim youth media and mediated practices constitute a cultural vanguard in the new millennium.

Devout contemporary youth may engage with Muslim media and cultural products not only because these things are *halal* (permitted within the faith) but also because they bestow "blessings." For example, a Koranic script table lamp available at http://www.islamicity.com/bazaar site promises that: "Blessings, Great Looks and Affordability come together . . . " This is "Allah online" (Lawrence 2002), exemplifying the late modern "resacralization" of the public, commercial sphere (see Grace 2004: 48) at a global level. It is claimed that commodified cultural forms such as *nasyid* (traditional Muslim) music (Barendregt 2006: 184) invite youthful consumers in the region to position themselves as members of the Islamic *ummah,* rather than as citizens of nations. According to Hassan (2002), *ummah* is an "all-encompassing unity," where "loyalty to the Islamic ummah overrides any other ethnic, linguistic and geographical loyalties" (94–95). Because of technology, Muslim countries and enclaves in different parts of the world are in much closer contact than ever before. While this is strengthening to the sense of *ummah* in some ways, it also highlights in an unsettling way the variations and hybridity of Islam in the world (Hassan 2002: 110). Media, lying as they do outside the formal mechanisms of the state, play an important role in this process (Starrett 2003: 80).

REFLEXIVITY ENGAGEMENT OF
YOUTH WITH THE MEDIA

Reflexivity is central to contemporary theorizing about reflexive modernity. In late modernity, "the self is reflexively understood by the person in terms of his or her biography" (Giddens 1991: 53). Theorists of "reflexive modernity" advance the idea that we face increasing uncertainty as we move towards a "post-traditional society" (Giddens 1994) in which fixed sources of meaning such as religion, gender, class, marriage, lifetime employment and the nuclear family diminish. This environment of uncertainty encourages the practice of reflexivity to manage one's existence in the risk society (Beck 1992). At the level of personal practice, reflexivity may be understood as a kind of feedback loop of self-evaluation through which we reinvent ourselves to deal with social and economic challenges. This entails self-conscious awareness and self-surveillance, reflection on the self and the presentation of the self. It is claimed that contemporary young people now live their lives more self-consciously—actively planning or projecting themselves imaginatively as individuals into a future adult existence (Nilan, Julian and Germov 2007). However, this claim needs to be mitigated when speaking about youth from non-Western countries since the process of late modern individualization is far from complete.

In Southeast Asia the sense of oneself as a freely choosing isolated individual has not been paramount in cultural traditions. Indeed the *ummah* is antithetical to Western individualism. There is also a traditional tendency in the region to collective praxis. Even today as I conduct research with young people in Indonesia, if I ask in Indonesian about their engagement with media, I am unlikely to obtain a personal response that uses "I"—the first person singular. This is partly linguistic and partly due to talking with a foreigner, but it is also cultural. The first person plural word for we (*kami*—where the interlocutor is excluded) is the most common pronoun used to tell me about media engagement as discursive and collective, respectfully referencing the perceived views and practices of fellow age-peers. For example,

> We can learn something from TV *sinetron* [soap operas]. Maybe because TV *sinetron* nowadays mostly feature a glamorous life style. I think this can motivate us. Sometimes, as teenagers, we have a fantasy about being like those people. So as individuals we can get a positive effect from *sinetron* like that, obviously it can increase our motivation to study hard so that we can become successful people like them. (Rosdiana, female, 18, Muslim mixed male/female focus group, Central Mosque, Makassar, January 2002)

Rosdiana does reference the individual once above, but this merely indicates that not all of the collective "we" she refers to will get a positive effect from watching *sinetron*. In giving account of the engagement of Indonesian teenagers (presumably like herself) with television *sinetron*, she indicates the sequential reflexive process of thinking imaginatively (*sering berangan-angan*) about living the depicted wealthy lifestyle, which then becomes a source of self-motivation for studying harder to succeed. This highlights the problem with theories of media engagement that focus on the construction of individual subjectivity and/or identity. For instance, the teenage computer "geek" in Western accounts is usually depicted alone at a terminal in his bedroom. Yet in Indonesia few homes have internet access. Local internet cafés automatically provide seating for up to three at a single terminal. Young people freely (even joyfully) admit to loyally following the fashions and tastes of their peer group and/or religious community, and to imitating *kakak*—older siblings, cousins, friends and associates. Indonesian youth derive greater pleasure from belonging to, and following, their crowd than from going their own way.

This does not mean that there is no evidence of late modern reflexivity; for instance, I often hear the phrase *introspeksi diri* (self-introspection). Nevertheless, the feedback loop of evaluation about the presentation of the self does not seem to happen primarily through silent, private reflection, or personal reflective blogging in MySpace, but is lived and talked out endlessly with siblings, cousins and friends. The process of reinvention of the self to deal with social and economic challenges, of actively planning or projecting oneself imaginatively into a future adult existence, occurs as intense social practice between age peers, even more so than it does in the West.

In Southeast Asian countries the certainties of past tradition have been decidedly altered by marked economic and political change and globalization. Yet in Malaysia and Indonesia many aspects of tradition remain strong, and most young people remain firmly located in their family networks and local communities. Moreover, there has been a cultural strengthening of religious discourses across the region, providing evidence of re-traditionalization. "Re-traditionalization means the *collective* future consciousness takes over" (Beck 2002: 11; my emphasis). To shore up the future in uncertain times, past traditional practices and understandings may be collectively recovered and re-invented (see Smith-Hefner 2005). In short, rather than looking for evidence of de-traditionalization or its apparent polar opposite, re-traditionalization, it is preferable, as Heelas (1996: 3) suggests, to view de-traditionalization as co-existing alongside re-traditionalization in Islamic media form and content in the region.

SETTING THE SCENE: YOUTH MEDIA IN THE REGION

October 2007 saw the release of the Indonesian teen "chick-flick" film *Cintapuccino,* which fuses the popular theme of *cinta* (love) with an international icon of trendy café culture—the *cappuccino*. The film follows a standard formula of girl (Rahmi) meets boy (Nimo), loses boy, finds boy again, just when she is about to be married to the new love in her life (Raka). The publicity photo was of a young woman sitting between two young men at a modern café bench. They are drinking cups of coffee. The trailer asked: *"Bagaimana Rahmi menghadapi dilema ini?"* (What will Rahmi do?) *"Menguap"* (yawn) wrote one MySpace blogger—*filmkritik*—about the movie. The sixteen lines of dismissive commentary by another MySpace blogger on the day of the film's release are summed up in his/her final word—*"cuek!"* (I really don't care). At the same time, KAMMI—a significant Muslim university student association—posted on its website a condemnation of *Cintapuccino* for encouraging young people to think about *bergaulan bebas* (free sex) and urged Muslim youth to avoid viewing the film. The cinemas were full in the first week of showing.

The example of reactions to *Cintapuccino* illustrates the climate of negotiation and debate over entertainment and leisure for Muslims that informs the development of Muslim youth media in Southeast Asia. As Mowlana says of Iran, "the audiences will turn to foreign satellite television programmes or seek alternative means of entertainment elsewhere" unless popular culture is "Islamicised" (1997: 207–8). Regional media and popular culture products created to solve this problem in Southeast Asia sit alongside the "plenitude" (McCracken 1997) of Western or Western-style youth media and cultural products available. It is common to find that a transregional company/media industry (or subsidiary) has developed a Muslim product to sit alongside its mainstream youth product.

So we find that against Coca Cola there is *Zam Zam* or *Mecca* Cola; against Revlon and Maybelline there are *Wardah* and *Trustee* face, hair and body products (guaranteed *halal*); and designer-label, alcohol-free, *halal* French perfume. An alternative to pop, heavy metal and dance club music is *nasyid*—even rap, reggae and beatbox varieties of *nasyid*. Cover-up Islamic clothing is tweaked in the direction of modern trends (denim, flounces, lace, pinafore style) with toning sequined headscarves. Cell phones can be personalized/Islamized with *nasyid* ringtones, wallpapers, Koranic verses, and so on. The Muslim answer to YouTube (http://www. youtube.com) is HalalTube (http://www.halaltube.com)—powered not by NEC, according to the website, but "by Allah."

Rather than children playing capitalist *Monopoly* there is the faith-building *Quran Challenge*. Little girls can have a Muslim "Barbie" doll, either *Fulla* (designed in Syria, manufactured in China, retailing in both Malaysia or Indonesia) or *Razanne* (designed in the United States, manufactured in China), complete with a range of headscarves and body-concealing outfits, with coordinated prayer mat. Boys can play with the new teenage Muslim superhero *Vimanarama*, who battled a subterranean army of fossil demons in his original outing as a comic book character. *Vimanarama* is available online as an action figure with skull cap and prayer mat. As a final example, in 2005 the Arab satellite TV network MBC created a version of *The Simpsons* to broadcast during Ramadan in both Arabic and English. In the Arabic version, main character *Omar Shamshoon* is Homer Simpson without the beer and bacon who still works at the local nuclear power plant. *Badr* (Bart) is still a cheeky prankster but he prays five times a day. And, yes, Marj's towering beehive hair-do is shrouded in a headscarf. In Indonesia in October 2007, the Muslim-adapted version of *The Simpsons* showed on ANTV during the *Lebaran* holiday, dubbed into Indonesian.

These examples suggest, firstly, that there is a substantial eager market of middle-class Muslim consumers for such products. Secondly, Muslim children and youth can have the same things as their Western counterparts—only *halal*. Thirdly, the majority are Western products that have been Islamized.

ISLAMIC YOUTH PRINT MEDIA—AN
EXAMPLE FROM INDONESIA

Trendy teen magazines for Muslim Indonesian teenage girls came into existence after 1998 in Indonesia, but were never very popular. Hamdani (2007) claims that really devout girls do not read trendy Muslim girls' magazines like *Muslimah*. And I have found that ordinary Muslim girls prefer to read mainstream girls' magazines like *Gadis,* because they are interested in gossip about *artis* and *selebriti* (Indonesian celebrities) and Western celebrities and pop stars. So it does not seem surprising that the market for a magazine like *Muslimah* was relatively low to begin with and fell to the point where publication ceased.

Muslimah covered some teen girl topics similar to the mainstream Indonesian girls' magazines *Gadis* and *Anneka*, but did so within *dakwah* (rules of Islam) discourse. The editors steered a path between keeping firmly to Islamic orthodoxy and encouraging frivolous pursuits. A 2004 editorial illustrates this negotiation:

God willing *(Insya Allah)*, we will continue to have your support, dear readers. Many wonderful things have happened since we began. From the beginning we grew and grew until we had to move premises. Our loyal readers know that there have been significant changes to our layout ... In this special birthday edition, as your guiding friend, we brighten your day with an inspiring spread from the world of Muslim women's fashion. We also debate birthdays. Three celebrities talk about birthday parties. In fact, dear readers, they all agree that money should not be squandered, only just enough spent to celebrate the day. In the future, *Muslimah* wants to continue to be a supportive friend to all our readers, so look out for us all through the year, identify with us, keep supporting us. Hey, you are the voice of our crusade, right? Whatever happens, our goal is the same, to promote the rapid expansion of Islam. Happy reading! *(Muslimah* 2004: 4)

The chatty tone is conveyed in the translation. Youth slang terms such as *banget, lho, tapi, kok, nggak, nih* were used. The hybridity of the text is striking. Mixing teen talk, promotional hype, and invocations of *Allah,* the editorial ends with a clarion cry for young readers to position themselves within the global Muslim "crusade," to see themselves as engaged in "the rapid expansion of Islam"—by reading the magazine and wearing the fashions. However, the authenticity of commitment to the collaborative project of faith was dubious. Discussing the publication of *Muslimah,* Hamdani (2007: 106) notes "a rumour in circulation that the PT Variapop Group also owns Tabloid Pop, a porn magazine" (see http://www.lenijuwita.wordpress.com for the same claim). As news of this circulated *Muslimah* finally stopped publication.

Another Muslim teen girl magazine in Indonesia is *Annida,* which treads a more orthodox religious line. Yet *Annida* too is struggling. So how do young Muslim women engage with a magazine like *Annida?* Between August and late November 2007 I undertook fieldwork and data collection in the city of Solo in Central Java. While based at Sebelas Maret University in Solo I was given a desk and chair in the main lecturers' office of the Department of Media and Communications. The following excerpt from my fieldnotes describes an early visit from three second year female Media and Communications students. I was shown a copy of *Annida:*

Around midday I was descended upon by Fatimah, Tutik and Hidayat, who pulled up chairs at my desk ... Fatimah had with her a Muslim girls' magazine called *Annida.* It seemed to have a lot more about *dakwah* than *Muslimah.* I said, "What is that you are reading, Fatimah?" and she told me in English that it was a magazine for Muslim female students who want to travel overseas. She showed me a dog-eared (obviously well-read) article about a young Muslim Indonesian woman wearing the *jilbab* who had studied and travelled in Europe by herself.

She pointed to a page full of photos of the young author on holiday snapped in Amsterdam, Paris, Hamburg, Copenhagen and so on. Fatimah and Tutik talked excitedly to me in Indonesian about this article and their own travel plans. Hidayat was making a list to show me—of countries she would like to visit.

Later I could find no evidence that *Annida* was intended specifically for "Muslim female students who want to travel overseas"—this might be a mis-translation. However, there is no mistaking what was of interest for Fatimah and her friends, aged nineteen to twenty: travel and study abroad. Later discussions with Fatimah revealed that what inspired her about the sprinkling of overseas study and travel articles in *Annida* was the idea that "an Indonesian girl like me who wears the *jilbab* can do that, can go there, and go to those places. I really want to see those countries." This response indicates a reflexive awareness on her part of the implicit conservative feminine subject position offered to young Muslim women, that they should stay close to home under the guidance of their parents until they marry. But Fatimah is inspired by the image and story of the girl who wears the *jilbab* and yet travels independently to foreign countries.

Later, looking through *Annida* together, I asked her, "What about the stories? There are lots of stories. Do you read them?" She replied, "Sometimes. But I just love to read about Muslim female students who travel overseas." It was clear that Fatimah and her friends spent a lot of time talking about their favourite topic—actively planning and projecting themselves imaginatively into a future young adult existence of overseas study and travel, and that they made use of the media text *Annida* as a special (Muslim) cultural resource for doing so (see Kim 2006). However, in their collective, selective reading, they seemed to pay relatively little attention to other kinds of articles, images and instructions in the magazine, including short fiction.

This may have been because the "heroine" (and author) of the "real-life" travel adventure narratives was a competent and confident young Indonesian woman they perceived to be very much like themselves. And the messages of the travel narratives—venture forth, be independent, have fun, learn new things, meet new people—were neither morally didactic nor theologically ambiguous, unlike the warning messages offered by short fiction, which is perhaps why Fatimah and her friends were not drawn to read the stories in *Annida*.

In the February 2007 issue of *Muslimah*, Muti had finally broken free from the control of her evil uncle. She gets a job at a photo-copy shop, but then during a routine delivery, two men try to abduct her into a car at knife-point. She manages to escape. Later, talking with her room-mates at the *kost* (boarding house) where she lives, her friend Endang says, "The thing is, why did these men want to kidnap you? Did they want to sell you? Nowadays there are many more cases of girls being kidnapped for prostitution overseas" (Dala F 2007: 111). Muti instantly thinks this could be true.

> Muti listened, feeling suddenly frightened. That could be a possibility. Up until recently [when she put on the headscarf] men had been struck with amazement at her beauty. However, now she didn't wear smart clothes, expensive perfume and cosmetics as she had before. But still she was very beautiful. Could Endang's suggestion possibly be true? That the men who had been following her wanted to make her into a prostitute? (Dala F 2007: 111)

This is rather contradictory because although now Muti wears the Muslim headscarf and covers up her body in flowing garments (the accompanying pictures show this), and by her own admission no longer wears make-up, she is still so beautiful that (in the story) bad men might want to turn her into a prostitute. So the logic of this is that putting on the large *jilbab* and full Muslim dress has not diminished her compelling effect on men and she is attacked anyway. This might not seem an attractive message for young Muslim women who believe, for instance, that they can travel the world with the protection of their Koran, their headscarf and cover-up clothing.

Moreover, there is a great deal of contrast between the victim subject position of Muti in the fictional text, and the agentic, independent subject position of the headscarf-wearing teen authors of the "real-life" study and travel abroad articles so favored by Fatimah and her friends. The narrative of a young Indonesian woman who fearlessly wears her *jilbab* into foreign places is a far more positive and rich source of textual reference for the reflexive construction of a successful future self than tortured, wilting fictional heroines like Muti.

MUSLIM VISUAL MEDIA IN SOUTHEAST ASIA—AN EXAMPLE FROM MALAYSIA

The example from Malaysia deals with a completely different genre of media text, and moves the focus to young men and their media text preferences. Malaysia has long had a local film industry, but there have not been many attempts so far to produce a popular yet sophisticated Muslim-themed film for export. The discussion below looks at two Malaysian-made Muslim-themed films.

When *nasyid* music group *Raihan*, "one of Malaysia's most popular pop groups" (Barendregt 2006: 171), decided to create the Islam-meets-science-fiction film *Syukur 21* (Thanks be to God in 2021) for release during Ramadan 2000, perhaps they believed it would be a popular film because they are so popular. The futurist film is set in the hyper-modern Asian super city of Raudah. Devout Muslim citizens live in peace and harmony with no crime. Children learn to recite the Koran from hand-held computers. There is a lot of praying. Fifty-year-old Kamal (divorce looming) has been living and working in the United States of America in multimedia programming. He is posted to Raudah, rediscovers his Islamic roots and his life is transformed. *Syukur 21* was directed by Eddie Pak, who does not regard it as a success. Although the film initially attracted audiences in Malaysia during Ramadan 2000, subsequently it failed to recoup production costs. Malaysian reviews dismissed it as tedious and cheesy. Producer David Teo does not regard it as a success either, although originally he thought it might "crack the box-office" in neighboring countries like Indonesia and Thailand (Lee 2006). But this did not happen. Teo has decided the answer for Malaysian export viability is action movies. His latest action movie *Rempit* is about a truly transregional youth pastime: illegal street motorbike racing.

Although *Raihan* is now as popular as ever, the same cannot be said of *Syukur 21*, which is now seen only on television during *Ramadan*. The faltering trajectory of *Syukur 21* is similar to the decline of *Muslimah* in Indonesia. Firstly, both texts addressed a niche audience of devout-but-trendy young Muslims that may not exist in substantial numbers. Secondly, both texts were limited by their didactic mission to encourage respectable conformity within the *ummah* at every turn, a tricky formula when it comes to engaging the wider cross-section of Muslim youth who dislike being moralized at and are used to being entertained.

A current attempt at an export-oriented Islamic visual media product out of Malaysia is the animated film and series about Saladin. The target audience is Muslim children world-wide, aged ten to twelve, although given the taste for cartoons and animation in Asia (Lent 2006), it is likely an older demographic will swell the audience for this action-packed war epic. Saladin is *Salah Al-Din Yusuf Ibn Ayyub,* the twelfth-century Kurdish-born Muslim warrior leader who drove the Christian armies from Jerusalem after eighty-eight years of Crusader rule and united the Muslim world, becoming one of the most significant caliphs. Saladin clearly stands for all Muslims. The slogan "Saladin—in Man's darkest hour, he was the beacon of hope" implies a specifically Muslim mankind.

The (currently unfinished) thirteen-episode series and film will be marketed in Indonesia, India, Pakistan, Turkey, the Middle East, North Africa, China and the West. So far the six-minute trailer for the Saladin film has won two animation awards in Asia. The Saladin text signifies a synthesis of de-traditionalization and re-traditionalization in the specific context of Muslim Southeast Asian media production. It uses a popular contemporary high technology process—3-D digital animation—to depict a heroic period in the past, the Golden Age of Islam. Like many other Islamic media products aimed at youth, it invites young Muslims to proudly position themselves within the *ummah*. Examples of online responses considered below indicate that this was the case to a certain extent. However, a reflexive and even antagonistic process of identity meaning-making was also going on in responses to the Saladin text.

The trailer shows a dramatic battle scene between Saladin's lightly clad army and well-provisioned Christian enemies at sea. Saladin's athletic, smartly led warriors are victorious over the encumbered, rigidly armored Crusaders, who sink helpless to the seabed when their ships are burned. The trailer features the usual kinds of startling computer-generated visual effects, and a soundtrack of dramatic vocal harmonizing and synthesizer sounds. Although it is likely that the real campaign warrior Saladin would have been muscular, with a tanned unshaven face, here he is very pale, slender, fine-boned and thin-faced, clean-shaven except for a neat fringe of beard. Referencing the cosmopolitanism of contemporary Islam he looks neither like a Kurd nor a Malaysian, nor an African, nor an Arab, nor a Turk, nor a Pakistani. His Anglo enemy King Richard is red-faced, huge, overweight and square-jawed—a stereotypical philistine cum Western bully army commander. Neither character shows much facial expression. Saladin's lightly pitched philosophical voice-over commentary on the battle is in English, with an Arabic accent.

The synthesis of the traditional and the contemporary cosmopolitan in the depiction of Saladin was offensive to some of many online young commentators (almost exclusively male). As one Malaysian blogger complained:

> Why does Saladin look like something out of Disney or Dreamworks (kind of a Prince-of-Egypt white-guy version of the man, I feel)? And why does he have to speak English with an "Arabic" accent? I mean, Chinese characters in English cartoons don't speak with a "Chinese" accent, so why should this renowned 12th century Kurdish Muslim warrior speak with that "Middle-Eastern" accent? (anon. http://www.mrbrown.com August 2006)

Another online comment, referring to the nineteen-year old Saladin in the cartoon, complained, "I think they should have drawn a beard onto Al-Ayyubi" (anon. http://www.muslimhiphop.com December 2006). In the end, though, as another blogger pointed out, "No matter how historically inaccurate the animated feature turns out to be, it's a monumental step for a country many Muslims once considered to be an outpost of the ummah" (anon. http://higher-criticism.blogspot.com October 2006). And as Vanzwan wrote on YouTube, "Good job!!! Excellent!! *Mmg mantap* proud to be a Muslim and Malaysian . . ." (http://www.youtube.com December 2006). Another wrote:

> God, I'm so amazed!!! Make me wanna go back to drawing instantly!! Hopefully this will be a great new start not jz for Malaysians to develop our own animation industry but to educate our kids with the real spirit of Islam in their heart. (Audishah http://www.youtube.com March 2007)

It proclaims both a nationalist and a Muslim project identity through engagement with the Saladin trailer. Other comments indicated nationalist pride with a touch of cultural cringe. "As a Malaysian, this is the first time I feel proud of my country film. Of course its not as good as Hollywood animation but indeed it is very impressive and it is even Islamic . . ." (Zenx6 http://www.youtube.com March 2007). Yet other YouTube comments on the Saladin trailer praised Allah while asking whether the final film or series could be downloaded free. For example, "Nice. Allah u Akbar . . . I hope when this series comes out that someone uploads it . . . subhanallah" (ImmortalPredator http://www.youtube.com January 2007). In summary, responses online to the Saladin trailer indicate that the film and series may appeal in a different way from *Syukur 21* to a much larger audience in Malaysia, and perhaps in the region. This may be because it offers reflexive engagement through invited pride in a heroic collective identity, while offering action-packed animation entertainment.

Yet this was not the way all young commentators responded online to the Saladin trailer. A highly emotional argument broke out between young Turkish and Kurdish commentators who (reading selectively) insisted on pulling the Saladin story into the realms of ethno-nationalism. Their exchanges elicited the following angry response (reproduced verbatim from a longer message), posted by a young male Malaysian blogger. He was very upset that the unifying Muslim symbol of Saladin had been transformed into an ethnic dispute:

> Wtf with all you ppl? Who fuckin care if he's Kurds or Arab or any other races? It won't change the world!!! It's because of you ppl the reason why Muslims won't be united. I would say fuck with that imagination! Keep on hating and killing each other!!! That's what you guys know the best isn't it?? Fuck with your pride and fucking history!!! LEARN THE BASICS OF ISLAM!!! PATHETIC PEOPLE! Disgrace to all Muslims . . . (Feaddy22 http://www.youtube.com January 2007)

This extreme response and the online argument it refers to indicate that the engagement of youth with Muslim media texts is, finally, as little determined by the intentions of producers as any other form of media. The meanings that these young male online commentators derive from the Saladin trailer are quite obviously their own, yet they refer implicitly to collective identities of various kinds. In its way, the strongly worded response above is just as reflexive an example of media engagement as any of the other postings, because the writer is actively positioning himself as the defender of the *ummah* against the perceived fracturing *risk* posed by nationalistic concerns. This almost instantaneous cross-national Muslim youth dialogue is only possible because of technology. Because Muslim countries and people in different parts of the world are in much closer contact now than ever before, this highlights in an unsettling way the variations and hybridity of Islam in the world (Hassan 2002: 110). Young Muslims online now make sense of their lives not only through local engagements of faith, but through the cultural experience of Islamic practice and discussion on a global stage. The anger expressed in the posting above constitutes not so much reflexive self-surveillance in the Western sense, but a form of reflexive surveillance of community in which self and *ummah* seem to be indistinguishable.

CONCLUSION

In the light of contemporary debates about late modern media engagement, this chapter has emphasized through example the limiting nature of Western theories of media engagement that focus on the construction of *individual* subjectivity and/or identity. It has also implied the simultaneity of de-traditionalization and re-traditionalization in Southeast Asian youth media trends. It has also indicated the way that Muslim media are used as cultural resources by young people in the region to constitute identity claims.

The Indonesian example above indicates that contemporary young middle-class Indonesian Muslim women now live their lives more self-consciously—actively planning or projecting themselves imaginatively into an exciting future adult existence—yet still primarily in a group context. The Malaysian example indicates that the constitution of the *ummah* through the popular culture consumption of Muslim male youth tends to be a fractured process where ethno-local collective identities often come into play. Both the Indonesian and the Malaysian examples point to the phenomenon of selective engagement by young consumers with Muslim media texts, where apparently minor elements or aspects of the whole text are focused upon and drawn out into wider projects pertaining to collective, rather than individual, identity projects. In both cases, these are contested discourses within pan-global Islam: the first example implies debates about the proper position of women, and the second example points to ethno-local disputes between different Islamic cultures that threaten the *ummah.*

In closing, it is worth noting that the specialized Muslim youth consumer market in Southeast Asia seems to have existed more in the minds of media producers with the money and/or the faith than in actuality, if we are to judge by the many failures of targeted Muslim media products to thrive. In looking for explanations, one only has to stroll the streets and shopping malls in the region after high school lets out for the day to see, for example, that girls who wear the headscarf do not exclusively band together as friends. Groups of male friends, too, vary in their piety. The strict exclusive groupings of Islamist youth constitute only a tiny minority of young media consumers compared to the masses of Muslim youth of varying degrees of piety who occupy mutually convivial urban space. When Muslim youth do engage with specialized Islamic youth media products, they do so utilizing creative processes of selection and synthesis, working reflexively, and most often collectively, with those media texts to build their own social worlds and future lives.

REFERENCES

Barendregt, B. (2006) "Cyber-*nasyid:* Transnational Soundscapes in Muslim Southeast Asia," in T. Holden and T. Scrase (eds) *Medi@sia: Global Media In and Out of Context,* London: Routledge.

Beck, U. (1992) *Risk Society: Towards a New Modernity,* London: Sage.

———. (2002) "The Cosmopolitan Society and Its Enemies," *Theory, Culture and Society,* 19(1): 17–44.

Brenner, S. (2005) "Islam and Gender Politics in Late New Order Indonesia," in A. Willford and K. George (eds) *Spirited Politics: Religion and Public Life in Contemporary Southeast Asia,* Ithaca: Cornell Southeast Asia Program Publications.

Dala F, A. T. (2007) "Cinta Untuk Muti" [Love for Muti], *Muslimah,* February: 108–11.

Giddens, A. (1991) *Modernity and Self-Identity: Self and Society in the Late Modern Age,* Cambridge: Polity.

———. (1994) "Living in a Post-Traditional Society," in U. Beck et al. (eds) *Reflexive Modernization: Politics, Tradition and Aesthetics in the Modern Social Order,* Cambridge: Polity.

Grace, G. (2004) "Making Connections for Future Directions: Taking Religion Seriously in the Sociology of Education," *International Studies in Sociology of Education,* 14(1): 47–56.

Hamdani, (2007) "The Quest for Indonesian Islam: Contestation and Consensus Concerning Veiling," PhD thesis in Pacific and Asian Studies, Australian National University.

Hassan, R. (2002) *Faithlines: Muslim Conceptions of Islam and Society,* Oxford: Oxford University Press.

Heelas, P. (1996) "Introduction: Detraditionalization and Its Rivals," in P. Heelas et al. (eds) *Detraditionalization,* Oxford: Blackwell.

Kim, Y. (2006) "The Body, TV Talk, and Emotion: Methodological Reflections," *Cultural Studies & Critical Methodologies,* 6(2): 226–24.

Lawrence, B. (2002) "Allah Online: The Practice of Global Islam in the Information Age," in S. Hoover and L. Clark (eds) *Practicing Religion in the Age of the Media,* New York: Columbia University Press.

Lee, D. (2006) "Teo's Movie-Making Tao." http://www.star-central.com/default.asp

Lent, J. (2006) "Comic Art in Asian Cultural Context," in T. Holden and T. Scrase (eds) *Medi@sia: Global Media In and Out of Context,* London: Routledge.

McCracken, G. (1997) *Plenitude: Culture by Commotion,* Toronto: Fluide.

Mowlana, H. (1997) "Islamicising the Media in a Global Era: The State-Community Perspective in Iranian Broadcasting," in K. Robins (ed) *Programming for People: From Cultural Rights to Cultural Responsibilities,* New York: UN Television Forum.

Muslimah (2004) no. 25, August, Jakarta and Kuala Lumpur: PT. Variapop Grup.

Nilan, P., Julian, R. and Germov, J. (2007) *Australian Youth: Social and Cultural Issues*, Melbourne: Pearson Education.

Smith-Hefner, N. (2005) "The New Muslim Romance: Changing Patterns of Courtship and Marriage among Educated Javanese Youth," *Journal of Southeast Asian Studies*, 36(3): 441–59.

Starrett, G. (2003) "Muslim Identities and the Great Chain of Buying," in D. Eickleman and J. Anderson (eds) *New Media in the Muslim World: The Emerging Public Sphere*, Bloomington: Indiana University Press.

3 Reimagining Tradition
Globalization in India from MTV to Hanuman

Vamsee Juluri

Since the implementation of economic liberalization policies in the early 1990s and the rise of satellite television, India has witnessed a media and cultural transformation on a scale so profound that it raises many questions for students of globalization, media, and audience studies. One of the biggest challenges worth noting is the fact that the enormous growth in media in this time has not resulted in a simple process of Westernization. Instead, most global media corporations have been forced to localize their programming in some form or another, even as the substantial local media industries in India such as the Hindi film industry (popularly known as "Bollywood") held their own and confronted globalization in a number of ways. As a result of these localization strategies, the Indian mediascape has come to be marked by narratives and discourses that seek to join the foreign and the domestic, the global and the national, the modern and the traditional, and the scientific and the religious.

There is no dearth of examples of such seemingly contradictory articulations in the media and everyday life in India. When an Indian-American space shuttle astronaut's return from a mission is delayed, the news channels show Indian school children attending religious ceremonies to pray for her return. When the time-honored festival of Dasara rolls around, organizers see no harm in setting up a Harry Potter–themed canopy in which to worship the goddess. The global and the local, and the modern and the traditional, appear to occupy a position of not just harmony, but of a happy triumph even. A best-selling book in India promises in its title to show "The truth about why the twenty first century will be India's" (Varma 2004), and much of that truth is seemingly about the adaptability of Indians to remake their traditions and cultures for a changing world. It is therefore no surprise that surveys of Indian youth have repeatedly found that young, middle-class Indians espouse traditional values such as respect for elders, family, and marriage on the one hand, as well as more contemporary or modern values such as competitiveness, aspirational mobility, and consumerist pleasure, on the other (Chawla 2005; Gahlaut 2005).

Such examples raise the question of whether globalization in India has been a process of mere cooperation, or one of cooptation instead.

Scholarship on Indian media in recent years has focused on the broader context of the rise of right-wing political and cultural forces in India in the wake of economic liberalization (Rajagopal 2001). In an especially telling narrative, Sunil Khilnani (1999) describes how a group of religious ascetics visited the site of India's nuclear tests in 1998 to gather the dust from there, ostensibly to "peddle" it as a sacred symbol of Hindu India's resurgence after centuries of conquest by alien invaders of different faiths. While vested political acts such as these may warrant criticism for their symbolic attempt to infuse religious identity into politics, the question of the media's role in reimagining tradition for the global age may be better served by turning the focus of inquiry from the actions of political parties and their religious propaganda ploys to the specificities of media institutions, texts, and audience reception practices. This chapter therefore seeks to shift the attention of media studies of globalization in South Asia from politics in general to a closer look at the meanings that arise in relation to important issues like tradition, religion, nation, and the world, particularly in media consumption.

My aim in this chapter is to highlight the discursive contours of this media transformation and address some pressing questions about cultural imperialism, globalization, and audience studies in the process. I begin by outlining some theoretical questions about tradition and global modernity, and go on to discuss three examples of how tradition is reimagined in global media consumption, using three case studies. The first case addresses the phenomenon of "pop nationalism" that arose in the mid to late 1990s, and evaluates the ways in which young viewers interpreted national and global discourses on music television channels like MTV and Channel V. The second case examines how the family was reimagined as a site of investment in post-liberalization India in the reception of *Hum Aapke Hain Koun,* a very successful and popular Hindi film that wed consumerism, religion, and old-fashioned values in a compelling manner in the minds (and hearts) of its viewers. The third case is based on an ongoing study and explores how religion is being reimagined in a new genre, the animated mythological.

THEORIZING GLOBALIZATION, TRADITION, AND MODERNITY

It may be useful to clarify the use of the term "tradition" in this chapter, as it tends to imply either a belief in an essentialist, ahistorical, unchanging past, on the one hand (a politically conservative viewpoint), or a cynical view that holds all tradition as invented, fabricated, and somehow politically nefarious (a common pitfall of a politically liberal viewpoint), on the other. Given the natural proclivity of critical cultural studies approaches towards the latter, the following discussion does engage with the idea of tradition as being (re)invented constantly (Giddens 1990), but without reducing all claims of tradition to a politically conservative conspiracy. I therefore approach the use of the term "retraditionalization" (Mohammadi and Mohammadi 1994) somewhat cautiously in the context of post-global Indian media consumption, especially since my concern is not so much with the terrain of official, sanctioned, or institutionalized (and politicized) "tradition" (as seen, for instance, in the propaganda of right-wing political parties), employed as a reaction against globalization, as it is with the ways that the non-modern and the modern negotiate with each other in popular media reception practices.

The need for such an approach arises not only from the encounter of audience studies with global media studies (Murphy and Kraidy 2003), but from a deeper problem with how the question of tradition, especially in the context of so-called traditional, developing, or third world societies, is treated in Western academic discourses. While the dominant paradigm of international communication in particular and the social sciences in general conceived of tradition as an inherent impediment of third world nations to their development and modernization (especially in the heyday of such studies in the 1950s and 1960s), the critical approaches in international communication also tended to see tradition in rather static and passive terms, despite their good intentions. Thus, the cultural imperialism thesis, while remaining apt and compelling in its relevance in terms of its warnings about the political economy of media globalization, may be rightly faulted for its view of third world audiences as being merely victims of global or Western media (Buell 1994).

It is important, in other words, to acknowledge the values and investments that the "traditional" may carry in the meanings made by audiences, even as these meanings may be seen as the ways that they negotiate determinate conditions of modernity. I therefore approach the traditional in the following sections not so much as either an opposite of modernity or even as a self-conscious category for audiences, but as a way of engaging with non-modern ideas and practices that underlie their reading of media discourses.

Such an engagement is useful not only as a way of acknowledging the agency of postcolonial media audiences in discussions of media globalization, but also from the point of view of reexamining the assumption of cultural imperialism as a simple process of Westernization. As the following case studies indicate, the advent of global media in India since 1991 has not merely replaced traditional, indigenous, or national culture in any sweeping homogenizing sense with a monolithic Western or global one. This is evident not only in the localization strategies of global media institutions (Chadha and Kavoori 2000), but also in the ways that audiences interpret and negotiate meanings of media texts that attest to their abiding investment in notions of family, nation, and religion. However, neither the relative agency of audiences in negotiating meanings nor the seeming capitulation of Western-owned media corporations to local market tastes are causes for celebration. In the following sections, I outline the ways that media consumption has negotiated the meanings of important terms such as family, nation, and religion as part of the broader process in which tradition is reimagined in globalization.

REIMAGINING THE NATION: MTV AND CHANNEL V

In the wake of the Gulf War in 1991, the Hong Kong–based Star TV network began to provide MTV along with a handful of channels that were quickly picked up in India. However, the first concerted effort to localize began in 1994, with the start of Channel V, a part of the Star TV network (which had itself been acquired by News Corporation). MTV returned to India in its local avatar, known as MTV India, shortly thereafter. Both channels vied to appear more Indian than the other (Juluri 2003). The localization strategy encompassed a number of dimensions, ranging from the use of Hindi film songs as music videos to the use of American and Canadian VJs of Indian heritage, and the exoticization of Indian everyday life in promos (such as the popular South Indian film cowboy character Quick Gun Murugan and quirky Indian-English phrases like "V are like this only").

The imperative for localization was manifold. It included a recognition of the potential of Indian film culture as a source of programming for the audience, as well as the peculiar demands that the demographic, and in particular, the generational nature of Indian audiences were presenting. Channel V, for example, decided to present itself as a youth channel in attitude, but a family channel in demographics. One implication of this strategy was that music television acquired a form that seemed to be exotic and nonreverential enough to appeal to the young, but also played it safe by emphasizing themes such as patriotism. The best example of this phenomenon was the music video of singer Alisha Chinai's "Made in India."

"Made in India" was not only the first ever pop song (not from a movie) to attain commercial success, but its lyrics and video narrative provided what turned out to be the first global narrative for Indian audiences. The video tells the story of a princess who is wooed by suitors from different countries, and she turns them all down to select a man who comes in a box labeled "made in India"; a not subtle allegory, perhaps, for the ways that Indians were thinking about globalization. By the late 1990s, pop nationalism had manifested itself quite widely on music television, and, in conjunction with other media discourses, seemed to advocate a view of globalization not as a foreign invasion but instead as something good for India, a way for India to take its rightful place in the world.

An interesting feature of this phenomenon was the ways that young music television viewers identified with these discourses. In my study of music television audiences (Juluri 2003), participants expressed a distinction between "patriotism," which they thought of as something the government ordered people to exhibit, and the "feeling" of "being Indian," which they found in videos like "Made in India," as the following comments suggest:

> They tell us about worshipping the nation but not about the feeling, the Indian feeling. (Translated from Telugu.)

> Not a patriotic song, but has a lot of meaning in it.

> When you see the song, the feeling comes . . . [that] . . . among all the husbands in the world it is the Indian husband who loves the most. (Translated from Telugu.)

It is also interesting that participants described their national identity in terms of familial and relational values, such as "being a good husband." While acknowledging that audiences did indeed feel represented by narratives such as this, the question remains: Did audiences also accept the terms on which these narratives offered them representations seemingly of themselves, terms that are not only ideological, for instance, in their naturalizing of a consumerist view of nationalism, but are also troubling in their visual repertoire? I have characterized the look of these music videos as "self orientalism," and suggested that the ways that music television audiences interpret being Indian is sincere in its yearning but ideologically flawed in its acceptance of the many disturbing terms of its discourse. Thus, even as audiences may desire to interpret globalization in traditional terms such as commitment to marriage, they are brought into a newer discursive regime in their engagement with the media.

REIMAGINING THE FAMILY: *HUM AAPKE HAIN KOUN*

Even as music television cashed in on the enduring popularity of Indian cinema, the latter remade itself sharply in response to a number of global forces during the 1990s. These forces ranged from the stylistic impact of MTV on film songs to the rise of a new genre of youth-oriented films that were accurately described as the "Riverdale" phase of Bollywood, in a reference to the popular *Archie* comics series (Joseph 2000). Despite these seeming changes in the direction of global media trends, the narrative thrust of Indian cinema veered strongly in the direction of family and tradition in the mid-1990s (a trend that is sometimes attributed to the nostalgia of the growing Indian global diaspora for such themes).

Hum Aapke Hain Koun (Who am I to You?), released in 1994, was an immensely popular and successful movie that was in many ways a good indicator of how popular sentiment in India was dealing with the vast changes globalization had brought in since 1991. The movie barely registers the presence of the growing global consumer culture in India (a pet dog drinks Coke, and the protagonist's brother, we are told, travels abroad to set up a business partnership), but instead focuses on the rich, festive, and entirely pleasant setting of a wedding in a wealthy family, with many relatives, friends, and servants in attendance. Participants in my study of the reception of this film (Juluri 1999) often compared the experience of watching this movie to being at a wedding, and the convivial atmosphere in the theaters, with their festive and well-dressed audiences, certainly supported this observation.

If the localization of music television enabled audiences to interpret globalization as the resurgence of the nation in a global arena, the unabashedly happy narrative and setting of *Hum Aapke Hain Koun* allowed a rediscovery of the family within a broader idea of the tradition in which family is located—an important resource for Indians during a period of globalization and rapid modernization, as the following comments indicate:

It was all about family values in a changing society.

Not too many families are happy these days.

[The family in the movie was] traditional with a modern outlook.

They [the family in the movie] have taken modern amenities, but are rooted in tradition.

These statements suggest that the characters in the movie, and their actions, were being perceived as an idealized vision of families in a time of globalization; they could reap its benefits (the protagonists are a wealthy business family) and enjoy consumerist pleasures (songs about chocolates and ice cream), but unlike the nefarious and feuding business families of TV soap operas, remain loyal, respectful, and entirely loving to one another.

While the values and sentiments implied in audience interpretations of *Hum Aapke Hain Koun* are commendable, drawing on a social philosophy of selflessness and sacrifice (an important element in the narrative), the social context of selfish, individualistic consumerism in which its reception took place belies its easy celebration. One fall out, for instance, of this movie was the fact that wedding ceremonies in India began to be greatly influenced by the depiction of the idealized, wealthy, harmonious weddings in this movie. Despite the wide variations in customs and ceremonies across regional and caste communities in India in terms of wedding practices, the specifically North Indian, Hindu, upper-caste practices depicted in the movie began to be widely emulated. As one participant noted, "everyone wants their marriage to be like *Hum Aapke Hain Koun*."

Hum Aapke Hain Koun was in many ways a classic example of tradition being reinvented in a new idiom, in this case, one of wealth and spectacular consumerism. The naturalization of class differences and wealth in reception was in evidence during my study, and it is notable that while most middle- and upper-class participants identified with the wedding customs (although they were from very different communities than the fictional protagonists), working-class participants distanced themselves instead. Even if they expressed these distances in ethnic rather than class terms, it is apparent that the grounds of privilege on which *Hum Aapke Hain Koun*'s utopia rests were more or less accepted as normal by the middle and upper class participants. As I show in the final section of this chapter, this change in the understanding of privilege is perhaps the most important consequence of the ways that audiences are reimagining themselves as a consequence of globalization.

REIMAGINING RELIGION: HANUMAN

Some of the most important implications of globalization have to do with the question of religion. Although the connections between economic globalization and the rise of right-wing political forces claiming to represent religious identities have been often discussed, what is relevant in the case of media globalization in India is the broader and deeper ways in which religion continues to play out as a form of culture, more than anything else. As Rachel Dwyer's (2006) timely study of religion in Indian cinema shows, there are many more ways in which religion figures in Indian media than as a mere conspiracy perpetrated by the recently ascendant right-wing parties.

The most telling case study of this phenomenon is the rise of a new genre in television and film, the animated mythological. Mythology movies and television serials have a strong history in Indian popular culture. The Indian film industry was dominated by the mythology genre during the first half of twentieth century (and even longer in South India), and since the 1980s, epic myths such as the *Mahabharatha* and *Ramayana* have been a popular and prolific feature on state and private television. While the older mythology movies were closer in their inspiration to the values of Mahatma Gandhi and the freedom struggle than to right-wing political forces (Dwyer 2007), present-day animated mythologicals raise a number of questions about how the stories of religion are being reinvented and experienced in a society in which the religious and non-religious are not clearly separated to begin with.

In 2005, a feature-length animated movie entitled *Hanuman,* about the beloved monkey-god, released to widespread success. It heralded a new genre of animated mythologicals that retold the familiar stories of Hindu gods and goddesses, but derived much of its form from the Western style fantasy and superhero genres. Hanuman was now experienced, especially by children, not only as a deity but also as a friendly superhero-like figure, with stuffed-toy merchandize available in the many new shopping malls of India. Since *Hanuman,* a number of other myth-inspired animated movies and TV serials have been made, including the rather aptly titled *My Friend Ganesha,* about the cherubic elephant-god, and a sequel to *Hanuman* was also in production in late 2007.

How young audiences interpret these films and TV shows (and perhaps soon, video games too) will no doubt have many consequences for religion and culture in a rapidly globalizing world. One indication from my ongoing study of the mythology genre in India is that there is a narrative shift from the older movies to the new animated superhero-type films, and this shift may have important epistemic implications for the audiences of these films as well. *Hanuman,* for example, presents its story with a rather didactic first-person voiceover ("my birth was indeed unusual," "knowledge and devotion is the mission of my life") in which the names of the gods, their relationships, and a lot of other details are presented as if these are somehow more important than the story, or the ethical message of the story (which were what were valued perhaps in popular mythology). At the same time, the film also seeks to make the deity/character more contemporary, for instance, featuring a child-Hanuman surfing over the rings of Saturn and effecting American colloquial sayings ("Yum!").

Some of these changes are perhaps what led one of the participants in my ongoing study, the father of a young girl who is a fan of the film, to comment that the film "fails to rise above its own story-telling." This comment echoes a number of comparisons made by participants between *Hanuman* and the older mythology movies, pointing perhaps to the ways in which the particular reinvention of popular religion in the era of globalization is facing a number of contradictions between the pulls of commercialism on the one hand and a more popular cultural expectation of a deity's representation on the other.

> Animated versions are more like fiction, whereas the old Telugu mythologicals are more real, and make you feel that yes, Rama and Krishna existed.

> These movie makers make a mistake in underestimating the sophistication of our Indian audience and their intelligence. Even children understand valor, fairness, devotion and value it more than mischief and cuteness, however much advertised.

The mythological is seen by some participants as indeed closer to reality or history than fiction, and the animated version is seen as somehow bringing it closer to the latter. While the questions of faith and belief that this finding raises are too complex to be discussed in this chapter, what is of relevance here is the fact that despite their belief in the "reality" of mythology or religious stories, participants do not necessarily impose their faith in any one definitive or monolithic account of the same. They are, in other words, open to the idea of traditional stories about the gods being retold for their children, despite their reservations that commercialism somehow leads to a dilution of the values they would like to see the stories reflect. Another participant, also a parent, writes about the Hanuman toy:

> I've seen the soft toy . . . I think it's rather cute. No problem with this . . . children adore Hanuman and I am sure he's better to have as a security blanket than a teddy bear. My daughters in any case, have a small god picture under their pillows when they sleep.

While there is no indication in my study thus far of parents trying to impose one meaning or another on their children's relationship with deity-toys, what is useful to consider is the broader consequence of religion being reimagined because of globalization. While critics have pointed out the political consequences of religious TV serials being capitalized on by right-wing political parties since the 1980s (Mankekar 1999; Rajagopal 2001), it remains to be seen if the new forms of mythology will disturb or support the emerging hegemony of the post-global consumer culture in India. One way of looking at this question is through the questions of definition that Ashis Nandy (1983) writes about. If, indeed, the new mythologies demand from viewers a discursive identification with definitions and labels, (as Hindus, or as Hindu superheroes, for example) then perhaps the political dangers are imminent. However, if these stories remain narrated in non-normative fashions, as ideals for values like "devotion" and "valor," as participants believe, then their use may remain politically unmotivated, and perhaps even culturally desirable. In the following section, I examine how the broad politics of definition are playing out in India since globalization.

CONCLUSION

The global has come to be experienced, imagined, and invested with meaning in the everyday lives of Indian media audiences in a manner that belies an assumption of either simple cultural imperialism (in which local culture or tradition is swept aside by Western culture) or audience resistance (in which local audiences have successfully appropriated Western culture to their own so-called traditional ends). The costs and consequences of media globalization in India call for a more nuanced understanding of how media consumption takes place under historical conditions of unequal privilege and power. For example, music television audiences seem to believe that globalization is good for India because the whole world is watching Indian music videos, or that liberalization has reduced class differences, because poor people are often presented (in caricatured form) in music television promos.

This phenomenon may be part of a broader reorganization in common sense, especially among younger Indians, who have found in the new media discourses a sense of self devoid of social location and accountability (Khilnani 2005). Given the all too real ground of enormous differences in privilege that have created very different experiences and understandings of globalization for India, it remains to be seen whether the ways that tradition is being reimagined will lead to a false sense of cultural security based on labels and slogans of identity, even as the ethical and social substance of that identity are lost. Is the present phase of postcolonial modernity in India merely the articulation of the worst of both, feudalism and consumerism? Is "tradition" doomed to remain the province of conservative social and political forces, even as these collude and conspire with the agents of globalization and modernity in self-serving ways, or are there other spaces for the negotiation of meaning available?

What is at stake in this process is a lot more than just either tradition or modernity; for under conditions of hegemony what we may be seeing in India is a crisis in understanding that goes beyond any one media discourse, or any one episteme. Even as the audience interpretation of popular media notions of nation, family, and religion may come from hopes and possibilities that do not deserve sanctimonious condemnation, the nature of the media discourses produced since globalization in India, and their social and political context, suggest the emergence of exactly such a crisis. The problem is therefore not so much whether audiences are misunderstanding in a simplistic sense either their traditions, or their modern futures. The problem, instead, is aptly described by Indian journalist P. Sainath (2007) in his Magsaysay award citation: "India's press today is creating audiences who have no interest in other human beings."

REFERENCES

Buell, F. (1994) *National culture and the new global system*, Baltimore: Johns Hopkins University Press.

Chadha, K. and Kavoori, A. (2000) "Media Imperialism Revisited: Some Findings from the Asian Case," *Media, Culture and Society*, 22(4): 415–32.

Chawla, P. (2005) "The At-Home Nationalist," *India Today*, 31 January: 10–12.

Dwyer, R. (2006) *Filming the Gods: Religion and Indian Cinema*, New York: Routledge.

Gahlaut, K. (2005) "The Yippie Generation," *India Today*, 31 January: 6–9.

Giddens, A. (1990) *The Consequences of Modernity*, Stanford: Stanford University Press.

Joseph, M. (2000) "Riverdale Sonata," *Outlook*, 1 November. http://www.outlookindia.com

Juluri, V. (1999) "Global Weds Local: The Reception of *Hum Aapke Hain Koun*," *European Journal of Cultural Studies*, 2(2): 231–48.

———. (2003) *Becoming a Global Audience: Longing and Belonging in Indian Music Television*, New York: Peter Lang.

Khilnani, S. (1999) *The Idea of India*, New York: Farrar Strauss Giroux.

———. (2005) "The Bubble Syndrome," *India Today*, 31 January: 16–17.

Mankekar, P. (1999) *Screening culture, viewing politics: An ethnography of television, womanhood, and nation in postcolonial India*, Durhan: Duke University Press.

Mohammadi, A. and Mohammadi, A. (1994) *Small Media, Big Revolution: Communication, Culture and the Iranian Revolution*, Minneapolis: University of Minnesota Press.

Murphy, P. and Kraidy, M. (2003) *Global Media Studies: Ethnographic Perspectives*, New York: Routledge.

Nandy, A. (1983) *The Intimate Enemy: Loss and Recovery of Self Under Colonialism*, New Delhi: Oxford.

Rajagopal, A. (2001) *Politics after television: Hindu nationalism and the reshaping of the public of India*, Cambridge: Cambridge University Press.

Sainath, P. (2007) "The 2007 Ramon Magsaysay Award for Journalism, Literature, and Creative Communication Arts: Citation for P. Sainath." http://www.sajaforum.org/2007/08/awards_p.sainath.html

Varma, P. (2004) *Being Indian: The Truth about Why the 21st Century Will be India's*, New Delhi: Penguin.

4 Reinventing Nationalism
The Politics of *Malaysian Idol* on Culture and Identity in Postcolonial Malaysia

Joanne B. Y. Lim

We [Malaysians] have become a model Islamic nation, one that has managed to achieve a balance between physical and spiritual development. (Badawi 2006)

As Malaysia celebrates its newfound "fame" as a model Muslim society in a post-September 11 world with the inception of *Islam Hadhari* (or Civilizational Islam), there seems to be an increasing need (especially on the part of the nation-state) to maintain a set of morals and ethics to accompany a "global mindset." In seeking the people's mandate, the country's prime minister Abdullah Ahmad Badawi introduced *Islam Hadhari* during the 2004 general elections, giving emphasis to the building of a "progressive" nation through "mental revolution and cultural transformation" in order to embrace the challenges of globalization. These recent changes and challenges within the political sphere of Malaysia resonate through the country's media industry, which is still subjected to state control and which continues to serve as a pedagogical and propaganda machine of the nation-state (albeit more subtly than before). Indeed, media (especially television) programs are incorporated into the rhythm of everyday life, where values portrayed through the media create family values, which then become new national values. While Ko Fu Yen (2007) describes a similar phenomenon in Taiwan during the sixties, I am suggesting that Malaysians are still experiencing such a phenomenon through state-led imagination and transformation into modernity. If the television set served as a symbol of civilization in the sixties, the reality genre today becomes a tool for Malaysians to revisit its own "civilization," to undo and correct "past mistakes," to re-learn the notion of civilization, and to re-educate the nation towards forming a new generation of "civilized Malaysians" in line with the much celebrated concept of Civilizational Islam.

As articulated by Homi Bhabha (1994), much of the distinction and tension within postcolonial nations are not actually between globalization and nationalism. It is the way in which nationalisms are appropriating and approximating part of the structures, economies, and discourses of globalization, and transforming themselves in that way. The argument lies in the fact that on the one hand there is globalization, and on the other hand there is the "new nationalism." Nonetheless, both globalization and the new nationalism are constantly in a profound transitional and translational state. Evidently, the nation is still very much alive, although it survives in a complex, compromised situation. Rather than living in a state of content with mere traces of the nation, following the work of Partha Chatterjee, the postcolonial nation, now freed from the rule of the colonial difference, has begun to appreciate nationalism as a tool that brings forth modernity to the citizens of the "new nation" in a way that colonialism never could.

Hence, the idea of the "imaginary" that had been emphasized in Anderson (1983) and Giddens' (1990) reading of globalization and national identity becomes less compelling, because nationalism is far from a "distant imagining" nor is it "distant" from the routine of everyday life—it is in the everyday life (and in the ordinary person who participates in a reality program) that nationness is being recycled, retranslated, and transformed to reinforce and reinvent the nation, nationalism, national subjectivity and national identity. In other words, it is also a site of cultural contestation because there is now a possibility of knowing fellow members of society, meeting them, and even "hearing" them through a seemingly insignificant television genre.

In presenting this argument, I have chosen to highlight the vastly popular television format that has visibly influenced the "identity" of both audiences and broadcast stations. The politics and implications of the Western-inspired reality TV genre discussed in this chapter exemplify the complex relationship between globalization and nationalism, and the dialectic consequences of globalization. With the participation of "ordinary" people, a genre that draws upon the idea of "reality," and a casual (or covert) surveillance format that audiences (and the public in general) are now accustomed to, the blurring of boundaries between entertainment and everyday life in reality TV becomes somewhat "ideal" for the spread of both globalization and nationalism that simultaneously constructs a desired "national identity," one that is reflective of the popularized notion of *Bangsa Malaysia* whilst in keeping with the "global culture."

Although the advent of reality TV signals the inevitable flow of Western television (and technology) into this third world country as a predictable result of globalization, the outcome of its presence (determined through analysis of the popular *Malaysian Idol* program and ethnographical material collected from 120 respondents between 2006 and 2007) can be read as articulations or dynamic responses and resistances to global forces, especially true of a country attempting to embrace globalization in the "Islamic" way—a new Islam that is friendly to global capitalism, rendering support to progress, development and (positive) changes whilst ensuring that efforts towards embracing globalization are constantly in accordance with Islamic values. Indeed, this form of governance hardly mirrors that of many other Islamic countries as it does not reject modernization yet is firmly rooted in the values and injunctions of Islam. Nevertheless, according to Abdullah, with rapid modernization and the desire to be classified among the developed world, globalization could lead to cultural fragmentation and a weakening of traditional social values and an inevitable loss of identity if issues such as world unrest and population displacement are not addressed. Hence, in the following discussions, I suggest that a genre often dismissed as mere entertainment (especially in the West) can play a vital role in addressing and responding to such concerns.

While there is much determination on the part of the nation-state and the multi-ethnic postcolonial society itself to identify and construct Malaysia's national identity, it undeniably remains a "site of struggle and contestation," a problem space in which different forces contend to "fix" their own definitions and interpretations of the concept. As Thompson (1978) asserts, "culture is a struggle between ways of life" constituted by the friction between competing interests and forces. Here, reality programs provide a "space" for competing minority interests and forces to "voice" their definitions and meanings of the concept of national identity, although one should not overlook the possibility of the genre as a vehicle for dominant political definitions. Nonetheless, while the media is potentially the primary source of strong national identification in this modern society, it is not my intention to suggest that national identification is solely dependent on the media because factors external to the media (such as present social and political stability) also play an important role, including the extent of democratization given to the media by the nation-state.

The importance of reality TV in relation to national unity is evident in the different stages of a globalizing process: the emphasis on "national identity" in the face of political globalization; the onset of "national integration" following the intensification and diminishment of ethnic and racial domination; and the stage of constructing a "national symbol" in the advent of the homogenizing and pluralizing of cultural identities, values and institutions. Hence, this chapter is structured according to three key elements that form a dialectical struggle between globalization and nationalism: national identity, national integration and national symbol, as described above. Although scholars argue that the process of nation-building and the transformation of national identity in Malaysia are mostly couched in the discourse of a dominant "nation-state paradigm," this chapter aims to analyse the articulation and representation of the three key elements where alternative "voices" have begun to challenge or reinvent the official definition of those terms, and promote the emergence of a new nationalism (albeit not necessarily liberated from state dominance or Western cultural hegemony).

With reference to Aihwa Ong's (1999) construction of globalization as producing nationalisms that take on a binary construction of "East" versus

"West," this chapter interpolates the contours of recent Malaysian nationalist intensifications through a popular cultural text on the search for an "idol," whose "idol" qualities are registered through the global iconicity of other "similar yet different" (American/pop) idols—the idol, like the genre itself, becomes a site of cultural contestation: the reconstitution of the idol as a national subject depends upon the designation and disavowal of both "Malaysia" and "the West." Between modernization and national integration, reality TV is often either essentially divisive and may neutralize any impact that is attributed to integrative goals or is to some extent preserving the "traditional" by enabling its survival through a Western-imported television format. More importantly, there seems to be an opportunity to promote these alternative (or new) definitions of national identity resulting from an inter-ethnic environment existing internally and externally of the television text.

THE CHANGING FORCE OF REALITY TV

The Malaysian media industry, particularly television stations, have only recently managed to "revive" the popularity of locally produced programs among local audiences, owing much of its success to the Western-inspired reality genre. As a third world developing nation striving to meet the demands of globalization and modernity, Malaysia's ability to assimilate a "global trend" into a local culture proves to be a milestone, amidst the concern that globalization threatens cultural identity (which Ien Ang argues is a misnomer). Indeed, there is a heightened sense of concern about the fact that reality TV has its origins in the West, especially for a postcolonial nation motivated to uphold its *Look East Policy* and eager to reject all forms of "dependence" on the "contaminated" West. The adapted programs are criticized for having "borrowed extensively from Western culture . . . [T]hese shows could have a negative impact on viewers because some of the action wandered from the norms of local culture" (*The Star* 2005a: 29). A newspaper report entitled "No Hugging, We're Muslims" quoted the country's deputy prime minister Najib Tun Razak's assertion that "hugging scenes are not suitable . . . they must sing decent songs, and must act decently . . . this is not a question of young or old people hugging. This is about religion. It is forbidden in the religion" (*The Star* 2005b: 6). His comments echo the concerns of many religious leaders in the country, especially Muslim leaders who claim that certain elements in the format appear to be "un-Islamic" and contradict traditional and cultural values of the nation. Subsequently, the deputy minister of the Energy, Water and Communications Ministry announced that the ministry would decide on the kind of reality TV shows that would suit the Malaysian society better and reflect "Asian values."

As mentioned earlier, instead of merely another entertainment form, reality TV becomes one of the possible (even necessary) sites of "unraveling" the postcolonial into the global, and serves an imperative role in the construction of a link between the popular and the society belonging to this postcolonial body. Hence, the popular in the form of reality TV is not merely a commodity or a postcolonial nation's response to globalization, but also a creator of needs, desires and fantasies that preserve the status quo. My reading of the reality program *Malaysian Idol* through the rubrics of globalization and nationalism is informed by several pivotal shifts in Malaysia's political, economic and cultural landscape over the past five years since the inception of the reality genre in the country's mainstream television: the rise of locally produced programs in line with the ongoing *Buy Malaysian* campaign (as opposed to consuming wholesale Western imports), the popular Short Message Service (SMS) voting system used during prime time news segments to obtain public opinion in matters pertaining to political, economic and social issues, and the increasing number of "ordinary" people recognized as icons and role models in society.

Jameson's (1981: 84–5) concept of allegory as a third world culture is also useful as a basis in approaching this text, as he states that all third world literature and cultural constructions are "necessarily" national allegories—everything that happens means something else. Hence, the reality genre may "stand for the nation—it is a means by which the nation can represent itself to itself and to its subjects." Through this perspective, *Malaysian Idol* and the idol himself can also be seen as a tool to build imaginary bonds that work to hold a particular nation or society together as a community by creating a "cinematic" yet recognizable experience of their fears, anxieties, aspirations and pleasures through this popular form, in order to "recognize themselves as a singular body with a common culture."

Indeed, it is in the idol that a common culture emerges; as articulated by a focus group participant, a reality talent show winner is often regarded as a "role model" or should at least possess role model qualities: "the (Malaysian) Idol is a role model . . . showing people how to do the right things . . . and to do things properly" (*Malaysian Idol* voter, age twenty-four). Daniel Lee's (*Malaysian Idol 2* winner) rise to fame was fueled not solely by his singing talent, as would have been expected of a talent show winner: "He is intelligent, being a university student, smart and cute. Young and old adore him." For the majority of audiences who voted for Daniel, talent show winners need to go beyond talent itself to prove that they "possess the whole package."

Contrary to the most basic definition of the word "idol" (referencing the Oxford dictionary), which is a mere image, a figment of the mind (fantasy), or a false conception (fallacy), focus group participants who were asked to define the word "idol" in relation to the program and its winner used the following attributes: inspiring, dedicated, original, a "real" leader. A fifty-two-year-old viewer expressed that he wanted his five-year-old son to "be like Daniel when he grows up . . . because he is a true role model." Clearly, the idol is an actual, authentic, genuine person who is very "real" to the respondents, but more interesting, the emphasis that he possess "role model qualities" suggests that national values and "common culture" are much sought after and appreciated by Malaysians in an acceptable image that they can be proud of naming their idol.

DESIRING TO BE SIMILAR YET "DIFFERENT"

As Aihwa Ong (1999: 18) suggests, "Globalization . . . has national and transnational forms of nationalism that not only reject Western hegemony but seek to promote the ascendancy of the East." In striving to be "not West," the nation-state takes pride in its implementation of the *Look East Policy* spearheaded by former Prime Minister Mahathir Mohamad, which discourages any dependent-type affiliations with the West, including any hints of Eurocentrism in Malaysian cultural consciousness. In dealing with this popular form, there seems to be caution in the extent of engagement with the concept of liberalism—in as much as the post-colonial nation struggles to sustain its cultural and religious "heritage" against former colonial powers, there seems to be resistance towards both returning to the past and any hindrance to moving forward and to being "at par with those of Europe and North America" (Mohamad 1991). Clearly, this is not a discourse of desiring to be less modern but, rather, an attempt to be "differently" modern—"at par" but not a "replica." The relationship between tradition and the effects of globalization on Malaysia produces an "alternative modernity" (Chatterjee 1993), one that forces a de-centering of Western theories on globalization and (post)modernity. Hence, instead of an outright ban on the Western format, the program (excluding several Western-like elements) has found acceptance and even popularity among society and the nation-state.

Without indulging too much in "hugging" and "inappropriate dressing," numerous local reality programs have incorporated other aspects of the reality format along with themes of nationalism. For example, participants of *Malaysian Idol* were given weekly tasks to select songs based on certain music genres. Participants were required to perform songs in both English and Malay to showcase their versatility and their potential to shine for local and international markets. Their costumes also reflected the genre; the high of nationalism was portrayed when participants dressed themselves in traditional costumes belonging to other races. Here, the reality program is used not only to increase the appeal of local programs and nationalism amongst Malaysians but more importantly, as a means to promote the inclusion of Malaysia and Malaysianness in the globalized cultural and entertainment industry. As articulated by a thirty-one-year-old viewer: "It is a more special and satisfying experience compared to watching the American version of the program, especially when you see participants appreciating our national culture and identity even whilst singing rock and R and B songs . . . Yes, *Malaysia Boleh* [Malaysia Can]—we copy well but shine in our own Malaysian way too."

The ability to relate to the participants "because they come from ordinary backgrounds, they could be anyone . . . your neighbor . . . even yourself" (focus group participant, female, age twenty-eight) also increases the power and popularity of reality TV participants among the Malaysian society, which extends beyond the program itself. Participants are often seen promoting nationalistic causes such as unity, racial tolerance and integration, and community service campaigns such as a national-level anti-drug campaign held in 2006. Under the rationalization of *Islam Hadhari,* Jaclyn Victor's (*Malaysian Idol* first winner) participation as an ambassador in a public service program has been deemed reflective of her role as a non-Muslim citizen who is carrying out the seventh *Islam Hadhari* principle, "the protection of the rights of minority groups and women" through humanitarian work. An article reads: "Indirectly, she becomes an icon to encourage the public to be involved in humanitarian work to help those who are in need . . . In the long run, the positive influence of these products [participants] of reality TV makes the program a proactive approach rather than a threat to society" (Islamhadhari.net 2006). Due to their strong impact on youths, reality programs are deemed by some to be useful in contributing to the success of state campaigns, while still maintaining their hold as a popular entertainment form.

Indeed, the political and economic structures of the Malaysian society have been cited as the locus where the roots of ethnicism are firmly entrenched (Tan Chee Beng in Kua 1985: 132). While it was previously problematic for cultural workers—producers, scriptwriters, directors, actors—to articulate and represent alternative definitions and interpretations of a national identity, the inclusion of the Malaysian society as alternative "cultural workers," often encouraged to "have their say" in reality programs through voting, forming fan clubs and actually taking part in the competitions, increases opportunities to promote a national culture based on cross-fertilization of various cultures. For example, it was highlighted during focus group discussions that Daniel retains and reflects cultural and moral values depicting a "civilized Malaysian"—he is indirectly regarded by his fans as a "progressive" individual who embraces globalization through his ability to integrate and assimilate himself into a Western-copied reality program yet "does not become completely Western" (focus group participant, male, age thirty), In contrast, his competition, twenty-seven-year-old Norhanita Hamzah, who many claim possessed better vocal abilities, was "discriminated against" because of her background as a pub singer and because her dressing "did not reflect the Malaysian culture" as her performance wardrobe included tank-tops and figure-hugging dresses that were deemed "too suggestive" compared to Daniel's suit, tie and leather shoes. Unlike the "model-son, perfect-elder-brother figure" portrayed by Daniel (whose forte includes ballads and pop songs), Norhanita depicts a more

Western-influenced celebrity and in one interview said: "I'd like to do a rock album, but with gothic pop influences." Her background as a pub singer influenced audience preferences, regardless of her vocal talents. The concern about what people would think about the projected image is seemingly an important criterion in determining who should be "idolized" in Malaysia. Evidently, the outcome (and winner) of the reality program bears much cultural and political significance because the chosen "idol" reflects the values of the nation and has the power to influence how "Others" view "us." So audiences take into consideration the fact that the idol will represent the country in the World Idol competition.

Such claims correspond with the need to reject Western hegemony and promote the ascendancy of the East, which is often achieved by linking the discourse of nationalism to studies of postcoloniality that describe nineteenth-century nationalism as being legitimated through the construction of the West as a space of contamination (Chatterjee 1993: 120). The participants become tools that (re)produce and are repository of complementary and contradictory place-images—Malaysia and the West as spaces of modernity, Malaysia (through Daniel) as the space that values tradition, and on the other hand, the West (Norhanita) as a space of contamination and artificiality. Hence, to dismiss the winners of *Malaysian Idol* as products wholly determined by cultural industries is to neglect the possibility that these "ordinary individuals" are not only created and constructed by audiences but have become sites of struggle for "ordinary people" within society—the youths, the repressed, the working class, and a nation caught between the demands of globalization and the struggle to preserve elements of "national identity" and Malaysianness. Nonetheless, the genre remains a "copy" of the West, but as Bhabha (1994: 86) argues, mimicry contains— both possesses and delimits—racialized difference, making the differences of East and West something that is "almost the same but not quite." In order to be effective, the colonial mimetic text "must continually produce its slippage, its excess, its difference." In other words, *Malaysian Idol* will only remain popular as long as there are contradictions or remnants of the West embedded within the program, be it through the participants, their choice of songs, or the clothes they wear.

CONSTRUCTING A NATIONAL SYMBOL

> Let us all as one be reminded that all Malaysians would live together as members of one big family. (Tunku Abdul Rahman, January 15, 2008)

The initial concern for national integration is seen to require an emphasis on common traditional symbols, or the construction of symbols that are made to seem commonly traditional. The "showcasing" of cultural activities and symbols of the various ethnic groups as one family (that is, the

Malaysia Truly Asia campaign) extends beyond the purpose of tourism and serves as an imperative method to promote national unity amongst its society. Rather than conservative national symbols such as presidency, the state religion, and a particular favored language (Boyd-Barrett 1988), adopted from the remnants of Western colonialism in Malaysia as a means to promote national integration, efforts are undertaken to diverge from any further emphasis on Malay-Muslim hegemony (Loh 1992). For example, the term *Malay language* as the national language has been recently changed to *Malaysian language* (Bahasa Malaysia) and is said to have positive "psychological effects" on the nation. Apart from the Malaysian language (widely used on *Malaysian Idol*), the notion of *Bangsa Malaysia* (Jeshuran, 1993: 203–23) has been a vital expression of unity within this multiracial postcolonial society, where emphasis is placed on the sense of belonging to a single "national race." As twenty-two-year-old Daniel asserts, "We define ourselves simply as the persons we are rather than by race, culture or religion. Once you open your heart to people, understanding those aspects just comes naturally without the need to constantly remind yourself, and I think that's what being a Malaysian is about," adding that his Malaysian idol status can be his channel to communicate his cultural ideals as well as represent what it means to be a Malaysian (Phang 2007).

While having participants from different ethnicities is hardly a valid measure of racial harmony, national unity is somewhat evident in *Malaysian Idol* through emphasis on the notion of "family." "The making of a good role model stems from proper upbringing and strong support of family members. It doesn't happen overnight and neither does it happen in four months . . ." (focus group participant, male, age twenty-seven). Hence, the families of participants are often highlighted in the programs, for example, with occasional appearances of family members in video footage acknowledging their supportive attendance at concerts. Another example of promoting the idea of unity through reality TV is in Daniel's association with the color pink, which has since become a "unifying" symbol for his fans and a recognizable identity marker that serves to provide a sense of belonging to a collective group: "My fan club, the Pinkies . . . follow me everywhere during my promotional tour. They are very united, and always do things together!" (Chow, 2007).

Fans who gathered at the launch of his first self-debut album in November 2005 carried a large pink banner that read: "United under one roof as a family because of Daniel." This exemplifies the intensity and importance of "unity" and the need for a "unifying symbol" in a multi-cultural postcolonial country where individuals recognize the power of collective groups to influence change and reinvent the idea of nationalism and national identity. Recognizing that the politics of reality TV, its participants, and popular culture itself affect change in society, Prime Minister Abdullah Badawi, together with pop stars (including Malaysian reality TV host and participants), promoted the "Unity Band" (a red rubber wristband printed with the words "I [heart] MY") as a national symbol of unity, with the tagline "Together we are stronger" in conjunction with the fiftieth anniversary celebration of the country's independence in 2007. Malaysians were urged to celebrate their "uniqueness" as part of their identity and to consolidate this identity by wearing the Unity Band, which signifies:

> An embodiment of what we stand for: distinct in diversity, united in nationality. A proud badge of our uniqueness. The colour red symbolises the blood that runs through our veins; no matter how we may differ in race, religion or creed, one factor unites us. And that is Malaysia . . . [The Unity Band] celebrates what makes us great—our enduring spirit and unity. (Unity Band UB50 Malaysia)

Here, the Unity Band proves to be an important identity marker for the nation while indirectly implying that "uniqueness" should be celebrated, albeit within a certain "boundary" being promoted as "unity."

Alongside the Unity Band, a symbol integral to satanic religion called the "Il Cornuto" (an infamous hand gesture that represents the devil himself—most evident in rock music) was re-modified and incorporated into a national "unity symbol." The symbol (displaying two fingers to form a shape of the letter "U") was evidently supported by the prime minister, who joined other government officials and youths in displaying the hand gesture at a Gegar (Rock) U! "Unity in Music" concert attended by university students and reality TV participants in August 2007. The hand gesture can also be read as symbolic of the love-hate relationship between the East and West with regards to the discourse of globalization and national identity, as the seemingly "negative" symbol belonging to the West is recreated into a positive one in Malaysia. Consequently, the notions of nation, nationalism and national identity were reinvented and reinforced through the emergence of this new "unity culture"; where racial integration has become more sought after than racial toleration; where the first prime minister Tunku Abdul Rahman's emphasis on living together "as one big family" and the national anthem (sung by pop stars instead of the traditional national choir) has since been included in the daily seven o'clock prime time news on a private entertainment channel. Finally, a recent illegal street demonstration on 10 November 2007 received the following response from a member of society via SMS to a local newspaper: "It isn't our culture to create chaos in our country. If you want to behave like people in other countries, go there and do it, not here. We treasure our peace!" (*The Star* 2007: 48) .

CONCLUSION

Indeed, like many other developing countries, Malaysia fears the kind of culture that the media encourages, even produces, and is struggling to find its own "voice" without having to succumb to extensive changes brought about by the perceived threat of imperialism and globalization. Yet through the constructed image of the idol, this form of popular culture gives the nation hope of realizing *Vision 2020*—when the country is expected to achieve its status as a "developed" country in line with globalization and modernity. While being carefully monitored for signs of deviation from the teachings of Islam, the Islamization-liberalism dialectic in Malaysia exists on a level that allows for the penetration of globalization into the country's technological, cultural, and media "scapes" (Appadurai 1996). After all, as Daniel asserts, "No matter how developed we've become, there's a need to understand and stay true to who we are" (Phang 2007).

Through the highlighted texts, I have discussed how the idol and the Western-borrowed reality format construct the new Malaysian as both 'the symbol of sacrifice and the symbol of progress within the discourse of modern nationalism, signifying obedience and tradition on the one hand and liberation and modernity on the other (Rao 1999: 319). The idol's nationality and globalism—both of which attempt to constitute Malaysianness—depend, in part, on measuring and denying any trace of the "West" in their ideals, values, and cultural politics. The West for reality TV participants is discursively constructed as a place of colonialism, modernity and artificiality, one that is always in dialectic with discursive constructions within notions of "Malaysianess." Hence, *Malaysian Idol* is both a figure of geographical excess and of interstiality and the idol is Malaysian in so far as he is not bound to tradition and does not resemble the Western idol and does not desire to be Western. The idol is invested, then, in negotiating strategies of emplacement and belonging for Malaysianness. Nonetheless, the *Malaysian Idol* brings with it the possibility of heterogeneity among Malaysians, homogenizing them into a kind of "global Malaysian" embodying a distinct Malaysian modernity, linking Malaysians "collectively" across class, race, region and religion.

It is also evident that the Malaysian idol is idolized because he is Malaysian; as a site in which Malaysianness is reinforced and reinvented, the idol's national inscription is always dependent upon the threatening presence of an Other space outside these boundaries, namely the "West." Nonetheless, the formulation of "the nation" as "not West" signals that the "Malaysianness" of the idol and the program depend on "the West" as a key term of exclusion. Indeed, it can be argued that the program format relies on certain stereotypes of "the West" and "Western" cultures that in turn produce a stereotype of Malaysian idol qualities. However, out of this "localized" reality program emerges a problem space, in which Malaysia and the West are necessarily "tethered" to each other (Bhabha 1994: 25). In spite of efforts carried out by the postcolonial country to exclude the West in matters of culture pertaining to the nation, the West, through this problem space, cannot remain completely outside the discursive geography of Malaysia. Finally, although the Western-borrowed reality genre may seem to intensify tensions and contradictions between Malaysia and the West, it has managed to challenge and "transform" otherwise "ordinary" individuals into significant resources for the learning of culture, nationalism, and national identity. Indeed, popular culture in the form of reality TV is not merely the implication of globalization on a postcolonial nation; rather, it constitutes, creates and produces the postcolonial nation that in effect implicates the discourse and politics of globalization. As made evident in this chapter, it is actually beyond the scope of entertainment that certain "realities" emerge from the study of reality TV in Malaysia, as the genre claims to reveal social, psychological, political, historical and cultural "truths," depicting the rhythms, systems and structures of everyday life.

REFERENCES

Anderson, B. (1983) *Imagined Communities: Reflections on the Origin and Spread of Nationalism*, London: Verso.

Appadurai, A. (1996) *Modernity at Large: Cultural Dimensions of Globalization*, Minneapolis: University of Minnesota Press.

Badawi, A. (2006) *Islam Hadhari: A Model Approach For Development and Progress*, Selangor: MPH Group Publishing.

Bhabha, H. (1983) "The Other Question," *Screen*, 24(6): 18–36.

———. (1994) *The Location of Culture*, New York: Routledge.

Boyd-Barrett, J. O. (1988) "Cultural Dependency and the Mass Media," in M. Gurevitch et al. (eds), *Culture, Society and the Media*, London: Routledge.

Chatterjee, P. (1993) *The Nation and Its Fragments: Colonial and Postcolonial Histories*, Princeton: Princeton University Press.

Chow, E. T. (2007) "Daniel in Idol-Land," *The Malay Mail*, 13 June.

Fernandes, L. (2000) "Nationalizing 'The Global:' Media Images, Cultural Politics and the Middle Class in India," *Media, Culture and Society*, 22: 611–28.

Giddens, A. (1990) *The Consequences of Modernity*, Cambridge: Polity.

Hardt, M. and Negri, A. (2001) *Empire*, Cambridge: Harvard University Press.

Islamhadhari.net. (2006) *Reality TV: Mengancam*. http://www.islamhadhari.net/v4/wacana

Jameson, F. (1981) *The Political Unconscious: Narrative as a Socially Symbolic Act*, London: Methuen.

Jeshuran, C. (1993) "Malaysia: The Mahathir Supremacy and Vision 2020" in *Southeast Asian Affairs 1993*, Singapore: Institute of Southeast Asian Studies.

Kabilan, M. and Hassan, Z. (2005) *Readings on Ethnic Relations in a Multicultural Society: Promoting National Unity and the Practice of Noble Values*, Serdang: Fakulti Pengajian Pendidikan UPM.

Kamali, M. (2006) *Principles of Islamic Jurisprudence*, 3rd ed, Islamic Texts Society.

Kilborn, R. W. (1998) "Shaping the Real: Democratization and Commodification in UK-Factual Broadcasting," *European Journal of Communication*, 13: 201–18.

———. (2003) *Staging the Real: Factual TV Programming in the Age of Big Brother*, Manchester: Manchester University Press.

Kilborn, R. W. and Izod, J. (1997) *An Introduction to Television Documentary: Confronting Reality*, Manchester: Manchester University Press.

Ko, F. Y. (2007) "Television Sets and National Culture in 1960s Taiwan," paper presented at the Inter-Asia Cultural Studies Conference, Shanghai.

Kua, K. S. (1985) *National Culture and Democracy*, Kersani: Petaling Jaya.

Loh, F. (1992) "Modernization, Cultural Revival and Counter-Hegemony: The Kadazans of Sabah in the 1980s," in J. Kahn and F. Wah (eds) *Fragmented Vision: Culture and Politics in Contemporary Malaysia*, Sydney: Allen and Unwin.

Marshall, P. (1997) *Celebrity and Power: Fame in Contemporary Culture*, Minneapolis: University of Minnesota Press.

Mohamad, M. (1991) "The Inauguration of the Malaysian Business Council," keynote address at the launch of the Malaysian Business Council, Kuala Lampur. (The speech text can also be found at the "Official Website of the Prime Minister's Office of Malaysia," http://www.pmo.gov.my, (specific URL: http://www.pmo.gov.my./WebNotesApp/PastPM.nsf/a310590c7cafaaae48256db4001773ea/d6e802eaef5e4bfd4825674a00182dcc?OpenDocument)

———. (1999) *The Way Forward: Growth, Prosperity and Multiracial Harmony in Malaysia*, London: Weidenfeld & Nicolson Ltd.

———. (1994) *Blurred Boundaries: Questions of Meaning in Contemporary Culture*, Bloomington: Indiana University Press.

Ong, A. (1999) *Flexible Citizenship: The Cultural Logics of Transnationality*, Durham: Duke University Press.

Phang, K. H. (2007) "Global Aspirations: Young Malaysian," *The Star*, 15 August.

Rahman, T. A. (2008) TV Broadcast.

Rao, S. (1999) "Woman as Symbol: The Intersection of Identity Politics, Gender and Indian Nationalism," *Women's Studies International Forum*, 22(3): 319.

The Star (2005a) "Concern Over Local Reality Television Shows," 3 August.

———. (2005b) "No Hugging, We're Muslims," 13 August.

———. (2007) "Why Protest?" 12 November.

Thompson, E. P. (1978) *The Making of the English Working Class*, London: Penguin.

Unity Band UB50 Malaysia. (2007) http://www.ub5o.com.my

5 Media Consumption and Incomplete Globalization

How Chinese Interpret Border-Crossing Hong Kong TV Dramas

Anthony Y. H. Fung

Hong Kong is located at the southern apex of China. It is a former British colony and now an international finance center heavily saturated with global culture and with capitalist values. While the globalized conceptions of democracy, freedom, capitalism and free economy have either been artificially implanted into the social structures during colonial rule or subtly dissolved and assimilated into the local culture through cultural and mediated contacts with the West, such Western ideologies are foreign to Hong Kong's motherland China. The border-crossing nature between Hong Kong and China in terms of information flow, ideologies, consumable goods, popular images and worldviews thus addresses the problems of globalizing China through a politically marginal but globalized city in Asia.

This paper focuses on Guangzhou, which is the major Chinese city nearest to Hong Kong. These two cities are linked not only by a national railroad and a highway, but also by transborder television airwaves, which are geographically unbounded. The reception of television frequencies in South China foregrounds the issue of in-flow of Hong Kong values, culture and norms, which are highly globalized, Westernized and capitalistic. Nowadays, residents in South China are exposed to the Hong Kong Cantonese programs, however, not via direct border-crossing reception. Rather, in the light of a legal vacuum for the border-crossing signals, it is the Guangdong Cable Network that intercepts the signals and channels the Hong Kong programs to Guangzhou and nearby areas. The Guangzhou audience, living in an information-closed environment, watch the same, capitalist-value-embedded programs from two Hong Kong broadcasting channels, Television Broadcast Ltd (TVB) Jade and Asian Television Ltd (ATV) Home, except that some of the news episodes—mainly political news and news related to China—are occasionally banned because of the sensitivity of an issue on the mainland. Inserting its own advertising in between these Hong Kong programs, the cable network earns huge advertising revenues up to RMB 1,500 million (Xinhuanet.com 2004).

Marketing data shows that before 2000, 70 percent of Guangzhou citizens watched Hong Kong television programs daily, overwhelming all local televisions. Although the audience share of Hong Kong television stations lowered to one-third (31.6 percent), these stations are still the most popular and important sources for programs and entertainment outside China (Xu et al. 2006). The reason is obvious. Many television programs in China have not yet detached from their propaganda mission and hence have little local appeal, even though nowadays the local programs have traces of commercial elements to retain viewers' attention. Even if the local audience might prefer to watch the ideology-laden programs, they have to deconstruct symbols and semiotics within the programs to derive pleasure (Lull 1991). Hong Kong television programs thus easily become a way for people to know the outside world and hear alternative voices and, above all, find an alternate way to be entertained.

As the border-crossing cultural flow is relatively uncontrolled, one can wonder what the long-term effect on the local culture in South China will be. Using the examination of how Guangzhou people interpret Hong Kong television series as a departure, the paper explicates how such interpretation is conditioned and constrained by the social structure. Theoretically, this paper sheds light on how the local decodes global content under a strong presence of nationalistic influence. Questions of how the external and global (Hong Kong) television soap operas affected, distorted or transformed Chinese values and how the Chinese resisted or adopted such influence give us a clear case of how globalization is taking place in China. How global viewings would affect a relatively closed society, its social system and its people's national identity is an empirical question that has yet to be pursued (Barker 1999).

Methodologically, the researchers, initially as a pilot study in 1999, collected Guangzhou audience responses to Hong Kong television dramas through focus groups. As an outsider, I started out by employing a mainland China marketing research company (White Horse Research) to recruit interviewers and the interviewees. After gaining a more substantial understanding of the audience and the system, the researchers conducted a more systematic study between September 2003 and January 2005. They selected twenty Guangzhou people from a range of socio-economic backgrounds and occupations and conducted interviews face to face.

The narratives collected in the study provide insights into the question of hybridization between the indigenous and external cultures; they also address the issues of autonomy of the local agency and global international ideology. That is, whether the Guangzhou audiences are able to decode the "global ideology" of Hong Kong TV beyond a framework of hegemonic ideology. The study argues that local audiences develop a critical consciousness to evaluate the capitalist values and global ideologies and that such criteria may also challenge their own cultural and political systems.

THE MISSING DIALOGUE BETWEEN
GLOBALIZATION AND NATIONALIZATION

Globalization, in the simplest and most common connotation, means that certain global values—political, economic, and cultural—have been so thoroughly circulated that ultimately national borders are dissolved and local cultures are homogenized. These global values, however, are legitimately referred to as Western values and culture (see, for example, Cvetkovich and Kellner 1997). However, the question of a non-direct Western influence from an intermediary agent, in this case, Hong Kong, has not been substantially studied. There is a lack of empirical evidence regarding this kind of mediated border-crossing influence. Naomi Sakr (2002) found that in the Middle East border-crossing satellite television could liberate viewers from government control of national media. Daya Thussu (1998) argued that even through the imagination of consumers worldwide, the virtual empires of the electronic age could have a profound effect on national media systems and cultural sovereignty.

Discussion of globalization often centers on the dialectics between the local and the global (Featherstone 1990). Challenges to the globalization thesis and the micro-processes of local-global struggle have raised two theoretical issues. First, globalization does not mean that local culture is completely paralyzed, subdued or suppressed. The autonomy of local processes is visible in the cultural sphere, and the image of a single dominating center and a dominated periphery is no longer the reality (Thussu 1998). Local resistance may exist or coexist with globalization in some forms of global localism (Dirlik 1996). The question is to what extent does globalization take root in the indigenous culture? Second, globalization means neither homogenizing all aspects of a local culture from a single global origin nor assuming that the localization of culture is uniformly against the global culture. Amidst the process of globalization, the global "West" certainly constitutes a major force. While the sources of globalization are always from multiple origins and multitudinous, the processes of reception of globalization are also multiple. As the local culture and the national culture are homogeneous, globalization may have different impacts on the local, the national or the interactions of both. This gives multiple consequences to the globalization process.

The current trend in studies on globalization tends to reduce the argument to a juxtaposition of the global with the local and then equate the local with the national. However, the political subordination of the local under the national is by no means a given (see, for example, Sinclair, Jacka and Cunningham 1996). While we may conceive of localization and globalization as polar opposites, the presence of nationalization may complicate the whole phenomenon if we have to chart the relationship between the local and the national, and between the national and the global. As the position of the national is understood geopolitically or geoculturally as being closer to the local, its influence on the local may be even more potent than the global. In other words, any global effect of television on the local may be filtered by the nationalization process, as in the case of national policy, or any local acculturation of the global may challenge the national.

Given the solid and real presence of the national in most nation states, the scarcity of studies on the dialectics between nationalism and globalization and, in particular, an assessment of the local influence by the dual national and global ideologies in a concrete historical context, becomes an unanswered theoretical gap in the field. This paper aims to present a strong case that the Guangzhou audience appropriates the nationalistic discourse to resist the international capitalist economy, and indirectly appropriates the global view to contest national control.

AUDIENCE, TELEVISION, AND GLOBAL VALUES

External incorporation of televised and globalized programs is often found to stimulate consumption and promote consumer values. Political economists argue (see, for example, Schiller 1996) that many multinational media and corporations apparently highlight the neutrality of messages and information, but in fact deliver their ideologies through those messages to different parts of the world. The so-called "market-choices" desired by the public are, in fact, not perfect choices, but pre-selection and pre-filtering by producers. Studying how audiences interpret the icons and symbols of Donald Duck, Dorfman and Mattelart (1975) concluded that audiences have the power to resist the hegemonic message, which in the final analysis supports the economic profits and ideology of cultural capitalists.

The analysis of political economy (see, for example, Schiller 1996) may over-emphasize the effect of capitalism on global media. However, even taking a more liberal interpretation, we still cannot deny that media corporations are prone to carrying the explicit or implicit "propaganda" of different parties—commercially, the advertisers, and politically, the government. Given the interplay between political and economical constraints, the content of the culture industry has to pander to the tastes of the capitalists and government officials (Murdock 1974; Herman and Chomsky 1998). Between autonomy and commercial interests, when television broadcasting channels encounter economic problems, they often sacrifice autonomy for commercial interests (Caughie 1982). The question is, when the consumer or capitalist value-laden programs are transferred to other states, how do these values challenge the indigenous culture? The effect depends very much on the local's acceptance of and resistance against these different worldviews or ideologies.

Audience research by Liebes and Katz (1990) showed that different countries have different interpretations of the American program *Dallas*. The result hardly supports the globalization thesis. Some audiences believe that the television images are totally unreal, while some interpret and judge the values of these images based on their cultural experience. Some studies (for example, Hodge and Tripp 1986) argue that dominant and subversive ideologies can co-exist. The culture is not determined by a certain producer or capitalist, rather it is overdetermined by different structures and institutions (Williams 1980). Cultural studies scholars (for example, Fiske 1986; Hall 1977) believe that even though we are living under a hegemonic society, the audience are not dupes and are able to make their own choices and to assert their identities. The very nature of televised production is already polysemic. Audiences can excorporate the seemingly one-dimensional television to re-construct their own desires (Grossberg 1984).

To articulate the problems of the reception of the television dramas in the eyes of Guangzhou people—whose worldviews are being strongly framed by the socialist system—Gramsci's analysis of hegemony (1971) may provide an appropriate framework. Gramsci believes that every social group is able to build up their own typical knowledge. They use their own knowledge to understand the world and rebuild "reality." In other words, the hegemony model implies that different groups or classes coexist with their own worldviews under a nationalistic political leadership. Based on that, when the local citizens receive messages from external media—the site for political struggle—audiences interpret and articulate these media discourses based on their own worldview, knowledge and moral standard. These "standpoints" are also framed by the environment, such as various nationalistic discourses. This implies that the dominant global ideas from the external programs would not prevail, not only because of the strong presence of the nationalistic effect, but also because of the fact that social groups' interpretation favors the vested interest and values of the national system.

Wober's challenge (1998) to traditional media and television analysis also echoes the same theme. Wober believes that current media cultivation studies of television (Gerbner 1992) have neglected audiences' personal interest. The audiences may resist foreign programs, but after a long period of time, these external media allow them to understand a kind of worldview that is widely accepted by another society, and hence may cause them to re-evaluate their own daily life and status. This means that although they do not decode the mediated ideology, they are aware of the differences between their ideological worldviews and others. Such cultural exposure thus may destabilize the existing nationalistic ideologies that they are accustomed to.

BRIDGING PROGRAM CHOICES AND CLASS STRUCTURE

Among all programs available, prime time television dramas or soap operas are what the Guangzhou audience appreciated most, as the contents of dramas are very different from that of the structural, inflexible and unentertaining mainland local productions. Their preference for and awareness of a specific television series depended very much on their perception of the class ideology of the program and their own class status. Constrained by and intertwined with their cultural, social and economic geographies, the local people were inclined to choose programs in which the social class of the important fictional characters did not deviate notably from their self-perceived class image. Early in our focus group one of the participants said:

> *File of Justice* and *Healing Hands* [which are two TVB programs] are comparatively better than others . . . I do not like [these programs] because there are characters who are either living just beyond the poverty line or those who enjoy luxurious life. There is always a big gap between the characters and me. I prefer middle-class stories.

Both *File of Justice* (1994) and *Healing Hands* (1999), the Hong Kong version of the American *Ally McBean* and *ER,* respectively, are in fact western-values-oriental-transformed middle-class stories. *File of Justice* dramatizes various dilemmas and consequences of legal sentences and *Healing Hands* explores predicaments that might result from professional medical decisions. Producers inserted into each series elements of middle-class lifestyle: love between middle-class professionals, politics within the legal and medical institutions, and, subtly, the fictional characters' consumption of clothing, food and expensive automobiles. Presumably, the audience in the interview fantasized about the professional characters in the series and positioned themselves within the boundaries of the middle class. Even if they did not admire the lifestyles and personalities of every character on the soap operas, nonetheless, such programs provided them with a frame in which their class characters are manifested and defined. The audience had to re-evaluate, ponder, and criticize, images of fictional characters in the soap operas that used to be irrelevant and remote from their social imaginations.

THE ONE-DIMENSIONAL IDEOLOGY OF HONG KONG TELEVISION PROGRAMS

Imbued with a strong critical awareness of class ideology, the audiences, in general, were unequivocal about their social loci, appropriateness and their critical ability to evaluate the programs, and in fact, they didn't hesitate to point out the "inappropriate" episodes, narratives, plots and characters. In as much as the criteria of "class reality" dictate the program choice, Guangzhou people are particularly aware of the common capitalist messages repeated, distorted and exaggerated in these programs. A female interviewee in her mid-thirties said:

I feel that all television drama programs are the same. The plots and the actors [of all Hong Kong series] are all similar. All the [characters such as] professionals, doctors and lawyers . . . go to bars for their leisure time to discuss their love affairs. They all work very short hours and have a long time to engage in private matters. They have to have expensive racing cars and drink red wine.

The interview suggested that the images of major fictional characters are drawn from the imagination of the middle-class, who establish their identities through conspicuous consumption during their spare time. What they refer as to "the same" is the one-dimensional, capitalist ideology of the program. In fact, just as the audience indicated, the production of these programs is based on producers' social imaginations of the middle classes, and they use the latter as the pivotal line of the television stories. Another audience member expressed that she is a bit impatient with the capitalist consumption manifested in these dramas.

I have recently watched *Women on the Run*. The program wanted to create a program like Western *Sex and the City*. I haven't watched the real one [*Sex and the City*]. But the Hong Kong dramas still have the same formula. For example, Bonnie Chan (a fictional character in the drama) starts her own PR firm. Her image is constructed by her elegant dressing, famous brands and her spending. I think money is not everything. A woman's success should count other things. The reality would not resemble [the plots or characters] at all.

Living in such a Chinese society, with a strong sense of class structure, interviewees can easily "discover" this ideology conveyed by the plots or characters such as Bonnie Chan. Another interviewee said, "On television, either you are rich or poor. The poor live in squalid conditions [whereas] the family members of the middle-class are framed to live in an extreme large house and lead a luxurious life. I think this is too much exaggeration, and I do think there are in-between classes [between the rich and the poor] that are omitted." These kinds of "omissions" reveal that the capitalist values in these programs exclude alternative ones that have no power to gain from exposure in these episodes.

FANTASIZING ABOUT THE REAL AND UNREAL

On the whole, the local people's dislike of, if not outright opposition to, the soap operas connected them to very basic values hidden in their thoughts. An acceptable program for them is one that reflects accurately the real social and situational contexts of Hong Kong. Educated in the socialist system under the Communist Party, the local audience simply equated good programs with their ability to reflect the class structure and materialistic form of a society. Given their primary assumption that the soap operas should serve as the mirror of reality, they expect to employ television programs as a "blueprint" or reference guide to help them comprehend this society. They anticipated they could discover the class structure of Hong Kong society by reading the television texts. One of the participants said:

> I know that television is a kind of entertainment. But television pro-grams should also more or less reflect our everyday life. Producers should have extracted happenings or situations from our daily lives and piece them together as scenes in the stories. Of course, this is not 100 percent. There are more glamorous sides of the rich people on TV. But in general, it is plausible that television stories are a true reflection or reminiscence of a place's culture. I think audiences are the same. [They are] able to come out with a true picture of Hong Kong.

According to this interview, the audience believes they have the ability to grasp, re-configure and finally depict a realistic picture of Hong Kong through reading the border-crossing television. While fantasizing about the materialistic superiority of the capitalist society of Hong Kong, ironically, the audiences are aware of the fact that uncritically embracing the material-istic way of life in Hong Kong is unrealistic for them, not because they can-not fantasize about the unrealistic way of life in Hong Kong, but because they are incapable of actualizing this consumption in their own context. Another respondent said:

> I don't know how true the program is [in terms of] reflecting the Hong Kong realities. But I think our mainland people should not learn these things because [the kind of consumption in Hong Kong] is unrealistic for us. All the people now search for highly remunerative jobs. This is not practical. The more we watch, the more depressing [sic] we are.

Artificially annexing the materialistic desires of Hong Kong onto the Chinese people immediately creates a dissonance for the subjects: mimick-ing the materialistic consumption of the people in a more advanced econ-omy, the audience would soon find that the "false" desire is somewhat unreachable. Rational Chinese audiences soon remonstrate against the unrealistic reception of Hong Kong television.

NEGATING THE UNREALIZABLE

From the outset of the border-crossing viewing, although they experi-enced pleasure at the entertainment, rationally, the interviewees seemed unduly reticent about the foreign culture. Given the foreseeable negative consequences of emphasizing the imbalanced economies of the two cultures, audiences were quite self-reflexive and critical of this content. For the Chinese audience, crimes, robberies and murders in the Hong Kong dramas are the manifestation of unequal social status, while social problems are the undesirable result of pursuing materialistic need that emerges from fantasizing desires. The Chinese audience also conceived that viewing Hong Kong programs contributed to accumulation of materialistic desires that could lead to their own serious social problems. While not suggesting that Chinese audiences entirely cease watching Hong Kong programs, the respondent warned that they should be vigilant to the blemished attractions of capitalism. A female respondent shared a similar opinion, pleading that the capitalist values that accompanied border-crossing television is inimical to the development of their children:

> The Chinese [mainland] programs have a stronger education value. The program indirectly guided our children along a correct path. At night, I usually watch ATV. Then I will ask my son to go into his room to do homework. I don't want him to absorb Hong Kong people's notion on money. Students should not squander all his money on brand names and consumption. Such faulty consciousness on money will eventually lead to wickedness, violence and crime.

With a nationalistic education that inculcated a strong sense of class consciousness, Guangzhou people clearly reflected the notion that inveterate class ideology embedded in the Hong Kong television programs is undesirable. They had a strong vision that this could create social instability and aggravate class conflict. For these audiences, exposed to border-crossing television—unlike the simplistic audiences suggested in the literature—watching television involves painstaking mental work. In a nutshell, their viewing is a mode of habitual, constant and conscientious shifting between being immersed in mediated pleasure and sifting through unrealistic as well as undesirable constituents.

HONG KONG VALUES AS A GLOBAL STANDARD

There is no doubt that the selective negation of Hong Kong television is an active reaction, but to the extent that the Chinese audience is also responding to their own socio-economic limitations we can also interpret such behavior as a passive refusal of the border-crossing ideologies. It is the perceived "deficiency" in the local context that prompted them to turn to something from without. The question is: What are the social functions of border-crossing television for the audiences, given the fact that fervent aspirations for the Hong Kong lifestyle, values and consumption are largely unrealizable for them?

Based on the data, I would argue that the Hong Kong values absorbed in these television dramas serve as a global standard or reference. For the audience of a relatively closed society, the articulation could be a path leading to social improvement. An interpretation of their responses to the socioeconomic conditions of Hong Kong illustrates their cultural benchmarking. Talking about individual characters in the dramas, a male respondent said he would like to be one of the male characters in *Court of Justice,* in which the middle-class solicitors are persuasive and confident. The reason for his identification is not just that these professionals live in a luxurious world with race cars, classy suits and huge flats, all the respondents think such professionalism is a highly recognized global practice. Another interviewee said, "Serving as a lawyer like those in Hong Kong or from the West—to fight for the virtue and truth is an ideal job."

Hong Kong television presented and prescribed a pseudo-world for the mainland Chinese audience. This pseudo-world might not be exactly reality, but it is an approximation of what happens in the Western world. In other words, the Hong Kong dramas become a standard for the mainland to follow. By viewing Hong Kong televised texts as a cultural standard, the audience does not entirely preclude the possibility of realizing the unrealistic global world. Under their specific social circumstances, first, perceiving that the television world is likely a miniature of Western societies, they think that the mediated texts could also be actualized and concretized in China, it's just a matter of time; and second, as the economic conditions in China improve, audiences do not see that "catching up" is out of the realm of possibility.

THE CRITICAL LENS: FROM EVALUATION TO SELF-EVALUATION

The sublimation of the televised text to a cultural standard inevitably leads to a secondary social effect. The projected changes on the mainland—in terms of the discrepancies both between people's material urges and socioeconomic development, and between their own normalized view of personal values, identity, and freedom and ideological control—may not match their program-induced social imaginations. With pressure from crude materialism and the border-crossing capitalist society, their exposure to the contradictory and yet pseudo-reality of the global world as presented in the Hong Kong dramas provokes self-evaluation of the system. This is a double negation, criticizing the cruel and unrealistic materialism as preached on border-crossing television and, at the same time, disqualifying their own local society by using others as cultural standards. After long-term viewing of media texts from without, the social agencies are then unconsciously bound to tackle local realities with the very same lens used to evaluate outside and distant reality.

However, this does not imply that with these standards they are intent on upsetting the status quo. In fact, rarely do they undermine their own community, neighborhood and relationships. Rather, the center of frustration and dissatisfaction diverts to the cultural and media terrain. One interviewee, living in a well-off and caring family said, "[television programs in China] speak our own language. I feel close and attached to them . . . but that television in China has too strong an ideology. I am not sure of their real effect either. How could that television [content] change our society?" In general, the audiences acknowledged that the cultural politics and ideology of their local television programs have substituted and overshadowed the real problems in the social structure, hence, failing to ground their criticism on the latter. The double negations are manifested as savorless and unpleasing feelings toward the cultural production of their hegemonic media.

[Hong Kong television soap operas are] quite different from those mainland productions. Although Hong Kong television soap operas are a bit unreal, they make us [feel] pleasant and comfortable. Actually, watching television is a kind of entertainment [for us] to spend our leisure time. We do not want to watch arts on television at all.

Another interviewee compared the Hong Kong programs to their own programs and said:

Hong Kong television shows us the world outside, and almost everything. I'm not saying that the West is always good, but at least our TV programs should use our own languages . . . from people's viewpoint . . . This is what we "miss" most in television programs in China. We are not duped audiences.

The everyday "languages" mentioned by the audience collectively symbolize much more than a materialist disparity, they also reflect a free and liberalizing worldview. It is beyond a capitalist pursuit and it is not just a degree of tolerance. Hong Kong experiences strong class inequality and alienation and atomization of relationships in an urban and capitalist setting The Chinese audience may be suggesting that they do not want their society to walk in the same footsteps. Nonetheless, what are salvaged in these televised texts, unquestionably, are the freedom and other liberalizing values that are essentially non-comparable and absent in the propagandistic nature of the Chinese television. This is a reconsideration and a revaluation—and even a critique—of the local nationalistic values, social norms and economic system under the silhouette of a capitalist system just across the border. At this moment, Guangzhou audiences' dissatisfaction might just be confined to the production of their own media. However, in the long term, there is no guarantee that such double negations and cultural criticism will not transform into a formal social movement that challenges the state. This is precisely what the authorities are anxious about.

CONCLUSION: MEDIA CONSUMPTION WITH INCOMPLETE GLOBALIZATION

Studies on cross-cultural television audiences have found no unanimous result on the effects of ideology embedded in programs. Results suggest that some individuals are dominated while some actively resist the domination. The empirical data of this study tends to support the latter, but it provides an important footnote to this process. Local audiences (Guangzhou audiences) in general are able to fantasize and derive pleasure from these border-crossing dramas and yet develop an alternative interpretation of Hong Kong television soap operas. However, instead of absorbing the prescribed capitalist values from Hong Kong television, as the globalization thesis would suggest, the Chinese audiences develop their own reading strategies. In this way, first, they are rational and critical and seem to be sensitive to the ideology reflected by the fictional characters, scenes and plots in the programs. In our case, the Chinese audiences criticize border-crossing television for its over-representation of the values and lives of the middle class, their consumption patterns and crude materialism, and their criticism is grounded in their realization of their own socio-economic status and perceptions of the difference between the two systems. Second, apart from pinpointing the possible negative consequences of the viewing, audiences do safeguard the values of Hong Kong television. From the Hong Kong television content, they presuppose that they are connected to the global trend, Western realities and even an advanced and utopian world, a world they are eager to join.

Exposed to what appear to be global values, it turns out that audiences have to use the same lens they use for the global world to evaluate their own values and culture. It is precisely these external values that give them an opportunity to reposition themselves. The mainland Chinese soon realize that capitalism and consumerism are irreversible trends, and the artificial truncation to the global is the reason why they economically "lag" behind Hong Kong. Such "difference" is due to an inappropriate national policy and their national system in the last instance. The people may not directly challenge their own system, but through criticizing their own local media production, they indirectly express their dissatisfaction with the hegemonic control of the national identity. This is not only a negation of their own media and Hong Kong's media but an indirect disavowal of their own system. In the long term, this accelerates and pushes for local political reform and development.

In this case, it is worth noting the "global forces" that drive them to be skeptical of their own system. Ostensibly, there is a discrepancy between what exactly is global and the perception of global on Hong Kong television. In this study, the local audiences are influenced not by direct globalized media but only by Hong Kong television texts, which are to a certain degree embedded with global values. The audiences did misinterpret these as global. The Hong Kong media are not global media; nor are these Hong Kong-produced television dramas representations of the West. After Hong Kong's hand-over to China, these television dramas are still sites of struggle between the authorities who deliberately imposed on them a Chinese identity, and the locals who defended their own Hong Kong identity, which is still very much influenced by the colonial legacy of democracy, freedom and individual rights (Fung 2004). Thus, what influenced the border-crossing audiences is not a complete version of globalization, first, because the cultural terrain of Hong Kong is not a replica of the global since it is being nationalized by China, and second, because the Chinese only absorb the global values through an intermediate agent. The media culture of Hong Kong in this case may be regarded as providing cultural interrelatedness or the "global acumen" that has been assimilated and incorporated by them (Hannerz 1989), but this culture, which has been subjected to the complicated process of hybridization or incorporation, is never the "global." No matter how receptive they are to the Hong Kong media culture, the Chinese audiences' understanding of the global is never complete. This is what I called incomplete globalization of the Chinese audience.

Such incomplete globalization, despite the suspicion of the degree of globalism, however, still performs important functions for the local. Given that the audiences in China are imbued with a strong national and class ideology, media texts from without might not rock their fundamental belief and provoke them to ponder the legitimacy of their own system. However, the geo-culturally closer Hong Kong television organizes for the local a set of relevant "global values" (though incomplete) to resist national control and domination.

From the perspective of social change, the contradiction between nationalism and this deviant form of globalization does influence this developing society. With this incomplete global value as a reference, the Chinese society may eventually adopt a form of consumerism or capitalism in its mode of operation, while retaining its self-perceived cultural values, norms and traditions. And they may also break through the nationalist control of the society in cultural politics, while not seriously destabilizing the whole system. Such cultural resistance, if not self-negation of their own system, may possibly lead the would-be consumer society to develop an alternative path of economic development that is different from the model of Western capitalist societies—but that has the same aspiration regarding various vague notions relating to freedom, human rights and democracy accompanied with these mediated discourses. The various forms of incomplete globalization in different countries in the region may also explain why Asian societies reveal a number of differing alternative development patterns.

REFERENCES

Barker, C. (1999) *Television, Globalization and Cultural Identities,* Buckingham: Open University Press.

Caughie, J. (1982) "Scottish Television: What Would it Look Like?" in C. McArthur (ed) *Scotch Reels: Scotland in Film and Television,* London: BFI.

Cvetkovich, A. and Kellner, D. (1997) *Articulating the Global and the Local,* Colorado: Westview.

Dirlik, A. (1996) "The Global in the Local," in R. Wilson and W. Dissanayake (eds) *Global/Local: Cultural Production and the Transnational Imaginary,* Durham: Duke University Press.

Dorfman, M. and Mattelart, A. (1975) *How to Read Donald Duck: Imperialist Ideology and the Disney Comic,* New York: International General.

Featherstone, M., ed. (1990) *Global Culture,* Newbury Park: Sage.

Fiske, J. (1986) "Television: Polysemy and Popularity," *Critical Studies in Mass Communication,* 3(4): 391–408.

Fung, A. (2004) "Postcolonial Hong Kong Identity: Hybridising the Local and the National," *Social Identities,* 10(3): 399–414.

Gerbner, G. (1992) "Violence and Terror in and by the Media," in M. Raboy and B. Dagenais (eds) *Media, Crisis and Democracy: Mass Communication and the Disruption of Social Order,* London: Sage.

Gramsci, A. (1971) *Prison Notebooks,* New York: International Publishers.

Grossberg, L. (1984) "Another Boring Day in Paradise: Rock and Roll and the Empowerment of Everyday Life," *Popular Music,* 4: 225–57.

Hall, S. (1977) "Culture, the Media and the Ideological Effect," in J. Curran et al. (eds) *Mass Communication and Society,* London: Arnold.

Hannerz, U. (1989) "Global Ecumene," in C. Breckenridge (ed) *Public Culture,* Chicago: University of Chicago Press.

Herman, E. and Chomsky, N. (1988) *Manufacturing Consent,* New York: Pantheon.

Hodge, R. and Tripp, D. (1986) *Children and Television: A Semiotic Approach,* Cambridge: Polity.

Liebes, T. and Katz, E. (1990) *The Export of Meaning: Cross-Cultural Readings of Dallas,* Cambridge: Polity.

Lull, J. (1991) *China Turned On: Television, Reform and Resistance,* New York: Routledge.

Murdock, G. (1974) "Mass Communication and the Construction of Meaning," in N. Armistead (ed) *Reconstructing Social Psychology,* Harmondsworth: Penguin.

Sakr, N. (2002) *Satellite Realms: Transnational Television: Globalization and the Middle East,* London: IB Tauris.

Schiller, H. (1996) *Information Inequality: The Deepening Social Crisis in America,* London: Routledge.

Sinclair, J., Jacka, E. and Cunningham, S. (1996) "Peripheral Vision. New Patterns," in J. Sinclair et al. (eds) *Global Television: Peripheral Vision,* New York: Oxford.

Thussu, D. (1998) *Electronic Empires: Global Media and Local Resistance,* London: Arnold.

Williams, R. (1980) *Problems in Materialism and Culture,* London: Verso.

Wober, J. M. (1998) "Cultural Indicators: European Reflections on a Research Paradigm," in R. Dickinson et al. (eds) *Approaches to Audience,* London: Arnold.

Xinhuanet.com. (2004, September 27) "TVB and ATV Jointly Decode the Problem of Advertising." http://big5.xinhuanet.com/gate/big5/news.xinhuanet.com/newmedia

Xu, C., Xiao, Y., Wei M. and Tsai, S. (2006) *Audience Rating Analysis and TV Management* (in Chinese), Guangzhou: Yangcheng Evening News Press.

Part II

The Rise of Asian Media

Regional Consumption

6 East Asian Pop Culture
Layers of Communities

Chua Beng Huat

Production, circulation and consumption of "East Asian" media products—films, pop music and television dramas and other programs—within the region including the People's Republic of China (PRC), Taiwan, Hong Kong, Japan, South Korea and Singapore (by virtue of its 78 percent ethnic Chinese majority population), are increasingly integrated into a loosely organized cultural economy, which can be substantively and discursively designated as "East Asian pop culture." In the Chinese-dominated locations of the PRC, Taiwan, Hong Kong and Singapore, which can be designated as a "Pop Culture China" sphere (Chua 2001), the history of pop culture flows, exchanges and consumption began as far back as 1930s, if not earlier, depending on the medium. To this established Chinese-languages pop culture media network were added Japanese pop culture in the early 1990s and, subsequently, Korean pop culture in late 1990s. The emergence of an East Asian pop culture stands significantly in the way of complete hegemony of the US media culture, which undoubtedly continues to dominate entertainment media globally. Indeed, at the beginning of the twenty-first century, discussions about media in East Asia have displaced concern over "cultural imperialism" of the West, namely of the United States, and focus on celebration of the "arrival" of East Asian pop cultures in the global entertainment market.

Several landmark achievements have led to that sense of "arrival." The earliest East Asian entries into the global pop culture entertainment markets are probably Japanese animation, *manga* and video games. These are, according to Iwabuchi (2002: 257), "culturally odorless" because they contain little explicit Japanese content; animation and *manga* figures have always been intentionally rid of Japanese features and resemble no particular ethnic group. These products continue to be the main stays of Japanese pop culture export to the world, with animation programs regularly dubbed into languages of local audiences. Since the 1990s, Chinese and Korean cinemas have entered global circulation, in both critical film festivals and commercial markets, juxtaposed against Hollywood's dominating presence. Beneath the global scale, since the mid-1990s, the most significant pop culture that circulates transnationally within East Asia is serialized television dramas, streaming routinely into the homes of audiences throughout the region; Japanese TV dramas throughout the 1990s, followed by Korean TV dramas in the early 2000s. The commercial success of these TV dramas is an almost exclusively East Asian phenomenon as they have no market in the West, except among East Asian diasporic communities watching DVDs.

SINGAPORE: SIGNIFIER OF EAST ASIAN POP CULTURE

The transnationalization and regionalization of East Asian pop cultures is most visible in Singapore because Singapore is primarily a market for and location of consumption of imported programs, since the small domestic population on this island-nation is unable to sustain a large media industry of its own. In the 1950s, when the PRC was closed to Hong Kong producers, it was also a site for Southeast Asian regional redistribution for Hong Kong cinema. In the mid-1970s, Singaporeans were introduced to the now global movie star Chow Yung Fatt, on the small screen in the serial drama *Men in the Net,* in which he played a PRC migrant struggling to survive in Hong Kong. At the same time, the Singapore audience was also watching Chinese costume dramas with themes drawn from "traditional" family politics dictated by the Confucian principle of filial piety, particularly, dramas based on the popular romance novels by the Taiwanese woman writer Ziong Yao. Now, Hong Kong and Taiwanese drama series of all genres constitute part of the daily programming of Singapore television stations.

Japanese action movies were popular in Singapore in the 1960s, but the flow was disrupted when the Japanese movie industry went into decline (Yau 2005). Japanese screen products returned very significantly with what has come to be called "trendy" television dramas in the 1990s—melodramatic romances of love gained, love lost, with plenty of agonizing twists and turns—among young urban(e) professionals. Japanese export of these trendy dramas to the rest of Asia was largely serendipitous. In spite of the very high cost of the very high quality productions, the "bubble economy" of Japan at the time was able to generate enough profits for the producers. Consequently, the early export of Japanese TV dramas was through very informal channels, including Taiwanese business people returning from Japan with DVD sets of the dramas for screening by unlicensed satellite television stations. Significantly, in spite of the popularity, Japanese producers continue to be slow and reluctant to export, in part because of piracy of media material in the region.

As Japanese popular television lost its vitality and appeal in the region, along came Korean TV dramas at the end of the 1990s, becoming routine broadcasts by the early 2000s. In contrast to the serendipity of Japanese TV drama export, exporting of Korean TV dramas is a conscious national industrial strategy. The inflows of Korean pop culture—music, films and

TV dramas—quickly came to be dubbed the "Korean Wave" (韩 流), following the PRC fans. Correspondingly, the importing of Korean dramas became a strategy for new or smaller or marginal television stations to establish their presence among local audiences. Singapore is again a good example of this strategy.

Since its establishment in the early 1960s, the television industry in Singapore had been monopolized by the state-owned MediaCorp, which operates four stations, one of which is dedicated to Mandarin programs. In 1999, the local monopoly newspaper publisher, the Singapore Press Holdings, ventured into commercial television with two free-to-air stations, one in English (Channel I) and the other in Mandarin (Channel U).[1] The English-language channel's locally produced programs were abject failures. The production studio was shut down in less than two years, with programming reduced to news and imported programs, primarily from the United States. On the other hand, the Mandarin channel was able to carve out and take away a significant segment of the audience from the already established state-owned television station, through broadcasting a combination of Korean dramas and local variety shows that look and feel like similar shows from Taiwan, which in turn are very similar to those from Japan. The general formula in all these variety shows seems to be high-energy, rapid-fire commentaries from the team of program hosts, whose entire focus is on making fun of and embarrassing whoever appears on the show.

The popularity of the Korean dramas on Channel U pushed the state-owned channel to also import such series. By late 2003, there was at least one Korean TV drama on one Singapore television screen every night. The two stations were engaged in constant bidding wars for the same dramas. This destructive competition stopped when the two companies decided to merge and reorganize their stations through product differentiation. While MediaCorp's Mandarin channel develop local programs, Channel U has repositioned itself as the "Asian pop culture channel," on which movies and contemporary TV dramas from Hong Kong, Korea and Japan, along with historical costume dramas and *wuxia* (武侠, martial art) dramas from the PRC—often jointly produced with a Hong Kong or Singapore partner—are freely mixed in the daily offerings, interspersed with local news, talk shows and occasional variety or game shows, making it a signifier of the idea of an East Asian pop culture.

OTHER INSTANCES OF CULTURAL ECONOMY INTEGRATION

In addition to Singapore, trendy Japanese dramas penetrated the rest of the East Asian markets through different channels. In Hong Kong, where more than 90 percent of the local audience were already captured by the two free-to-air television stations, TVB and ATV, Japanese drama was a significant vehicle for STAR TV, a cable television provider, to establish its presence and garner its share of the local audience. According to Iwabuchi, these promotional efforts of STAR TV were far more important than those of the Japanese producers. Similar situations prevailed with cable TV stations in Taiwan (2004: 7). In the PRC, the dramas are mostly distributed via pirated VCDs and DVDs and, with increasingly sophisticated computer-mediated information technologies, circulated by "communities" of fans: One fan downloads the episode from the television broadcast and another adds subtitles and uploads it for public access (Hu 2005: 176–80). The broad regional popularity of trendy dramas attracted much academic research, enabling comparative studies of the meaning-making activities of its consumers in different regional locations (Iwabuchi 2004).[2]

In 2004 and 2005, the most popular Korean drama series in locations where an ethnic Chinese population dominated was undoubtedly *Jewel in the Palace* (打长令), a fictionalized chronicle of the rise of the first female imperial court physician in the Chosen Dynasty in Korean during the fifteenth century. Ethnic Chinese audiences are familiar with historical dramas; indeed, historical dramas are almost the only genre of the PRC that is able to successfully cross national boundaries into ethnic Chinese regions. However, as a rule, such historical costume dramas are not exported because audiences in the rest of East Asia do not have the requisite knowledge of Korean history to sustain interest; hence, the Korean dramas that are exported are mainly contemporary urban romances. In the case of *Jewel,* the "close" cultural affinity between the Chosen Dynasty period and Chinese history was an important bridge to its success; for example, the shared calligraphic script facilitated "indigenization" of the series. Riding on this affinity, the Hong Kong television station made additional efforts to "indigenize" the Korean drama. For example, beyond the usual dubbing and subtitling, the station provided a brief supplementary narrative before each episode, giving the Chinese language equivalents of ingredients in food or medical preparations that were part of the story.

The series was first exported to Taiwan, dubbed in Mandarin, and was well received. Its popularity can be gleaned from the fact that some candidates for the national assembly election in 2004 turned up, with their entourage of supporters, on nomination day to register their candidacy dressed in costumes from the drama (Ko 2005). It was subsequently broadcast on TVB in Cantonese in Hong Kong, to record-breaking audience ratings. In 2004, the local Hunan satellite TV station obtained the rights from the Taiwan distributor, beating a national Shanghai competitor who was negotiating with the Korean producers, to air the series in the PRC. Strategically, the provincial Hunan station was able to use the popular series as the vehicle to propel itself into the PRC national broadcasting space (Leung 2005).[3] Finally, the drama series was broadcast in Singapore, twice on cable television and twice on the free-to-air Channel U, thus, covering all points in China's pop culture.

Japan is the most resistant to the penetration of popular cultures from the rest of the region. In the 1990s, there was a trickle of Hong Kong action movies, especially those of Jackie Chan, and popular music that flowed into a small aficionado market. This made it all the more remarkable when Korean television dramas suddenly exploded in Japan, with *Winter Sonata*. The series was released in January 2002 and quickly circulated with great popularity throughout East Asia, except Japan. It was first shown on NHK-owned cable television during the late night timeframe, in December 2003. Popular demand caused the NHK to show it again in 2004. Meanwhile, its popularity began to receive media coverage. Then, on 3 April 2004, the star of the series, Bae Yong Joon, arrived at the Tokyo airport and five thousand largely middle-aged female fans turned up to welcome him. Thus began the *Winter Sonata* phenomenon. NHK rebroadcast the series on terrestrial stations in April 2004, again picking up record ratings and leading them to rebroadcast it later in the same year. According to Mori (2005), NHK earned about 3,500 million yen (US $3.5 million) from *Winter Sonata* products, including 330,000 sets of DVDs and 1,220,000 copies of the novelized book. The series propelled Bae into superstardom in Japan, elevated to so-called "Yon-sama," "Prince Yon" among his fans.

Beyond the television screen, *Winter Sonata* also spawned several behavioral changes among its Japanese middle-aged female audience. Their active fandom brought into the limelight a group of media consumers who hitherto have been largely ignored by the media. Their very public celebration of the star, Bae, made them a media phenomenon, generating new ideological commentaries about gender politics. Like Korean drama fans from elsewhere in the region, the Japanese fans traveled as tourists to the sites where the television series was shot, transforming televisual sights to tourist sites and radically modifying the character of Japanese tourists to Korea, which had hitherto been a destination of sex tourism for Japanese men (Hirata 2005). The narrative and characters also changed the images and views of the Japanese female consumers, who might have viewed Koreans, including those who had been long resident in Japan, as ex-colonized, marginal people. Many began to imagine themselves as "cultural brokers" who would work to bridge the cultural and attitudinal gaps between the Japanese and the Koreans (Iwabuchi 2005). It should be noted that these intense reactions towards Korean TV dramas are not replicated elsewhere in the region and are explainable within the history of colonial/postcolonial relations between Japan and Korea; the latter was colonized for almost seventy-five years by the former.

The above instances—the popularization and consumption of Japanese and Korean television dramas in all the ethnic-Chinese dominant locations, the popularization of Korean dramas in Japan and of Japanese pop cultures of different genres in Korea—together substantiate the presence of an East Asian pop culture sphere. It also shows that the flows and exchanges are very unequal. Japan continues to be largely an exporting country to the rest of the region, the success of *Winter Sonata* in Japan notwithstanding. Korean pop culture is now a constant flow into the predominantly ethnic-Chinese locations; however, in these locations Chinese language(s) pop culture remains more widely consumed than imports, with occasional spikes for a very popular singer, film or drama series from Korea or Japan. The unequal flows and exchanges are consequences of demographics; the relatively smaller consumer populations of Japan and Korea make dubbing or subtitling of Chinese-language(s) programs a risky venture. On the other hand, the regional, massive ethnic-Chinese population makes dubbing and subtitling of Korean and Japanese programs financially viable, even lucrative, as in the case of *Jewel in the Palace*.

TRANSNATIONAL AUDIENCE COMMUNITIES

In the narrative above, East Asian pop cultural economy integration is discussed primarily with regard to television dramas because they generate most visible and stable consumer communities that facilitate audience research. Relative to television dramas, music and film make light demands on audiences in terms of time commitment; no more than a few minutes of consumer attention is required in the case of a song, and usually, no more than a couple of hours in the case of a film. In contrast, television drama demands audience viewing at regular intervals, usually once every week for one episode. Many other activities need to be sacrificed or at least displaced so a viewer can watch the episode each week; alternatively, efforts have to be made to video-record an episode if missing it cannot be avoided and time has to be found to watch that episode before the next installment. These demands amount to an active participation with what is on screen, drawing the audience into an intimate virtual relationship with the characters in the drama. The respective demands on consumers have determining effects on the different genres of pop culture that are studied academically. The sustained consumption practices in watching television dramas are a necessary condition that enables the analysis of receptions and responses, making it a major focus of media studies. In contrast, ideological analyses are the norm for film narratives and musical lyrics, in addition to particularistic analyses of "star" musicians and film actors and actresses, as in "celebrity" studies.

Several layers of audiences/consumers for pop cultures can be identified. First, and most obvious, is the local audience of local productions. Most pop culture products are in fact directed at the domestic market; for example, Singaporean television stations produced up to one thousand hours of dramas annually, very little of which is exported. Next are audiences located in the export markets, namely, transnational audiences. As media consumption is generally a solitary activity, including watching movies in a cinema—a very obvious exception being consumption of music in a dance club—institutional mechanisms are necessary to bring about among consumers an awareness of shared interest in viewership, that is, an awareness of a "community" of audiences.

An avid consumer often seeks ways to intensify the pleasure of consumption through active engagement with others similarly disposed. The most conventional mechanism that facilitates this is the "fan club," which organizes avid consumers with shared affections for a particular performance artist, drama series or genre of programs into a "community." While the term "fan club" suggests that the clubs are organized by fans for fans, they are in fact often established by the artist or the production companies as a means of sustaining consumer interest to extend the longevity of what would otherwise be an essentially ephemeral phenomenon. Fan club membership suggests a greater passion than conventional media consumption, desire for more than just a leisure activity that fills the remains of a working day. Fan clubs can be organized as "local" or "international"; furthermore, local fan clubs can be linked transnationally through different channels of exchange and communication.

The Internet has become one avenue for organization of transnational consumption of pop culture. The following is a summary of what happened to one of the Japanese television drama series, *Pride,* recounted by Hu (2005: 177–78):

> In January 2004, a Hong Kong fan, R, who is a skilled Japanese speaker, did the Chinese subtitling for *Pride,* a few days after the original broadcast in Japan. She thanks T and A for their supplies of the raw material, and when she made a mistake in the subtitling, she took care to insert a correction by thanking another fan for pointing out the mistake. The version of R's Chinese subtitling of *Pride* was extremely popular in the Hong Kong newsgroup through its online circulation by means of BitTorrent. [T]he marketing of another version of *Pride* produced by a Taiwanese-based leading pirated-Japanese-VCD company seems to be threatened, because R's version has already been so widely circulated among Chinese fans through the Internet. The inner passions for drama, fan friendship and performance/self-expression are displayed in the context of this Chinese translation/subtitling; being "acknowledged by a community of like-minded is a characteristically romantic structure of feeling."[4]

These online communities are highly organized transnational communities of consumers. The passion of a few language and technology savvy consumers/participants/members drives them to do the painstaking work of initiating and amending translation/subtitling of their favorite drama series, for the benefits of other members of the cyber-virtual fan community, beyond the clutches of profit-oriented market players and the legal constraints, including censorship, of the nation-state.

However, an artist or a drama series is "popular" precisely because they have statistically large numbers of audience/consumers, far exceeding passionate members of "hyperactive" Internet communities and other fan clubs. Indeed, this larger and wider number of consumers who conventionally watch the dramas as leisure and entertainment account for the "popularity" of the pop culture item in question. It is therefore necessary to conceptualize the idea of "community of consumers" beyond the restrictive boundaries of passionate fans. Qualification for "membership" in this larger potential "community" is no more than the act of consumption. As the potential members of this larger community are necessarily as widely dispersed across geographic space as the distribution radius of the pop culture products, the potential community would not be bounded by geographic boundaries but would be transnational and transcultural. The question is, through what processes and institutional mechanisms can this statistical presence constitute itself into a "community," since for these viewers pop culture consumption is largely a private affair, without any expectation or conscious effort to engage with fellow consumers.

One mode of realizing this larger community of consumers is through the media itself. The "popularity" of a singer, an actor or a drama series is produced, very significantly, by the wide media attention and coverage they receive; popularity is thus engendered by other constitutive members of the media culture industry—newspapers, magazines, television, radio and advertising. Take the entertainment page of any newspaper in East Asia as an illustration. The page can be conceptualized as a "community" space for the entire East Asian pop culture industry. The places that appear regularly on it are the production centers of Seoul, Tokyo, Shanghai, Beijing, Hong Kong, Taipei and very occasionally, Singapore. These centers define the boundaries of East Asian pop culture within the entertainment page; the page is thus a proxy for the geographical map of East Asian pop culture. The bounded page space is "peopled" daily by images of and information about East Asian artists. The likes of Bae Yung Joon in Seoul, Faye Wong (王菲) in Shanghai, Wong Kai Wei （黄嘉伟）in Hong Kong, Jay Chou (周结伦) in Taipei inhabit these pages at unpredictable intervals, more frequently in the rising phases of their careers and with diminishing presence when they are on the way out. The entertainment page is read by an unknown number of readers, who are also unknown to each other. A "community" is instantiated if two or more readers happen to be present at an event, during which they participate, as part of free-flowing conversation, in exchanges concerning one of the artists reported about on the page. Such instances make manifest the hidden presence of a "community of consumers" of East Asian pop culture as an "occasioned" and "occasional" community, befitting the practices of the overwhelming majority of consumers, for whom consumption is leisure and entertainment rather than a primary focus of everyday life.[5]

IDENTIFICATION AND DISTANCE

A central question of transnational audience research is how audiences identify with the narrative, the themes and characters of an imported drama
series. Audience identification with the narratives, characters and activities
on screen can be quite direct, especially but not exclusively during actual
viewing time. At the most immediate level, identification is disclosed in
audience comments such as "I can understand the character on screen and
why she acts the way she does. I would do the same if I were in her position because we are all human." One version of this identification is when
a drama fan reworks on-screen events, activities and characters into his or
her life. For example, this Hong Kong viewer comments:

> Many times in life I encountered obstacles, or often I feel frustrated at
> not being able to utilize my capabilities, hence I do identify with the
> male led in *Long Vacation* [a Japanese drama series]. But I find one
> thing quire reassuring in the drama. When Kimura Takuya summoned
> the determination to win the piano contest and eventually won it, it
> seemed that his "vacation" had ended. I hope my "vacation" will end
> like his. (Leung 2004: 94)[6]

A Singaporean viewer notes:

> Such things can happen anywhere in this world. It's just that it is filmed
> in Japan and the characters are Japanese. But when you are talking
> about love, sex, and marriage, it happens anywhere in the world where
> someone, out of a situation, has sex with someone else on a fateful
> night and then thinks about it and, you know, wonders, "Why did I do
> it?" (MacLachlan and Chua 2004: 147)

A less inclusive mode of identification than "humans as such" takes the
form of "I identify with the character and his/her actions because we are
Asians" and therefore "alike," against an unsaid, "we are not like non-
Asians." This generates and affirms a sense of "Asianness," despite the fact
that the culture of the production location is different from that in which
the audience is embedded. This idea of "being Asian" has been conceptualized by Iwabuchi in terms of "cultural proximity" (Iwabuchi 2002).

Research on transnational consumption of East Asian pop culture has
found that audiences at different locations differentiate themselves along
one identifiable dimension, namely, a linear trajectory of what might be
called "capitalism-driven consumerist modernity." With the exception of
Japan, rapid capitalist development in East Asia is a relatively recent phenomenon, initiated in the early to mid-1960s. At the level of everyday life,
the rapid economic development translates into material improvements
through the expansion of consumption. As a consequence, there has been

a readily observable frenetic pace of expansion of consumerism throughout East Asia, most recently in the PRC, after the marketization of its economy since 1978. This frenetic expansion is fueled partly by pent-up demands due to underdevelopment, especially for necessities and household products. In addition, it is driven by the desire to "catch up" with the standard of living of the developed capitalist economies.[7] "Modernity" for the masses in newly developed East Asia is thus expressed through consumerist culture. Along this line, Japan, as the most capitalist-consumerist-modern location, leads at the front, while less capitalist economically developed countries, such as the present PRC or Vietnam, bring up the rear, with locations such as Hong Kong, Taiwan, Singapore and South Korea in a difficult-to-differentiate "middle."

This linear placement explains the general structure of respective audiences' gazes on the other "Asians," for instance, the Taiwanese or Vietnamese audiences' future-oriented gaze in watching/reading Japanese TV dramas. Japan's present is the future of the rest of Asia, where capitalist consumerism is less developed (Ko 2004; Thomas 2004). In contrast, there is the nostalgic gaze of the Japanese audience: the present of the rest of Asia is the lost past of Japan, enabling the relatively small segments of Japanese fans of pop cultures from the rest of East Asia to retain their self-centeredness (Iwabuchi 2004). This linear vector along the road to capitalist consumerism becomes blurred as the location in question catches up with Japan in consumption power, as Korea, Hong Kong and Singapore have done.

However, watching/reading an imported drama is complicated unavoidably by the audience's awareness that the drama is "foreign" and that this "foreignness" is integral to the viewing pleasure. The mediation of foreignness raises hurdles to identification, while simultaneously making distancing from the narrative and characters on screen relatively easy. As soon as characters, actions and sentiments are contrary to an audience's sentiment, "foreignness/difference" surfaces to distance them from what is on screen. For example, apparently, Singaporean married women have a tendency to resist Japanese dramas' representations of sexual relations:

> [The Japanese] want to be first in everything. Their technology is first and this may affect them. They want to be advanced in everything . . . And unconsciously, it may influence their thinking, their attitude towards sex, their values. (MacLachlan and Chua 2004: 164)

"Difference" between "the Japanese they" and "Singaporean us" is emphasized repeatedly and unmistakably. Another Singaporean example: "I have a wish. I wish these Japanese dramas would not encourage our youths to accept those one-night love relationships so easily, sleep with each other and that's it. This is very unacceptable" (MacLachlan and Chua 2004: 165). Here, in contrast to the generalized, abstract categories of "human" and "Asian" that suppress "difference," the specificities of the "culture" of production location, presumed to be (re)presented by the TV dramas, are evoked to create "difference" and the basis of cultural distance. Obviously, the transnational audience moves between the two sentiments at will. Identification and distancing or cultural proximity and difference alternate intermittently rather than with either one sentiment being consistently sustained throughout the entire duration of watching an imported TV drama series. This alternating between two sentiments has consequence on the stable identity formation of TV drama audiences.

PAN-ASIAN "IDENTITY"

Undoubtedly, the passionate activities of fans in consuming a particular iconic artist and/or genre of pop culture signify the importance of the latter in their subjectivity. For example, the painstaking collaborative work done by Japanese TV drama fans in downloading, uploading, initiating and amending translation/subtitling of their favorite drama series in the cyber-virtual online fan communities is indicative of the presence and importance of a pan-Asian consumer community to the individual members. It is also the case that ex-consumers can readily recall, in fond nostalgia, the period of life when the consumption of pop culture was an important part of their daily life; the pop culture of "those days" has been etched into their memories and might have in some ways changed their personalities and their lives. For example, as mentioned earlier, one cannot deny the possibility that many middle-aged Japanese women may have permanently changed their attitudes towards Koreans as a consequence of watching the Korean TV drama *Winter Sonata* and idolizing its star, Bae Yong Joon.

No wonder, therefore, a persistent question arises: Will the transnational flow and consumption of East Asian pop culture lead to an emergent "pan–East Asian identity"? Evidently, similar East Asian physiognomy facilitates audience identification with the on-screen actors, characters and even themes, engendering the "I can understand the character because we are Asians" sentiment. However, other factors in media consumption mitigate the establishment of a stable "pan-Asian" identity among the consumers.

Firstly, as transnational Asian audiences view on-screen representations of each other along a linear capitalist-consumerist culture developmental sequence, they identify at least as much with a "capitalist-consumerist modernity" as with "Asianness." Secondly, the identification with an abstract "Asianness" is also constantly disrupted by the recognition of difference and distancing from the "foreign" culture represented on screen. Thirdly, individual identity formation is an unending process of layering and interaction of a constant stream of cultural knowledge. In this unending constellation of cultural inputs, pop music, cinema and television consumption are, for an overwhelming majority of audience/consumers, leisure activities, residual to the necessary routines of everyday life. Consequently, their impact on individual identity formation is on the whole rather weak. Finally, the "life" of a pop culture product and audience "loyalty" are equally ephemeral. In sum, any suggestion of "lasting" effects of pop culture consumption on individual identity formation would be difficult to establish.

POP CULTURE SPACE AND PUBLIC SPACE

Stuart Hall (1994) designates "popular culture" as the political arena that encompasses all the everyday life cultural practices of the masses in contradistinction to and contestation with the elite culture of a society. Within this larger popular culture political arena, consumer communities of imported pop culture are often confronted with an overwhelmingly bigger "non-consumer community." In such confrontations, the non-consumers readily use their overwhelming demographic majority to "anoint" themselves as the "people" and turn the contest into one of "defending" the "national" culture against foreign cultural "invasion" or "imperialism," often with the complicity of not only local pop culture producers but also the state. Three recent instances in East Asian pop culture illustrate this form of politics.

First is the case of Chang Hui Mei (Ah Mei), an aboriginal Taiwanese singer who was hugely popular in Pop Culture China. In 2000, she sang the Taiwanese national anthem at the inauguration of elected president, Chen Shui Bian, leader of the Democratic Progressive Party, which espouses independence for Taiwan from the PRC. This transformed her into a site for "Taiwan Straits" politics. The PRC government immediately forced sponsors to cancel her endorsement contracts, removed and suppress all her images from public places and imposed a ban on her performances. The PRC government clearly realized the impact of denying any Chinese language(s) artist access to its massive consumer power.[8] It took Ah Mei the next two years to work herself back to a concert in Shanghai. Then, in 2004, her sold out concert in Hangzhou was canceled by local police who "feared" a possible riot when a group of self-proclaimed "patriotic" Chinese students protested at the concert site against her supposedly "pro-independent" politics. However spurious this "nationalist" claim of presumably non-consuming protesting students might have been, it is a claim that was never discursively available to Chang's fans in the PRC.

Second, to be expected, the regional success of Korean pop culture has given rise to "anti-Korean" sentiments. For example, in Taiwan the counter-discourse "militarizes" Korean pop culture as the "Invasion of Korean Wave," suggesting a "violation" of Taiwan national territory. On the day that Bae Yong Joon visited Taipei to promote his movie, *April Snow,* self-fashioned "nationalist" Taiwanese rock musicians staged a concert to lambaste Korean pop culture and Bae himself (Yang 2005). In the PRC and Hong Kong media professionals, including the star of action-comedies,

Jacky Chan, protested against the extensive coverage by local media, which creates and enhances the "popularity" of every visiting Korean artist. In such instances, professional jealousy and self-interest hide behind the sign of the "national." In "expressing" and "representing" national interests as "cultural preservation," such protests exclude the fans of Korean pop culture from the nation as cultural "traitors."

Finally, the use of the "nation" and the "national" against the pop culture sphere also happens within the nation itself. For example, in Korea, in 2004, when it became public that earlier he had "cheated" conscription by faking his medical record, television actor Song Seung-Heon had to abruptly abandon the shooting of a drama series and return immediately from the shooting location in Australia to go into the military. Conscription is seen as the great "leveller" of inequalities among Korean men. Because of the Cold War legacy of a divided Korea, any attempt to escape conscription is tantamount to an anti-patriotic act. Media industry players and fans, at home and abroad, argued that Song was making very significant economic and cultural-diplomatic contributions to the Korean nation. Nevertheless, their request for him to complete the drama before entering the military fell on deaf ears.[9]

In these three instances, the pop culture sphere rubs up against the larger popular culture sphere. In the numerically and ideologically unequal contest that ensues, the sign of the "nation," and with it the imagined "national" culture, is discursively and strategically used by non-consumers to criticize and exclude the consumers of imported, foreign, pop culture as "less" than nationalistic; the "nation" is denied to the latter. Obviously, any theoretical desire to conceptualize a "pan–East Asian identity" from the transnational expansion of East Asian pop culture will have to recognize that such an identity, if it emerged at all, would be one of an "excluded" minority in any local contexts.

CONCLUSION

Transnational and cultural boundary-crossings of East Asian pop cultures have become routine and integral to the regular diet of regional media consumers, with occasional spikes for a red hot star, singer or television drama that create waves of excitement across the region. National and transnational communities of consumers have emerged, ranging from fan clubs to "occasioned" communities. Questions arise as to whether these consumer communities will in turn engender a "pan–East Asian identity" that might influence regional politics, which are still stuck deeply in international antagonisms resulting from memories of colonialism, World War II atrocities and the lingering Cold War.

Reviewing the expanding literature on regional audience reception, glimpses of a "pan–East Asian identity" are discernable. The apparent ease with which regional consumers identify with the on-screen faces, characters, activities and narratives of East Asian pop culture is reflected in the transformation of many of the East Asian artists into regional pop idols. However, identification and membership in consumer communities will always be ephemeral, as one fan grows out of it, a new one inducts him or herself, in quick succession, following the rise and fall of a constellation of popular artists, and making pop culture consumption poor ground for producing stable communities—too ephemeral to effect any significant influence, let alone changes, in the wider society. In particular, the previously mentioned middle-class Japanese women consumers of Korean TV drama, who imagined themselves as harbingers of change in "warming" relations between Koreans and Japanese, are unlikely to succeed, as they remain trapped within the *resentiment* of the region's international history and politics.

NOTES

1. "U" sounds similar to the Chinese word "尤," for excellent.
2. Iwabuchi notes the "intense sympathy many young East/Southeast Asians have come to feel toward the characters in Japanese dramas, and the way they have learned to cope with the meanings of their own modern experiences through the urban lives depicted in the Japanese TV dramas" (2004: 2).
3. Lisa Leung (2005) 'Mediating nationalism and modernity: the transnationalization of Korean dramas on Chinese (satellite) television'. Paper presented in the Workshop on East Asian Pop Culture: Transnational Japanese and Korean TV dramas, Asia Research Institute, National University of Singapore, 8-9 December.
4. Hu is quoting Streeter (2003: 649).
5. Chua (2006) provides a detailed analysis of newspaper entertainment pages as the imagined geography of East Asian pop culture.
6. The researcher adds her commentary, which reinforces the sense of "we are all human" (Leung 2004: 94–5).
7. For a comprehensive discussion of the rapid expansion of consumerism in newly rich Asia see Chua (2000).
8. In 2004, the PRC government similarly canceled the already granted performance permits to a few Singapore singers after the then incoming prime minister of Singapore, Lee Hsien Loong, visited Taiwan in his "personal" capacity.
9. For greater details on the cases of Chang Hui Mei and Song Seung-Heon, see Eva Tsia (2007).

REFERENCES

Chua, B. H., ed. (2000) *Consumption in Asia: Lifestyles and Identities*, London: Routledge.
——. (2001) "Pop Culture China," *Singapore Journal of Tropical Geography*, 22: 113–21.
——. (2006) "Gossips about Stars: Newspaper and Pop Culture China," in W. Sun (ed) *Media and Diasporas*, London: RoutledgeCurzon.
Hall, S. (1994) "Notes on Deconstructing 'The Popular,' in J. Storey (ed) *Cultural Theory and Popular Culture: A Reader*, New York: Harvester Wheatsheaf.

Hirata, Y. (2005) "Touring 'Dramatic Korea': Japanese Women as Viewers of Hanryu Dramas and Tourists on Hanryu Tours," in Chua Beng Huat and Koichi Iwabuchi (eds.) *East Asian Pop Culture: Analysing the Korean Wave*. Hong Kong: Hong Kong University Press, pp. 143–156.

Hu, K. (2005) "The Power of Circulation: Digital Technologies and the Online Chinese Fans of Japanese TV Drama," *Inter-Asia Cultural Studies*, 6(2): 171–86.

Iwabuchi, K. (2002) "From Western Gaze to Global Gaze: Japanese Cultural Presence in Asia," in D. Crane et al. (eds) *Global Culture: Media, Arts, Policy and Globalization*, New York: Routledge.

——. (2004) *Feeling Asian Modernities: Transnational Consumption of Japanese TV Dramas*, Hong Kong: Hong Kong University Press.

——. (2005) "When Korean Wave Meets Residents Koreans in Japan: Intersections of the Transnational, the Postcolonial and the Multicultural," in Chua and Iwabuchi (eds.) *East Asian Pop CultureL Analysing the Korean Wave*. Hong Kong: Hong Kong University Press, pp. 143–156.

Ko, Y. (2004) "The Desired Form: Japanese Idol Dramas in Taiwan," in K. Iwabuchi (ed) *Feeling Asian Modernities: Transnational Consumption of Japanese TV Dramas*, Hong Kong: Hong Kong University Press.

——. (2005) "The Festive Machine: Taiwan's 2004 Elections as Popular Culture," paper presented at the International Workshop on Political Elections as Popular Culture, National University of Singapore.

Leung, L. Y. (2004) "Ganbaru and its Transcultural Audience: Imaginary and Reality of Japanese TV Dramas in Hong Kong," in K. Iwabuchi (ed) *Feeling Asian Modernities: Transnational Consumption of Japanese TV Dramas*, Hong Kong: Hong Kong University Press.

——. (2005) "Mediating Nationalism and Modernity: The Transnationalization of Korean Dramas on Chinese (Satellite) Television," in Chua and Iwabuchi (eds.) *East Asian Pop Culture: Analysing the Korean Wave*. Hong Kong: Hong Kong University Press, pp. 53–70.

MacLachlan, E. and Chua, G. (2004) "Defining Asian Femininity: Chinese Viewers of Japanese TV Dramas in Singapore," in K. Iwabuchi (ed) *Feeling Asian Modernities: Transnational Consumption of Japanese TV Dramas*, Hong Kong: Hong Kong University Press.

Mori, Y. (2005) "*Winter Sonata* and Cultural Practices of Active Fans in Japan," in Chua and Iwabuchi (eds.) *East Asian Pop Culture: Analysing the Korean Wave*. Hong Kong: Hong Kong University Press, pp. 127–142.

Streeter, T. (2003) "The Romantic Self and the Politics of Internet Commercialization," *Cultural Studies*, 17: 648–68.

Thomas, M. (2004) "East Asian Cultural Traces in Post-Socialist Vietnam," K. Iwabuchi et al. (eds) *Rogue Flows: Trans-Asian Cultural Traffic*, Hong Kong: Hong Kong University Press.

Tsai, E. (2007) "Caught in the Terrains: An Inter-referential Inquiry of Trans-border Stardom and Fandom, *Inter-Asia Cultural Studies*, 8 (1):137–156.

Yang, F. C. (2005) "Rap(p)ing Korean Wave: National Identity in Question," in Chua and Iwabuchi (eds.) *East Asian Pop Culture: Analysing the Korean Wave*. Hong Kong: Hong Kong University Press, pp. 191–216.

Yau, S. K. (2005) "Interactions between Japanese and Hong Kong Action Cinema," in M. Morris et al. (eds) *Hong Kong Connections*, Durham: Duke University Press.

7 Discovering Japanese TV Drama through Online Chinese Fans

Narrative Reflexivity, Implicit Therapy and the Question of the Social Imaginary

Kelly Hu

The aim of this study is to explore Chinese fans' online practices in reflexive afterthought writing and their open exhibition and exchange of reflexive thoughts. Undeniably, there must be many reasons Chinese fans love Japanese TV drama. My main argument here is that the rich narrative reflexivity embedded in drama could be a very special attraction for some online Chinese fans, a point that generally goes unnoticed. Thus, I want to reveal the way in which Chinese fans discover narrative reflexivity as a series of specific traits, which then draws them on to engage in the activity of generating reflexive thoughts and carrying out implicit therapy on themselves through the practice of online discussions and writing. The Japanese TV drama to which I refer mainly evolved from the "trendy drama," which emerged in the late 1980s and is still popular today. It features characters and stories in a modern urban setting and is targeted at young Japanese audiences. The name "trendy drama" has its own historical meaning, as it marked a departure from Japanese "home dramas," which are made for Japanese women in their forties, fifties, and above (Iwabuchi 2004: 9–10). *Tokyo Love Story* (1991) may be seen as a landmark in the concept of the trendy drama—it deals with complicated love relationships and captures the rhythm of the city and the working lives of young people in their twenties and thirties.

Japanese TV drama has been popular in a number of Asian countries, including Taiwan, Hong Kong, China, Korea, Singapore, Malaysia and Thailand, since the middle 1990s. The Chinese community is certainly the largest audience for Japanese TV drama in the Asian region and in the West, as testified to by the wide circulation among the Chinese of pirated Japanese VCDs and DVDs worldwide and even the recent popular P2P digital uploading and downloading of Japanese TV drama on the Internet (Hu 2005). Undeniably, the Chinese community has constituted a niche market for Japanese TV drama for some time. However, paradoxically, the promotion of Japanese TV drama has never been the result of any corporate strategy to capture Asian markets (Toru 2004: 77).

There have been a number of studies on the reception of Japanese TV drama in East and Southeast Asia. For example, the Japanese scholar Koichi Iwabuchi has edited a book in English that brings together a wide range of studies on the transcultural consumption of Japanese TV drama in East and Southeast Asia (2004). In Taiwan, the Chinese-language journal *Envisage* has published two issues that focus on Japanese popular culture and the way it is sweeping into Taiwan, China, and Hong Kong (2002, 2003). Of particular interest were comments on the hunger for Japanese TV drama in Taiwan.

The obsession of Taiwanese audiences with Japanese TV drama partly stems from their longing for the advanced modernity portrayed in Japanese TV drama, as reflected in the higher standard of living, consumption trends, and eye-catching landscapes (Lee and Ho 2002: 36–45; Chiou 2002: 58–63; Ko 2004: 108). Due to "cultural proximity," Taiwanese audiences have "the perception of living in the same temporality" as Japan (Iwabuchi 2002: 153). Thai youth's consumption of Japanese popular culture, including their embrace of Japanese TV dramas, is related to the emergence of middle-class Thai youth in the 1990s. This has blurred the division between "Tokyo-Japan, an Asian metropolitan center, which is a location much more modern than their own" (Siriyuvasak 2004: 190). In addition, Dong-Hoo Lee indicates that the "trendiness" of Japanese TV drama is an advanced model for Korean TV drama to emulate and to adapt to "its own encoding process" of production (Lee 2004: 272).

Based on the above literature review, on the one hand, Asian audiences yearn for Japanese TV drama's presentation of a better capitalist/consumerist modernity than they possess themselves. On the other hand, they feel that they live side by side and keep pace with Japan because metropolitan lifestyle constructed in Japanese TV drama also echoes parts of their own real lives (Iwabuchi 2004: 9). I would extend such complicated feelings that arise in response to the middle-class materialism represented in Japanese TV drama to something else: the Japanese TV drama scripts, which are equipped with an abundance of narrative reflexivity, the focus of this paper.

Following Anthony Giddens (1991), reflexivity is an essential part of the making of the self and self-identity in a modern society. Scott Lash further summarizes different levels of Giddens' account of reflexivity. The first level is "structural reflexivity," in which agency "reflects on the 'rules' and 'resources'" of social structure, then reflects on "agency's social conditions of existence" (Lash 1994: 115). The second level is "self-reflexivity," in which "agency reflects on itself," which is a form of "self-monitoring," including the "autonomous monitoring of life narratives and of love relationships" (115–6). Both structural reflexivity and self-reflexivity emphasize the important role that the self plays in its negotiations with institutions and self-inspection. The reflexive project of the self, which consists in the sustaining of coherent, yet continuously revised, biographical narratives, takes places in the context of multiple choice as filtered through" modern institutions (Giddens 1991: 5). This reflexive project of the self aims at self-realization and the colonization of the future (Giddens 1991).

In an earlier, as yet unpublished paper, I argue that in many, if not all, of the Japanese TV dramas, there is a strong reflexive tendency implanted as a regular script formula that usually grasps precisely the inner reflexive process of the protagonists and the philosophy of life that they come to as a result of their personal and social experiences (Hu forthcoming). By narrative reflexivity, I mean that the narratives in the scripts of Japanese TV dramas have adopted the tactics of reflexivity, which are then widely applied to a wide range of re-examinations of the self and the self's relation to others and social issues, through which the protagonists achieve a kind of self-awareness, self-therapy, and self-control. The narrative strategies in Japanese TV drama testify to the way in which "a general feature of modern social activity" is its bond with "psychic organization" (Giddens 1991: 13).

In this study, however, I want to bring forward some additional examples of narrative reflexivity, as revealed by online Chinese fans, which will further reinforce my argument that this reflexivity is one of the distinctive characteristics of Japanese TV drama. Focusing on fan discussions of Japanese TV drama and fan reflexive writing through online fan websites based in Taiwan, I intend in this paper to explore the way in which online Chinese fans "discover" Japanese TV drama through their own eyes—they demonstrate how the narrative reflexivity of Japanese TV drama encourages them to reflect on life and inspires them with hope and comfort. In Lisa Leung's comparative study of the way in which local Hong Kong audiences and diasporic Japanese audiences living in Hong Kong receive Japanese TV drama, she makes the point that the two different audiences interpret both similarly and differently the message of "gabaru" (striving and struggling hard for something better) that is embedded in Japanese TV drama (Leung 2004: 90, 103). Leung notes that most Hong Kong and diasporic Japanese respondents loved Japanese TV dramas because "they make them think" and help them "reflect on the meaning of life" (2004: 94, 97). The responses of these respondents reaffirm one of the arguments of the present study—that narrative reflexivity in Japanese TV drama has the strong potential to stimulate audiences to be reflexive in developing personal growth.

In addition, I propose the way in which "implicit therapy" works through the power of narrative reflexivity. To put it simply, therapy is "engaged toward finding one's 'proper place' as an individual and a social subject" (White 1992: 11). The effort invested in looking for subjectivity and self-identity can involve a set of reflexive processes in self-affirmation and may achieve a certain degree of self-healing. I argue that narrative reflexivity in Japanese TV drama is also a therapeutic means by which some Chinese fans believe that the narrative encourages them to "manage problems, emotions, and fantasies" (White 2002: 313). I shall spell out more the reason that I refer to "implicit therapy" in relation to the narrative reflexivity of Japanese TV dramas later in this article.

My observations since 2001 of the online Chinese fans of Japanese TV drama began with a Taiwan-based website called "Dorama" (http://over-time.idv.com/), which was established in 1999 and still exists today. As it is a quite popular Chinese-language website, Chinese people from around the world, including those who live in Hong Kong, China, Malaysia, Singapore, the US, and Canada also visit the website. Although there is no data to show who the visitors are, it is reasonable to assume that the majority of people are in their twenties and thirties, are equipped with basic Internet capabilities and are of the generation that craves Japanese TV drama. "Dorama" is a well-developed digital platform that offers various functions to satisfy fans' needs for any information related to both older and the latest Japanese TV dramas. It has a database that covers Japanese TV dramas, actors, actresses, scriptwriters, various collections of fans' notes, an open discussion forum, and so on. The discussion board of "Dorama" is one place we can easily discover the way in which online Chinese fans generate reflexivity, although, as a source, it is often rather fragmented and information-oriented, as discussion topics come up in a somewhat irregular and uncontrolled way. Through the mediation of "Dorama," I was led to some fans' own websites, which are interlinked. In addition to the discussion board, the collections of notes that are specially selected by "Dorama"'s owner and the blogs that mainly contain fans' notes on Japanese TV drama are also helpful for grasping the way in which the reflexive writing of Chinese fans functions. Certainly, blogs are much better organized than the discussion board, and some of them even register a personal style.

Most of the online Chinese fans of Japanese TV drama, the principal subjects surveyed in this study, can be assumed to be Taiwanese in origin, as the fan websites that I have observed are all located in Taiwan. However, because these fan websites are apparently open to Chinese fans worldwide, the term "Chinese fans" can be given an inclusive meaning that also denotes Chinese fans living outside of Taiwan. The messages or notes left on the fan forums do not usually emphasize where the authors are from. Therefore, the term "Chinese fans" is considered to be non-exclusive, even though it is predicted that Taiwanese fans are in the majority.

NARRATIVE REFLEXIVITY AND IMPLICIT THERAPY

In addition to life-style, popular music and beautiful scenery, Japanese TV dramas provide a variety of perspectives. It not only brings out hope, but also teaches one how to face reality, how to define one's own life. (Junichi's wife 2003)

Japanese TV drama = life, or Japanese TV drama always makes me think of life. (Zhi-Shia 2004)

The magic of Japanese TV drama is amazing. When I came upon difficulties, the mottos from Japanese TV drama would emerge and make the decision for me. (Xiao-Yeh 2004)

I like the tenacious and earnest way that Japanese TV drama treats "life." Mm . . . I also want to seriously live my own life. (S-Ieng 2002)

I started watching Japanese TV drama only three months ago, when I became so sick that I couldn't go out . . . Japanese TV drama always expresses positive encouragement, such as the importance of knowing oneself and being honest with oneself, etc. . . . Japanese TV drama gives me the courage to fight my illness, appreciate my life more. (Typist 2003)

The above statements from online Chinese fans of Japanese TV drama may sound like uninvited audience testimonials, because, as mentioned earlier, the Asian audience has never been a profitable target for Japanese TV stations. They demonstrate that for some fans, Japanese TV drama is a specific category and carries an implicit therapeutic function. Interestingly, Chinese fans' reception of Japanese TV drama contradicts a Japanese scholar's criticism that Japanese TV drama merely presents "flat and superficial reality" (Mamoru 2004: 37). It also subverts general notions about melodrama. Based on her studies of Dutch audience engagement with the US TV drama *Dallas,* Ien Ang suggests that "the characters in a melodrama seem to be so taken up with their own violent emotions that there is no scope for reflection, intellectual distancing and relativizing" (Ang 1991: 62). Japanese TV drama moves in the opposite direction; although it is not devoid of emotional sentimentality or outbursts, it seldom goes so far as to be totally overwhelmed by emotions. Below I will discuss the way in which narrative reflexivity is the key point in making the transition to the trajectory of implicit therapy.

In Mimi White's book *Tele-Advising: Therapeutic Discourses in American Television* (1992), there is a comprehensive survey of various types of TV programs in the US and the way in which they are imbued with therapeutic discourses, mostly in the form of compulsory confessions. By listing examples that range widely from talk show programs to religious programs, soap operas, and shopping channels, White argues that American TV's therapeutic and confessional discourses widely "modify and reconfigure the very nature of therapy and confession as practices for producing social and individual identities and knowledge" (7). The therapeutic discourses referred to by White are apparent in their media representations, as therapy is dominant in the social imaginary of the United States. The therapy I discuss here in relation to Japanese TV dramas is "implicit," because these dramas neither encapsulate a precise therapeutic agenda nor correlate with psychological authorities and psychiatrists with PhDs in hand. They are unlike many American TV programs, which are immediately recognized to be in conspiracy with the popular American therapeutic culture. The therapy that is embedded in Japanese TV drama is also vague in a sense, as it is not a concept that is widely comprehended as a television discourse.

Consumerism has for some time been associated with a therapeutic ethos. Advertising often appeals to consumers with such therapeutic aims as providing happiness or physical and psychic health. T. J. Jackson Lears' study of US advertisements in the early twentieth century reveals that this therapeutic ethos was plotted in promotional strategies (1983). He argues that in advertising there was "a shift from a Protestant ethos of salvation through self-denial toward a therapeutic ethos stressing self-realization" (4). The emerging therapeutic ethos in American advertising was related to "the struggles between the individual's self and the burgeoning of capitalization, industrialization and urbanization." In such conditions, the therapeutic ethos in American advertisements promised "to cure the wounds inflicted by rationalization, to release the cramped energies of a fretful bourgeoisie" (17).

Lears focuses on the way in which consumerism has been endowed with a therapeutic function, whereas Giddens also points out "not just academic studies, but all manner of manuals, guides, therapeutic works and self-help surveys contribute to modernity's reflexivity" (1991: 2). These views of therapy have somehow liberated it from its legitimate status in the professional psychiatric disciplines by, in a sense, admitting that therapies have wider and multiple applications, although they may be unnamed or unrecognized. However, it seems that the consumerism as therapy that Lears discusses is less concerned with the therapy as the reflexivity of self-identity in Giddens' account and more a realistic vision of pure pleasure, satisfaction, and relaxation. It seems that consumerism emphasizes Giddens' contention that "therapy is not simply a means of coping with novel anxieties, but an expression of the reflexivity of the self" (34). He regards therapy as part of modern reflexivity and says that it "exhibits in full the dislocations and uncertainties to which modernity gives rise" (180). The therapeutic purpose ought to be accomplished through the reflexive process of the individual. Put in another way, the reflexive approach could potentially be therapeutic for any kind of mental stress or insecurity imposed on modern individuals. If this is the case, then we may conclude that, because Japanese TV dramas highlight reflexivity, they have the potential to heal.

The everlasting quest for self-fulfillment and the proper positioning of the self in late modernity are reconfigured in various scripts and constructed by the Japanese TV drama industry. The implicit therapy in Japanese TV drama can be roughly defined as discourses/life philosophies that are encouraging, inspiring, and comforting with an optimistic spirit of progress and the potential to serve as advice to help people overcome risks, unpredictability, and suffering. However, the implicit therapy does not work without inviting reflexive practices. As Giddens sees it, most therapies are concerned with "self-observation" or "taking charge of one's life" (71, 73). The implicit therapy elicited from narrative reflexivity in Japanese TV drama not only instigates emotional catharsis, but it also confirms the viewer's own capacity to manage and improve oneself. The Japanese television industry is sophisticated at incorporating the therapeutic styles of both consumerism and modern reflexivity—displaying a middle-class and metropolitan lifestyle, yet promoting the importance of self-reflexivity. Such reflexive and healing empowerment may undergo a kind of textual excursion from the television scripts to the fans' own meaning-making, which is tied to their own personal life experiences.

The following is one example that emphasizes how narrative reflexivity evokes implicit therapy. *Lunch Queen (Ranchi no Joou* 2002) is a TV drama with stories centered around a restaurant that insists on faith in the good quality of cuisine and food. In one episode, a father and daughter go to the restaurant for Japanese-style beef and rice. The father does not have enough money for two dishes, so he only orders a dish for his daughter. The waitress then generously treats the father to another dish. The father and daughter cannot help going back again to express their appreciation to the waitress (the female protagonist): "It is so delicious. I feel like having it all over again. It's made me want to try my best to live." The waitress is deeply touched and replies in tears, "I used to think the way you do. Thank you, please come again." This exchange seems to encourage both the poor father and the waitress to work harder for a better life. *Lunch Queen* simply reinforces a similar notion. The therapeutic effect of food has proved to be enormous, as shown by the words of both the customer and the waitress, who have been given new hearts by tasting this food. Again, however, it is not enough to emphasize how stimulating the delicious food is. Reflexive thinking about the sincerity of the lifestyle is the main requirement for reaching therapeutic inspiration. The script invites the audiences to identify with the philosophy of sincerity—to live and work with sincerity and professionalism is a new ethos of salvation today.

Let's take a look at some examples from online Chinese fans' reflexive notes. Setsuna has in her blog ardently recorded the classic lines from each episode of the Japanese TV drama *Operation & Love (Puropozu Daisakusen* 2007). The following is an example.

> I finally realized that the pain that derives from the hesitation of giving something a try will be much more unbearable than the pain caused by the failure I experience after I did it. Although I am not sure whether there is a key to open the door of a miracle, I have convinced myself to believe in it! (Setsuna 2007)

This quotation comes from the voice-over of the protagonist's inner monologue. This particular drama describes how a young man, Ken, attempts several supernatural "time slips" to go back in time to win his loved one's heart. He is an indirect and hesitant person who always misses the chance to confess his love to the young woman he has always been deeply in love with. After several trips back to the past, he achieves self-growth by gaining confidence to have a deeper look at himself and his life. Setsuna writes a short note after the transcript:

> In my opinion, to generate the courage to try something is necessary. At least I would not feel regret even if I did not succeed. Like Ken, I also doubt whether the key to the door of a miracle exists. But I have decided to believe there is a chance; otherwise, life would be without any hope.

Setsuna's adoption of a quotation from a drama is one of the typical methods by which Chinese fans produce potential self-reflexivity and advance reflexive writing based on their readings of the drama. Even though Setsuna does not reveal much about herself, these reflexive words have at least made her think more deeply about life and about how she identifies with the principle of trial-and-error.

Another fan, Peggy, comments on the drama *I'll be Back* (*Kimitoita Mirai no Tameni* 1999) and cites her favorite quotation from it (Peggy 2002). In this drama, the male protagonist dreams of his dead mother. In his dream, he reveals to his mother that he does not want to live alone without her. The mother says, "If you died, who would miss me then? . . . Because you are alive, I can eternally live in your mind." Peggy confesses that she is always afraid that beloved family members or friends will die and abandon her. But the words of the drama have had a great therapeutic effect on her—at least, she is now less fearful of losing those dear to her. She realizes that keeping people in one's mind is an alternative way of extending their lives, even though they no longer have corporeal existence in the world. By reinforcing the words she reflects on, part of her self has been transformed because of the reflexivity delivered through the drama.

These reflexive notes are apparently centered on re-reading the themes and motifs that are usually irresistibly enmeshed with the act of examining and re-interpreting the reflexive life philosophy that is created by the scriptwriters. Despite the fact that most fans do not disclose their wider life history in relation to the narrative reflexivity they discuss, their reflexive thoughts may to some extent be connected to themselves by a kind of self-projection. Every time they make an effort to keep reflexive notes, they must, to some degree, have digested, absorbed, and appropriated the drama texts into their own new forms of reflexivity, which also more or less contain a certain degree of implicit self-therapy. Such an act of reflexive rewriting helps to sustain and preserve the "emotional immediacy that initially attracted the fan's interest" (Jenkins 1992:

770)—that is, it establishes intimacy between the texts and fans' affection towards them.

THE OPERATION OF THE SOCIAL IMAGINARY

> The themes of Japanese TV drama are simple and easy to understand with a certain degree of depth in the exploration of and reflection on life. In comparison, Taiwanese drama, though it has extremely dramatic plots, lacks any motif or meaning to be delivered. (Myo-Miao 2003)

> What attracts me most is that the scriptwriters of Japanese TV drama take pains to conduct research for diverse professional script materials. This is what Taiwanese TV drama can never catch up with. (Mint Tea 2004)

> Hong Kong dramas are *always* [sic] about romance, with predictable formulae. Watching Japanese TV dramas makes you think. (Hong Kong respondent, quoted in Leung [2004: 101])

In these quotations, Chinese fans talk about the differences between Japanese TV drama and Taiwanese/Hong Kong TV drama. It would be too complicated to find out why the TV dramas produced in various Chinese societies do not generate the same rich levels of reflexivity as Japanese TV dramas do. I do not want to conduct a comprehensive comparative study here. However, I would like to offer some views in the hope that they may shed enough light for a basic understanding and perhaps encourage more advanced studies, even if they are not exhaustive enough to untangle the complexity.

According to John Tomlinson, the imaginary "is the product of an act of cultural creation which is fundamental to any subsequent system of cultural representation" (1991: 157). The questions of modernity "are bound up, not with an inescapable rationality, but with a social imaginary which is at the centre of the self-understanding of a culture" (160). If the TV industry can be seen as one of the modern institutions that have invented cultural narratives that embody the social imaginary that is part of a nation's modernity, then the massive production of reflexive scenarios by the Japanese TV drama industry corresponds with a social imaginary that reinforces the importance of reflexive introversion and the subtle observation of the self.

In Koichi Iwabuchi's study of the way in which Japanese reality TV adapts and repackages the American reality show *Survivor,* which originally highlights the conflicts among rivals in the new Japanese *Survivor,* he reveals how the producer insists on capturing the discovery of "the true self" by featuring "the life story of each contestant" (2003: 25). Interestingly, even though TV drama and reality TV are different genres, inward reflexivity is, in a way, similar to the spirit of seeking "the true self," as both are relevant to self-reflexivity. I argue that such reflexivity in Japanese culture may relate to another kind of "ethnic theorizing," such as the ubiquity of Japanese *kokoro* (heart), which was also largely applied in advertisements in Japan in the 1970s (Ivy 1995: 42). The heart is where one always returns and where one locates oneself through the journey of self-discovery. Brian Moeran has stated that *kokoro* could be articulated with "self-discipline," which I think is similar to reflexivity that evaluates the significance of self-monitoring through the reflexive effort done by the heart (1984: 262). On the one hand, such self-reflexivity, which contains introverted self-examination, is somewhat different from Giddens' account of modern reflexivity, which primarily highlights its linkage with "democratic involvement" and "expert systems" (Giddens 1991: 212, 213, 18). On the other hand, the inwardness of the self-reflexivity accentuated in Japanese culture does overlap with modern individuals constantly go through reflexive practices, which involves the transformation of psychic dynamics, which is also a means of coping with modern social reality.

The famous Japanese writer, Banana Yoshimoto, also points out that "Japanese people have the delicate sensitivity to feel the slightest thing—that is their wonderful quality" (Kawai and Yoshimoto 2002). As noted in Koichi Iwabuchi's survey of the reception of Japanese TV drama in Taiwan, Taiwanese audiences feel that Japanese TV drama is characterized by specific Japanese styles of "delicacy" and "elegance," which helps them to distinguish Taiwanese TV drama from Japanese TV drama (2002: 151). The perceptions by Chinese audiences of Japanese TV dramas echo the way that Yoshimoto, as a native writer, sees her own culture—there is a strangely inter-Asian (Japanese-Chinese) connection that allows similar comprehension of the social imaginary of Japanese culture. It is not my intention to make a culturally essentialist claim for Japanese culture. If the delicate mode of Japanese culture is not natural, then it has been widely and cunningly adopted and reinvented in the formulized and commercialized production of popular culture, including the reflexive TV scripts that center on urban stories. Reflexivity becomes part and parcel of the standardized consumer culture of Japanese TV drama, which invites their audiences to constantly labor toward self-reflexivity.

According to Kahn-Harris, Scott Lash points out that "reflexivity is more present in certain areas of modern societies than others" (2004: 98). I further argue that reflexivity may be observed in any modern society, but the degree of reflexivity and the forms and content of its cultural representations and practices may differ in different societies. Both Lash and Castells challenge Giddens' notion of reflexivity and comment that people of lower classes may become "reflexivity losers," as they lack "the accumulation of capital and the accumulation of information" that global elites are privileged to have easier access to (Lash 1994: 129; Castells 1997: 11). The inequalities in reflexive accumulation invite us to rethink whether Giddens' notion of reflexivity is universal and ubiquitous. What hint do we get from this case study of online Chinese fans?

From the viewpoint of Chinese fans, the reflexivity of life and the self as a social imaginary is sophisticatedly deployed in Japanese drama narratives, whereas this social imaginary does not seem to be well developed in Chinese-language TV drama. Hence, a social imaginary that centers on the reflexivity of life and the self, as represented in Japanese TV drama, is sought after and envied by some Chinese. This paper does not wish to promote a kind of blind prejudice against Chinese-language TV dramas. Chinese-language TV dramas should not be looked down upon as inferior, as they have their own specific appeals for practical purposes or logics of operations that represent their own social realities. The rich narrative reflexivity in Japanese TV drama does not guarantee that the reflexive content is absolutely right or ideologically unproblematic, but it only confirms the fact that there are high percentages of reflexive contents in these TV representations. In contrast, TV drama productions in Chinese societies, including Taiwan, Hong Kong, and mainland China, prefer the body-as-spectacle, emotional explosions, love-hate (sometimes revengeful) relationships in romance or family dramas, and competition among different corporations if the story is set in modern society. Straightforward dramatic effect, rather than inward narrative reflexivity, is more on the agenda for TV dramas made in Chinese societies. However, reflexivity of other kinds, including reflexive investment in knowledge intensity in the economic and technology sectors, may be more in accord with the feverish pursuits of the three Chinese societies by both government policy and people. The incorporation of introverted self-reflexivity into the popular literature of various kinds, including TV drama scripts, does not appear to be a mainstream social imaginary that is frequently practiced or valued.

Globalization combined with digital technologies in a way empowers marginalized audiences, such as these Chinese fans, to express aloud their reception of Japanese TV drama. The Internet, in particular, disrupts the limitations of time and space and offers channels for fans' self-displays as they rework the narrative reflexivity in their own terms. They construct alternative sub-cultural virtual spaces in which fragmented personal reflexive notes are circulated and the post-viewing experiences of feeling healed are exchanged and shared. These online Chinese fans tour the imagined Japanese landscapes portrayed in Japanese TV drama, through which they may also take various journeys of reflexive self-discovery when they watch different Japanese TV dramas. This is what Beck has termed the "globalization of biography"—one's life is endowed with inner mobility and multi-locations, either through real movement between different places or in media-supported travels through space (2000: 73, 75). "In a way, places become new opportunities for discovering and testing out particular aspects of oneself" (76). Different Japanese TV dramas constitute places to which Chinese fans virtually travel when they imagine and locate themselves in the scenes. This case study reveals that the practices of online Chinese fans are a transnational process of cultural transaction, cultural translation, and cultural appropriation. It also demonstrates that adventures in search of reflexive guidelines and healing empowerment need not be tied to a fixed locale or to the traditional bonds of family and community. Instead, they are globally mobilized through the convergence of audio-visual and digital technologies that cut across various geographical boundaries. Through their eyes, online Chinese fans discover and consume the Japanese style of reflexivity that is represented in TV drama and use it to build reflexive and therapeutic transnational biographies of their own.

REFERENCES

Ang, I. (1982) *Watching Dallas: Soap Opera and the Melodramatic Imagination*, London: Routledge.

Beck, U. (2000) *What is Globalization?* Cambridge: Polity.

Castells, Manuel (1997) *The Power of Identity*, Wiley-Blackwell.

Chiou, S-W. (2002) "Cultural Imagination: Japanese Trendy Drama in Taiwan," *Envisage: A Journal Book of Chinese Media Studies*, 1: 50–67 (in Chinese).

Giddens, A. (1991) *Modernity and Self-Identity: Self and Society in the Late Modern Age*, Stanford: Stanford University Press.

Hu, K. (2005) "The Power of Circulation: Digital Technologies and the Online Chinese Fans of Japanese TV Dramas," *Inter-Asia Cultural Studies*, 6(2): 171–86.

———. (forthcoming) "Can't Live Without Happiness: Reflexivity and Japanese TV Drama," in M. Yoshimoto et al. (eds) *Television, Japan and Globalization*, Honolulu: University of Hawaii Press.

Ivy, M. (1995) *Discourses of the Vanishing: Modernity, Phantasm, Japan*, Chicago: University of Chicago Press.

Iwabuchi, K. (2002) *Recentering Globalization: Popular Culture and Japanese Transnationalism*, Durham: Duke University Press.

———. (2003) "Feeling Glocal: Japan in the Global Television Format Business," in M. Albert (ed) *Television Across Asia: TV Industries, Program Formats and Globalisation*, New York: Routledge.

———. (2004) *Feeling Asian Modernities: Transnational Consumption of Japanese TV Dramas*, Hong Kong: Hong Kong University Press.

Jenkins, H. (1992) *Textual Poachers: Television Fans and Participatory Culture*, New York: Routledge.

Junichi's wife (2003) "A Scholar Says: Young People Easily Identify with Japanese TV Drama," online posting, http://over-time.idv.tw/.

Kahn-Harris, K. (2004) "The 'Failure' of Youth Culture: Reflexivity, Music and Politics in the Black Metal Scene," *European Journal of Cultural Studies*, 7(1): 95–111.

Kawai, H. and Yoshimoto, B. (2002) *Naruhodo No Taiwa* (in Chinese), Taipei: China Times Publishing.

Ko, Y-F. (2004) "The Desired Form: Japanese Idol Dramas in Taiwan." In K. Iwabuchi (ed) *Feeling Asian Modernities: Transnational Consumption of Japanese TV Dramas*, Hong Kong: Hong Kong University Press.

Lash, S. (1994) "Reflexivity and its Doubles: Structure, Aesthetics, Community," in U. Beck et al. (eds) *Reflexive Modernization: Politics, Tradition and Aesthetics in the Modern Social Order*, Cambridge: Polity.

Lears, T. J. (1983) "From Salvation to Self-Realization: Advertising and the Thera-peutic Roots of the Consumer Culture, 1880–1930, in R. Fox and T. Jackson (eds) *The Culture of Consumption: Critical Essays in American History, 1880-1980*, New York: Pantheon.

Lee, D-H. (2004) "Cultural Contact with Japanese TV Dramas: Modes of Recep-tion and Narrative Transparency," in K. Iwabuchi (ed) *Feeling Asian Moderni-ties: Transnational Consumption of Japanese TV dramas*, Hong Kong: Hong Kong University Press.

Lee, T-D. and Ho, H-W. (2002) "Beyond Tokyo Rainbow Bridge: The Imaginary Appropriation of Japanese Trendy Drama in Taiwan," *Envisage: A Journal Book of Chinese Media Studies*, 1: 15–49 (in Chinese).

Leung, L. (2004) "Ganbaru and its Transcultural Audience: Imaginary and Real-ity of Japanese TV Dramas in Hong Kong," in K. Iwabuchi (ed) *Feeling Asian Modernities: Transnational Consumption of Japanese TV Dramas*, Hong Kong: Hong Kong University Press.

Mamoru, I. (2004) "The Representation of Femininity in Japanese Television Dramas of the 1990s," in K. Iwabuchi (ed) *Feeling Asian Modernities: Trans-national Consumption of Japanese TV Dramas*, Hong Kong: Hong Kong Uni-versity Press.

Moeran, B. (1984) "Individual, Group and *Seishin:* Japan's Internal Cultural Debate," *Man,* 19(2): 252–66.

Myo-Miao (2003) "My Way of Living," online posting, http://www.readingtimes.com.tw/discuss/japantv/main.asp.

Mint Tea (2004) "Why do you love Japanese TV drama?," online posting http://www.readingtimes.com.tw/discuss/japantv/main.asp.

Peggy (2002) "Afterthoughts on *I'll be Back*," online posting, http://over-time.idv.tw/.

Setsuna (2007) "A Room for Japanese TV Drama," online posting, http://www.wretch.cc/blog/Setsuna2006&article_id=20805282#trackback3660981.

S-ieg (2002) "Leading a Life by Watching Japanese TV Drama," online posting, http://mypaper.pchome.com.tw/news/jpdrama/.

Siriyuvasak, U. (2004) "Popular Culture and Youth Consumption: Modernity, Identity and Social Transformation," in K. Iwabuchi (ed) *Feeling Asian Moder-nities: Transnational Consumption of Japanese TV Dramas*, Hong Kong: Hong Kong University Press.

Tomlinson, J. (1991) *Cultural Imperialism: A Critical Introduction*, Baltimore: Johns Hopkins University Press.

Toru, O. (2004) "Producing (Post-) Trendy Japanese TV Dramas," in K. Iwabuchi (ed) *Feeling Asian Modernities: Transnational Consumption of Japanese TV Dramas*, Hong Kong: Hong Kong University Press.

Typist (2003) "Are Japanese TV Dramas Good?" online posting, http://mypaper.pchome.com.tw/news/jpdrama/.

White, M. (1992) *Tele-Advising: Therapeutic Discourse in American Television*, Chapel Hill: University of North Carolina Press.

——. (2002) "Television, Therapy and the Society Subject; or, the TV Therapy Machine," in J. Friedman (ed) *Reality Square: Televisual Discourse on the Real*, New Jersey: Rutgers University Press.

Xiao-Yeh (2004) "Xiao-Yeh, Japan," online posting, http://www.readingtimes.com.tw/PROMOTE/0110/popu_pa0004.htm.

Zhi-Shia (2004) "How do you love Japanese TV drama?," online posting, http://over-time.idv.tw/.

8 Dialogue with the Korean Wave
Japan and its Postcolonial Discontents

Koichi Iwabuchi

Since the mid-1990s, East Asian media flows and connections have been intensified. Media markets have rapidly expanded and transnational partnerships have been closely formed among media corporations that pursue marketing strategies and joint production ventures spanning several different markets. The circulation of popular culture is no longer limited to the national borders but finds a broader transnational acceptance in the region, leading to the formation of new links among people in East Asia, especially the youth. This trend has shown no sign of letting up. Asian markets have become even more synchronized, East Asian co-projects in film and music have become more common, and singers and actors from around the region are engaged in activities that transcend national borders.

In this development, Japanese media culture took the initiative in the 1990s. However, many other East Asian regions, too, are creating their own cultural forms of international appeal within the social and cultural contexts specific to their countries, and media flows are becoming more and more multilateral. Most notably, in the early twenty-first century, Korean popular culture is sweeping over Asian markets. Korean TV series and pop music are now receiving an even warmer welcome in places like Taiwan, Hong Kong, and China than their Japanese equivalents.

Japan, too, is embracing the Korean Wave. Films, music and TV dramas from Korea have become widely and commonly received since the late 1990s. And it was especially the phenomenal popularity of *Winter Sonata* in 2003 that clearly marked the landing of the Korean Wave in the Japanese market, which has been hitherto exclusive to other Asian TV dramas.

This chapter aims to examine the complexity of the impact of the Korean Wave in Japanese society in terms of Japan's postcolonial relationship with Korea. The reception of other East Asian media cultures proves to be an opportune moment for Japanese audiences to critically review the state of their own lives, society and history. Comparing the reception of the Korean Wave, and *Winter Sonata* in particular, with the fervent reception of Hong Kong popular culture in the late 1990s, it will be suggested that while the sense of nostalgia is a key feature to the both cases, the nostalgia perceived by consuming Korean TV dramas shows a more dialogic possibility in that it urges (mostly middle-aged) female audiences to engage in active post-text encounters with Korea in ways that could change their perceptions of Korea and its colonial history in a self-critical manner. However, it is also crucial to consider how the media flows from South Korea have influenced, both constructively and unconstructively, the social positioning and recognition of resident Koreans in Japan, most of whom are the descendants of expatriates under Japanese colonial rule. By closely looking into this question, I will elucidate the possibility and the limit of Japan's ambivalent postcolonial engagement with Korea, which has been triggered through transnational media culture connections. This consideration highlights the importance for the study of trans-Asian media and cultural flows to go beyond the nation-centered framework by examining how the transnational intersect with the postcolonial so as to seriously scrutinize whether and how media culture connections foster the potential of transnational dialogues.

NOSTALGIA AND SELF-REFLEXIVITY

The Korean Wave is not the first instance where other Asian media texts have been well received in the Japanese market. Various kinds of films (mostly from Hong Kong) and stars such as Bruce Lee, Jackie Cheng and Dick Lee have been favorably received because they appealingly represent different kinds of cultural expressions and imaginings of being modern in Asia. Most recently, there was a Hong Kong boom in the late 1990s, which is still fresh in our memories.[1] A comparison of the reception of Hong Kong media culture in the late 1990s and that of the Korean Wave in the early twenty-first century elucidates both similarities and differences between them in intriguing ways.

While the scope and intensity of media and cultural flows from South Korea is not comparable to those from other Asian regions and countries, the Hong Kong boom and Korean Wave have something in common in that the well-received media texts represent modern cultural scenes in urban settings. While sharing the experience of negotiating with American—and perhaps to a lesser extent Japanese (see Lee 2004)—influences on production styles, Hong Kong and Korean media industries have developed their own styles of films, pop music and youth-oriented dramas that attain transnational appeal in terms of the representation of "here and now" in Asian urban contexts. They lucidly articulate the intertwined composition of global homogenization and heterogenization in a different way from those of Japanese media texts. For audiences, similar and different, close and distant, fantasizing and realistic, all of these intertwined perceptions subtly intersect so as to arouse a sense of cultural identification, relatedness and sympathy in the eyes of young people in East Asia under regional cultural dynamics (see Iwabuchi 2004 for the case of Japanese TV dramas).

It can be argued that one of the main reasons for the success of Korean TV dramas is their depiction of family matters and relationships, which enables them to appeal to a wider range of viewers than Japanese programs. Even for young viewers in East Asia, South Korean dramas are preferable to Japanese ones in terms of realism and their ability to relate to the characters and story lines. In my interviews with Taiwanese university students in 2001, I was told that Japanese series tended to focus solely on young people's loves and jobs, and this restricted the scope of their stories and thus audience identification. Korean dramas, on the other hand, while featuring young people's romances as a central theme, tend to portray the problems and bonds of parents and children, grandparents, and other relatives. This makes them look more similar to the actual lives of young people living in Taiwan. The restricted and closed relationships and daily lives of young people featured in the world of Japanese TV dramas have attracted many followers in the Asian region.

However, it is rather the sense of nostalgia that marks the adoring reception of *Winter Sonata* in Japan. This shows significant similarity and difference in the reception of Hong Kong and Korean media texts in that the main audiences are women in their thirties, forties, fifties and sixties who tend to express their nostalgic feelings for the things that used to be in Japan in their reception of Hong Kong and Korean media texts. In the case of Hong Kong culture, it reminded Japanese audiences of the vigor of the society that has supposedly been lost in Japan. This sense of nostalgia was strongly contextualized when Japan struggled with an economic slump after the so-called bubble economy, while other Asian nations enjoyed high economic growth from the early 1990s. In this suffocating socio-economic atmosphere, Japanese audiences' consumption of Hong Kong media culture was sharply marked by a nostalgic longing for lost social vigor.

This mode of reception shows a highly ambivalent posture in the appreciation of cultural neighbors. On the one hand, Japanese audiences' emphasis on the temporal difference rather than spatial one occasionally displays their failure and refusal to see other Asians as modern equals who share exactly the same developmental temporality. An awareness of "familiar" cultural differences through the consumption of Hong Kong popular culture arouses contrasting senses, a sense that Hong Kong's level of being modern still lags behind Japan, albeit slightly, and a sense of contemporaneity in living in the same temporality that promotes cultural dialogue on equal terms. This might attest to Japan's historically constituted double claim of being similar but superior to "Asia." Orientalist thinking that attempts to understand Asia's present by equating it with Japan's past good times occasionally resurfaces in the nostalgic appreciation of Hong Kong culture (Iwabuchi 2002: Ch. 5).

On the other hand, however, it also shows their appreciation of a different mode of Asian modernity on more than equal terms with Japan in terms of the negotiation with the West and the sophistication of cultural hybridization. Hong Kong's present was appreciated as a promising vivacity of another Asian modernity that looked in stark contrast to Japan's present. By realizing that Hong Kong is no less developed and modernized than Japan and positively identifying themselves with its sophisticated media texts, Japanese female audiences themselves tried to regain vigor and energy (Iwabuchi 2002: Ch. 5). By watching media texts produced in other parts of East Asia, Japanese audiences thus realize that they now inhabit the same developmental time zone as people in other Asian regions and that the peoples of Asia, while being washed by similar waves of modernization, urbanization, and globalization, have experienced these phenomena in similar yet different ways in their own particular contexts. This may prove to be an opportune moment for Japanese people to critically review the state of their own modernity. Belief in Japan's superiority over the rest of Asia—a condescending mode of thinking that, while accepting that the country belongs geographically and culturally to Asia, makes a distinction between Japan and Asia—remains firmly rooted in society, but such attitudes are being shaken as countries in Asia become more and more interconnected through popular cultural flows. Revived emotions induce self-reflexive attitudes in audiences and drive them to search for a better past, present and future.

This is analogous to the reception of *Winter Sonata* in Japan, but nostalgia projected onto the Korean TV drama is slightly but significantly different. While both nostalgias are socio-historically structured and self-reflexive, in Hong Kong's case nostalgia is projected more onto a societal loss perceived as such by individuals, but in the case of *Winter Sonata,* it is projected less onto the social vigor Japan allegedly has lost than onto personal memories and sentiments in terms of emotions of love and interpersonal relationships. This causes a crucial difference in the perception of coevalness (see Fabian 1983). In contrast to a highly precarious way of interpreting the cultural difference of Hong Kong in a temporal framework, the reception of *Winter Sonata* and other Korean TV dramas in general seems to more often escape the pitfall.[2]

It can be argued that Japanese audiences of *Winter Sonata* also perceive a temporal gap, given that most audiences are older women, compared to their Korean counterparts. Those middle-aged women are reminded of the pure passion for love and caring in human relationships, which according to them, they used to have in their youth. However, I found that the audiences do not seem to associate the temporal gap with that between the two societies, even if they compare *Winter Sonata* with Japanese dramas of the 1970s and 80s, precisely because the longing for things that used to be is induced more at the level of personal memories and love sentiments than at the level of social loss. If, in the Hong Kong case, the sense of nostalgia is closely related to the "discourse of vanishing" (Ivy 1995), discourses about social loss in the course of modernization, in the Korean case it has more to do with the personal recovery of vanished sentiments. And this longing is also related to the vanishing of discourse, the failure and incapability of Japanese media industries to produce media narratives that inspire emotions in a positive and humane manner. Most obviously, it is the pure, single-minded, loving, affectionate and caring interpersonal relationships depicted in *Winter Sonata* that attract Japanese audiences. Especially admired is the man's magnanimous tenderness, that subtly combines embracing leadership and sincere respect for the partner, who is attractively portrayed by Bae Yon-jung.

Interestingly the highly personalized longing provoked by the reception of the Korean drama has strong marks on the vivacity of post-text social praxis, which is crucially different from the Hong Kong case. Many audiences told me that they consciously tried to become more caring and gentle to others and respect family members after watching *Winter Sonata*. More significantly, compared to Hong Kong's case in which many audiences tended to consciously indulge in the act of consuming media images and did not pay much attention to directly connecting with the people and culture of Hong Kong, audiences of *Winter Sonata* are much more actively making contact with Korean culture, society and people. Fascination evoked in the media texts more directly and actively leads to interests in knowing and encountering "real" Korea. As detailed in Hirata (2008), no small number of them joins *Winter Sonata* tours to Korea to experience the drama scenes, experience local culture and people, and start learning the language. Furthermore, many audiences are learning the history of Japanese colonialism in Korea. The nostalgic longing evoked by *Winter Sonata* is less motivated by the will to identify with the modernizing energy of the society, but precisely because of this personal-oriented desire, it is more engaging and emancipatory. Personal is indeed political!

INTERNATIONAL CULTURAL EXCHANGE AND BEYOND

The historical relationship is an important factor in understanding the development of the Korean Wave in Japan and its difference from its Hong Kong counterpart. Particularly important here is the history of Japan's colonialism, which has long rendered the relationship between the two countries geographically and culturally close yet politically and emotionally distant. The recent upsurge of the Korean Wave in Japan, which is based on the contemporaneous appreciation of its cultural neighbor, can be seen as a positive kind of reaction to the postwar closure of bilateral cultural exchange. Japan did have a history of imperial invasion in Hong Kong, too. No small number of people in Hong Kong still hold a strong anti-Japan sentiment, as is clearly shown by the demonstrations over the dispute about the possession of the Senkaku Islands. The point is, however, how the (post)colonial historical relationship is perceived and discussed in Japan. It is not a historical fact but the public perception of history and postcolonial presence that is at stake in the consideration of the way in which the history of Japanese colonialism inscribes the manner of the Japanese reception of other Asian cultures. Japan's colonial relationship with Hong Kong has never been a big public issue in Japan—let me reiterate that this is not to say it is insignificant—but the perception that South Korea is a former Japanese colony and no small number of people in South Korea have a strong antagonism against Japan has long been widely held in Japan.

The bilateral relationship between Japan and South Korea has significantly improved since the late 1990s. The Seoul Olympics in 1988 were perhaps the first instance that changed Japanese images of South Korea, from a backward, still-undeveloped country to an urbanized modern country. The event attracted many tourists from Japan and activated grassroots exchange among the populaces. More significantly, two momentous events in the late 1990s greatly improved the cultural relationship between Japan and South Korea. One was the South Korean government's decision in late 1998 to abolish the long-term regulation policy of banning the import of Japanese culture. This announcement clearly signified a new epoch for the bilateral relationship and was particularly welcomed in Japan. The Japanese government has been interested in the potential of media culture facilitating cultural diplomacy, particularly in terms of its capacity to improve Japan's reputation and to make smooth Japan's historical reconciliation with other East and Southeast Asian countries.

Yet what has become prominent is not just the entry of Japanese popular culture into South Korea but, to an even greater degree, the flow of Korean popular culture into Japan. The two-way flow of popular culture has significantly contributed to the people mutually finding intimate human faces and the immediate attractiveness of cultural neighbors. It is also greatly enhanced by the other historic event, the co-hosting of the Fédération Internationale de Football Association (FIFA) world cup soccer tournament. The co-hosting process eventually resulted in a tremendous improvement in the cultural relationship between the two nations, at the official level as well as at a grassroots level. It engendered many government-sponsored events, media collaborations, such as the co-production of TV dramas, and various kinds of people's cultural exchanges.

Supporting this trend, some surveys showed drastic improvement in people's mutual perceptions and positive views about the future relationship between Japan and Korea, with Japanese responses apparently being more positive. Likewise, many audiences of *Winter Sonata* expressed that the drama had totally changed their images of Korean society, culture and people, which were hitherto negative. By experiencing Korea through post-text activities, they came to see the close ties the two countries have and to recognize as fallacy the Orientalist images of Korea that have dominated Japanese perceptions. According to a survey, about 60 percent of audiences came to have a better image of South Korea and 40 percent are paying more attention to the media coverage of the Japan-Korea political and historical relationship (Hayashi 2004).

While this development can be seen as a transient boom and whether media consumption of *Winter Sonata* will lead to a substantial understanding of Korea is highly doubtful, if we look closely into the audience reception as detailed in Mori (2008), the change cannot be easily dismissed. In the post-text activities that characterize the *Winter Sonata* syndrome, some even start learning what Japanese colonialism did in the Korean peninsula and realize how it still casts a shadow on the current situation. It probably will not lead to drastic political change in the short term, but the imagination and practice in everyday life is the basis of societal constitution. As Appadurai (1996) argues, the acceleration of transnational cultural flows, through the development of communication technologies as well as the escalation of the transborder movement of people, has dramatically transformed the role of social imagination in the texture of people's everyday life, in such a way that imagination summoned up by fantasy through media products is not simply privately owned but can be a collective one, so much so that "The imagination is today a staging ground of action, and not only for escape" (7). Through such a mundane practice of evoking imagination via media culture, audiences will indeed become active political agents.

Having said this, admittedly the caution is an important reminder against uncritical celebration of the role of popular culture in the enhancement of inter-national relationships. The tendency to place too high an expectation on popular culture's capacity to enhance inter-national relationships needs to be carefully examined. Being concerned mostly with relationships between nations could lead to the convenient use of popular culture to promote national interests. What is problematic here is that such discourses can only be put in the foreground if one does not attend to the complexity of transnational popular cultural flows that (re)produce not just dialogue but also unevenness (see Iwabuchi 2002, 2004). Most imperatively, such a view tends to subtly re-demarcate the national boundaries and disregard, and even suppress, the issues of existing differences, marginalization and inequality within each society in terms of gender, sexuality, ethnicity, race, class, age, region, and so on. The fact that what is being promoted is the exchange and dialogue between cultures that are dominant and popular in each country needs to be remembered. If we take cross-border dialogue engendered by media cultural flows seriously, we must go beyond the (inter-)national framework and consider how the complicated transnational circulations of people, capital and media texts crisscross local multicultural and postcolonial issues. Then, if we are to

take the Korean Wave in Japan seriously, we must examine the impact
it has had on the social positioning of resident Koreans in Japan who
have long been discriminated against as second-class citizens. Such an
examination would be a significant touchstone in the consideration of the
(im)possibility of mediated transnational cultural dialogue.

THE KOREAN WAVE AND THE RECOGNITION OF KOREAN RESIDENTS

Resident Koreans are those who migrated to Japan during Japan's colonial rule and their descents. At the end of the war, roughly 2 million
Koreans lived in Japan as Japanese nationals under colonial rule. More
than 1.3 million people returned to Korea, but about 60,000 Korans
remained in Japan due to the difficulty of finding a job and starting a
new life in Korea. Most of those who remained in Japan were the earliest immigrants who had firmly established their families in Japan and
lost a substantial connection with Korea. By implementing the San Francisco peace treaty in 1952, the Japanese government one-sidedly deprived
Japanese nationality to those Koreans who had stayed in Japan and subjected them to the rigid control of alien registration law. Koreans then
had two options, other than remaining stateless residents in Japan, either
to return to Korea or naturalize to Japanese. But neither option was persuasive to many, though some of them repatriated to North Korean after
1959, responding to Kim Il Sung's encouragement of repatriation. The
start of the diplomatic relationship between Japan and South Korea in
1965 made it possible for Koreans in Japan to obtain permanent resi-
dency if they became South Korean nationals. Still, those who supported
and identified themselves with North Korea remained stateless, neither
Japanese nor South Korean. In either case, as non-Japanese nationals,
resident Koreans had to be registered as foreigners living in Japan and
carry a registration card, which included fingerprints until 1991, when
their status as special permanent residents was fully acknowledged by the
Japanese government.[3]

Some might wonder why many Koreans did not naturalize into Japanese despite the fact that they eventually lived in Japan for good. It is
mostly due to the lingering structural discrimination against resident
Koreans and the Japanese government's authoritarian immigration policy's intent to keep the nation apparently "homogeneous." If they apply to
become naturalized, resident Koreans have to undergo a long, inhumane
examination about "properly Japanese" qualifications and are strongly
urged to adopt a Japanese name. Due to the strong assimilation policy, to
become a Japanese citizen Koreans are required to forget and hide their
descent. Thus, no small number of them choose not to become Japanese
citizens, and this decision has been an important part of their identity

formation in the resistance to the repression of the Japanese government. "Residing in Japan" (*zainichi*) is "an alternative to becoming naturalized" and the construction of their identity is centered on the sense of belongingness to Korean nations (Tai 2004: 356), though the number of Koreans who naturalize into Japanese has been increasing recently.

When we consider the impact of the Korean Wave in Japan, as suggested above, the presence of resident Koreans as (post)colonial subjects in Japan is decisively different from the Hong Kong case. The isssue at stake here is whether the presence of problematic (post)colonial subjects has been intertwined with Japan's favorable reception of popular culture from Korea, the country with whom they have ethno-historical "roots and routes," and how that reception has impacted local multicultural and postcolonial questions.

Ashley Carruthers (2004), in his analysis of the Japanese consumption of Vietnam exotic, argues that while it is a subjectless multiculturalism that tries to pleasurably domesticate multicultural situations in a highly consumerist manner, without seriously engaging with the presence of actual subjects, what marks the Japanese case is a striking tendency that exotic Vietnamese cultures are introduced, exhibited and promoted by Japanese people themselves. Here, the relative absence of Vietnamese residents in the Japanese public sphere as a significant other makes it much easier for people in Japan to consume Vietnamese culture as exotic:

> I wish to argue that there is another factor crucial to any understanding of the exceptional commodifiability of the Vietnamese exotic in Japan: the fact that the Vietnamese are not significant national others . . . Vietnameseness in Japan is not embodied in a threatening way. It can be safely conceptualized in the abstract, untroubled by the prospect of encountering the concrete "ethnic" subject and its strange cooking smells and noisy music. (Carruthers 2004: 415–16)

Perhaps this point is applicable to the reception of Hong Kong culture, too. The relative absence of Hong Kong subjects in the public sphere renders the consumption of Hong Kong culture idealized and commodified.

Yet, as Carruthers points out, this is never the case with Korean culture. "The commodification of Koreanness is disrupted by a general distaste for the national otherness represented by diasporic or hybrid Korean identities" (2005: 416). Resident Koreans have long been forced to live as second-class citizens in Japan and have suffered considerable discrimination and prejudice, and many of them have been forced to live by passing as Japanese, hiding their ethnic background and adopting Japanese names in public. Koreanness is not something that can be comfortably consumed as a mass exotic commodity in the Japanese public imaginary unless its origin is suppressed or "Japanized," as is often the case with celebrities who willingly or unwillingly conceal their ethnic descent in public. For resident

Koreans, the fact that their identity construction is neither Japanese nor Korean in a full sense has been a serious issue. It also evokes uneasiness for Japan since its postcolonial subjectivity never allows it to cheerfully forget the history of colonialism.

In this context, the advent of the Korean Wave and the improvement of the images of Korea in general pose intriguing question about whether and how it is related to the social positioning and recognition of resident Koreans. As Taylor (1994) argues, social recognition of difference is a significant aspect of the multicultural politics of the marginalized. Then, the question is how resident Koreans, whose otherness cannot be easily contained by subjectless multiculturalism, are recognized via the fetishization of Korean popular culture? Does the recognition work to empower or disempower resident Koreans? How are positive perceptions of South Korea through the Korean Wave related to the perception of resident Koreans in Japan? How is their untameable postcolonial subjectivity, which resists easy cultural consumption, repositioned within Japan through the positive consumption of Korean popular culture and the advance of bilateral cultural exchange?

There are no straightforward answers to these questions, nor can we generalize about the diverse experiences of resident Koreans. It cannot be denied that the rise of the Korean Wave and the betterment of Korean images in Japan have significantly improved the image of resident Koreans, and this has empowered no small number of resident Koreans. Some, especially the younger generations, have gained the confidence to live as Koreans in Japanese society without naturalizing into Japanese. Others have become more willing to bridge the two countries, using the avenues of popular culture, such as film and music, to convey their personal experiences of hybridized acculturation. Issues about resident Koreans have come to be more frequently dealt with, attracting more attention in public media spaces such as popular magazines and TV shows. While *All Under the Moon* (1993) was the first commercially successful film about resident Koreans in Japan (see Iwabuchi 2000), recent films such as *GO* (2000) and *Pacchigi* (2005) have been even better received.

At the same time, the impact of the Korean Wave still tends to be constrained by the attention paid to inter-national relationships, which overpowers the concern with resident Koreans. The sense of frustration is often expressed by resident Koreans themselves that Japanese people might embrace the Korean Wave but the structure of social discrimination and indifference has not changed. For many resident Koreans job opportunities are still limited and it is at times not straightforward to rent a room. The Japanese government is not interested in improving these situations; instead, it is solely interested in using the recent cultural exchange to ease the historically strained relationship between Japan and South Korea. In the above-mentioned survey (Hayashi 2004), about a quarter of respondents said that they had become more interested in resident Koreans and their history, which is not negligible but yet much lower compared to their increasing interest in South Korea. Even worse, according to *Asahi Shinbun* (21 August 2004), in response to the question about interests roused by the Korean Wave, only a few mentioned historical issues or resident Koreans.

Furthermore, it should be noted that the improvement of the image of South Korea is occurring simultaneously with the demonizing of North Korea. Since the North Korean government officially acknowledged their involvement in the abduction of Japanese nationals, there has been a massive and antagonistic media bashing of North Korea. Racist attacks have also been made against resident Koreans who identified themselves with North Korea.

The clear divide between the public perceptions of North and South Korea among Japanese has an influence on the recognition and naming of resident North and South Koreans. The naming of resident Koreans—*zainichi chousenjin* (resident North Koreans or resident Koreans in general, as *chousenjin* signifies ethnicity rather than national identification), *zainichi kankokujin* (resident South Koreans, to differentiate from resident Koreans who identify themselves with North Korea), or *zainichi kankoku-chousenjin* (resident North and South Koreans, including both kinds of political identification)—is highly political, as it involves the issue of political identification with two Korean countries. In either case, however, remaining as Korean nationals is important for many since it signifies resistance to disgraceful naturalization into a Japanese national, as explained earlier. Recently, resident Koreans have tried to be more open to diversity within their communities and to widen membership irrespective of an individual's nationality or national identification. The name *zainichi Korian,* which uses the square form of the English term "Korean," has often been used because of its apparent political neutrality, though it is often criticized for the very same reason. In addition, it also has the merit of allowing inclusion of those who have been naturalized into Japanese, since the emphasis is more on historically embedded "Koreanness" than on national identification or the kind of passport someone has.

However, with the advent of the Korean Wave, the reference to resident South Koreans (*zainichi-kankokujin*) has become used more often than before in Japanese media. The new categorization of South Korean nationals living in Japan does not just accompany the suppression of resident Koreans who identify themselves with North Korea. No less importantly, this manner of naming signifies the ahistorical recognition of resident Koreans who are apt to understand their existence in relation to the contemporary culture and society of the nation-state called South Korea, which now produces attractive media products. Crucial in this nationalized recognition of resident Koreans is the disregard of the collective historical memories and experiences that are shared irrespective of nationality and that have been passed down from generation to generation.

TOKYO BAYSCAPE AND THE REPRESENTATION
OF RESIDENT SOUTH KOREANS IN JAPAN

While there are positive effects of the Korean Wave on the social recognition and positioning of resident Koreans in Japan, there can be discerned a confusion in how their existence is seen through the prism of South Korea, which accompanies the segregation of shared historical experiences of resident Koreans. How the Korean Wave has constructively and unconstructively influenced media representation and recognition of resident Koreans is elucidated in a TV drama series, *Tokyo Bayscape* (Fuji TV, Monday 9–10 p.m.), which broadcasted from July to September 2004. The drama is about the romantic relationship between a third-generation resident South Korean woman and a Japanese man and their aspiration to overcome the obstacle of ethnic difference. The story begins with a scene in which the depressed heroine sends a message to a web site from a mobile phone, "Please find the real me." This is the key phrase and motif of the drama, signifying the woman's desire to be recognized and loved just as she is, a woman of Korean ancestry who was born in Japan. Production of the drama was clearly motivated by the recent popularity of Korean TV dramas and films, as the producer clearly acknowledged. The drama is epoch-making: it is the first TV drama series on prime time on a major commercial TV station that features a resident Korean as the protagonist. This testifies to another positive result of the Korean Wave, gaining representation for resident Koreans, whose existence has long tended to be disregarded in the mainstream media.

However, it is apparent that the drama uses the hindrance presented by a resident Korean merely to add the spice of conflict to the romantic relationship. In the drama, the story revolves around the anguish of a third-generation daughter whose economically successful second-generation father stubbornly insists on her marrying a resident Korean and opposes her wish to marry a Japanese man. He is much concerned with the historically constituted discrimination against resident Koreans in Japan. At the same time, he has a bitter memory of his dead wife's passionate but tragic relationship with a Japanese man before their marriage and of how she never got over her longing for him. To the father, the daughter appears to be fatefully repeating her mother's forbidden love relations with Japanese men. While a parent's opposition to his child's marriage to a Japanese national might to some extent reflect the real-life experiences of resident Koreans, the drama focuses exclusively on the personal distress of resident Koreans without giving due attention to the structured discrimination in Japanese society. The issue is reduced to the personal anguish of well-to-do Korean residents in Japan—the social and historical issues are separated from the personal. Furthermore, the stubborn closed-ness of the resident Korean community is blamed for the daughter's agony, as symbolized by the father being presented as ethnocentric and obstinate and thus unable to understand the developing relationship between Japan and Korea (Ogura 2004). It is as if resident Koreans were all responsible for drawing the sharp exclusive line between themselves and the Japanese.

In relation to this, the protagonist's distress is depicted as the sharp divide between the two nations, South Korea and Japan. Japan's relationship with South Korea and its people is again confounded with that of resident Koreans whose historically contextualized experiences and subjectivities are thus interpreted in terms of those of South Korean nationality. This is shown by the catchphrase of the drama, "The love that transcends the national boundaries between Japan and South Korea." The father of the heroine often states that there is a deep gulf between Japan and Korea that is sharply divided by the Sea of Japan. A Korean star of *Winter Sonata* even appears at the end of one episode to urge the audience that people of both nations can be best friends by moving beyond what happened in the past. This is a striking confusion between Koreans and resident Koreans in Japan, as one viewer sharply criticized on the web site:

> I think the issue of resident Koreans needs to be distinguished from Korean Wave in Japan. Maybe they have the same nationality. Yet how is it plausible to deal with those Koreans who have been brought up in South Korea and those third generation resident Koreans who have been brought up in Japan on a par? . . . It is very good in any case that the neighboring country South Korea is in the media limelight and the friendship between Japan and South Korea is being deepened. However, resident Koreans are someone living next to you, not in the neighboring country. They might be your neighbors, colleagues or friends, if you are not aware of this. No sea divides Japan and resident Koreans.[4]

Yet, looking into the official web site of the drama series,[5] most audience contributions seem to affirm the drama narrative of inter-national relationship between Japan and Korea: "Unexpectedly I am addicted to the drama, because it deals with the contemporary issues between Japan and South Korea we are currently embracing." "This drama aims to bring Japan and South Korea closer, isn't it? If so, unless the drama has a happy-ending, the relationship between the two nations will remain distant." "I am deeply impressed with the drama that depicts the lovers who struggle to overcome national boundaries." These messages suggest that many in the audience expect the drama series to contribute to the further improvement of the relationship between Japan and Korea, but at the expense of accurately representing the complexity of experiences and social positioning of resident Koreans, since these are reduced to those of South Korean nationals living in Japan.

Thus *Tokyo Bayscape* confers a kind of social recognition on resident Koreans that renders them easily consumable historical subjects by interpellating them as South Korean nationals. The positive image of South Korea that the Korean Wave promotes eventually works to again marginalize and suppress postcolonial complexity and nuisances embodied in the historical subjectivity called "resident Korean." This is an attempt to simplify and misconceive a precarious identity formation and life experience that resist clear categorization in any sense since these individuals are constructed in a situation in which they are forced to live with vague feelings of uneasiness and strain in Japanese society. Social recognition is given only when historical nuisance is tamed by and for the majority. While there are positive developments in the social recognition of resident Koreans in Japan, that recognition comes with an acknowledgment that the past is over and no longer determines the present, the past should not be remembered and engaged with but, instead, left behind.

The drama also displays the replacement of multiculturalism with a multinationalism that attempts to understand the issue of multiculturalism in terms of nationality as a unit of analysis (see Iwabuchi 2005). The existence of resident Koreans in Japan is seen from the viewpoint of the inter-national relationship between Japan and South Korea, which disregards those whose experience and identity formation are torn between the two nations. The existence of South Korean nationals living in Japan rather than resident Koreans can be publicly recognized because they are more tolerable foreign nationals who are safely separated from the past, present and future of the Japanese imagined community. The factual mark of difference in terms of nationality and passport, the lack of the right to vote and the lingering difficulty of marrying Japanese nationals are dealt with in the drama, but not in a way that fundamentally questions the myth of Japanese homogeneity that has severely marginalized resident Koreans. This is reminiscent of the Japanese government's recent encouragement of resident Koreans to acquire Japanese nationality. As Tai (2004) warns, even if the naturalization process becomes less rigid and resident Koreans can more easily "come out" by publicly using Korean names and/or acknowledging their ethnic roots, this does not ensure the acceptance of resident Koreans as full citizens. Unless the lingering social discrimination and the racially and ethnically essentialist definition of "Japanese" are truly overcome, "resident Koreans are encouraged to 'come out,' but only in a contained way." Naturalization with Korean ethnic marks would result in Koreans being assimilated "only as a second-class Japanese" (369).

CRITIQUE FOR THE FUTURE

My critical analysis of the impact of the Korean Wave on the social positioning and recognition of resident Koreans in Japan should not be taken as totally rejecting positive changes. Critique is, however, a necessary detour to further the potential of the emergent change and to actualize transnational dialogue through media consumption. Let me end my arguments by looking at such promising signs in resident Korean audience responses to *Tokyo Bayscape* on the web site. On the official site of *Tokyo Bayscape* that is organized by Fuji TV there are some insightful comments from resident Koreans. A young female states:

> I am also a third generation resident Korean and attending a Korean school. To tell the truth, I have some reservation about the recent Korean boom in Japan. I am frustrated with the craze of Japanese people who do not even know about our history . . . But *Tokyo Bayscape* changed my view. We should try to let such people know about ourselves!!

The positive suggestion to educate Japanese people about history and resident Koreans should not be regarded as a one-way appeal from resident Koreans. Such an attitude would easily lead to the evasion of responsibility by the majority, who are inclined to unthinkingly look to the minority to teach them what to do. Her comment should be read as an appeal for both Japanese and resident Koreans to work together. She might have been encouraged by the fact that the Japanese mass media produced a drama that dealt with the anguish of young resident Koreans as well as by reading various comments on the web site that are critical of the current situation in Japan. In any case, her expression of hope reflects a possibility of cultivating a new kind of alliance through the consumption of media culture. Similarly, other resident Koreans, who sympathetically identify themselves with the protagonists, express a sense of empowerment in watching the drama:

> I am myself a third generation resident Korean and had the same experience of the break-down of marriage with a Japanese man . . . I was also distressed about who I am, but could not tell my anguish of living as resident Korean in Japan to my Japanese friend. But I now feel being healed by the drama.

> I am also a third generation resident Korean. I am really empowered by the drama that having two homelands is a nice thing. (^^ Thanks a lot)

> I have never felt it wonderful to be born as resident Korean, but the drama encourages me to straightly face what I am. Thanks all the production staffs for giving me a touching story.

While these comments make us realize the significance of a drama that deals with the hitherto disregarded issue of resident Koreans, there are also critical comments suggesting that the drama fails to convey the complexity of the lives of resident Koreans, instead confounding South Koreans and resident Koreans and lacking historical depth:

I am ambivalent about the recent Korean boom. I am glad that many people have more interests in South Korea but they still continue to be uninformed of resident Koreans. The drama story is nice but it is still far from our reality, as it is depicted from Japanese points of view.

I had quite a mixed feeling when I first watched this drama ... My grand father was forcibly brought to Japan during the colonial rule. There are many children and grand children of such people living in Japan ... for the first generation resident Koreans it is not something of the past that finished. The recent Korean Wave has improved the relationship between South Korea and Japan. To further mutual understanding, the history needs to be more firmly grasped.

I am sure that the drama has let many Japanese people know about resident Koreans whose existence has long been out of the front stage of Japanese society (but, let me remind you, not as foreign nationals who are living in Japan but as resident Koreans who are living traces of tragic history). Still now, it is not easy for resident Koreans to rent an apartment. Fact is stranger than fiction. There are more intricate troubles and incidents in reality.

The divergent views on *Tokyo Bayscape* expressed by resident Koreans is a testimony of the diverse social positions and experiences of individuals who cannot be understood as a homogeneous ethnic group. However, whether positive or negative, the views are expressed by individuals who have long been positioned as second-class citizens in Japanese society. We need to learn about the complexity and depth of their issues by listening carefully to the voices of resident Koreans who find sympathy for their anguish and hope in the drama, without heedlessly celebrating its empowering effect:

None of my good friends knows about my ethnic root. I always fear that they would dislike me when the fact is known. I was really moved with the scene that Mika (protagonist) confesses her ethnic background and nationality to her lover. I had the same experience once. I was so moved to shed my tears ... I really wish a happy ending.

Needless to say, her tears do not simply testify to the positive impact of the Korean Wave nor to the moving narrative of the love story. It is the historical present of resident Koreans living with the lingering structure of social discrimination that gives a special power to the drama narrative.

Fulfilling the wishes of many audiences, the drama has a happy ending. Yet, the respondent's wish for a happy ending is not the same as that of Japanese audiences. Here lies the expectation for real life. No matter how much strongly resident Koreans are empowered by the drama and the Korean Wave in Japan, the crucial question still remains. How can cultural empowerment lead to actual social transformation? The above-mentioned appeal of "let's work together" by a resident Korean needs to be actively echoed by people whose social positions are more privileged. To grasp how transnational media flows intersect with postcolonial ambivalence, a critical examination of the social recognition of resident Koreans in Japan is an unavoidable detour. This study suggests that such an effort could produce the beneficial result of productively turning the collective imagination from private fantasy to a vehicle for transgressive dialogue and social change.

*A different version of this paper entitled "When Korean Wave Meets Resident Koreans in Japan: Intersections of the Transnational, the Postcolonial and the Multicultural" was published in *East Asian Pop Culture: Analysing the Korean Wave,* Chua Beng-Huat and Koichi Iwabuchi (eds), Hong Kong University Press, 2008.

NOTES

1. For a detailed analysis of the Hong Kong boom in Japan in the 1990s, please see Chapter 5 of Iwabuchi (2002).
2. Such a condescending view is more often than not found in the media discourse about the phenomena that aims to dismiss Korean TV dramas as the belated equivalent of Japanese dramas in the 1960s and 70s and to mock dissatisfied middle-aged women audiences who find a savior in Korean TV dramas that actually reflect the behind-the-time standing of the society (see Lee 2004). This is mostly evident in men's weekly magazines, while the depiction is more sympathetic to the experiences of audiences in the magazines whose target readers are women and whose articles are mostly written by women.
3. For a detailed discussion see Ryang (2000) and Tai (2004).
4. http://www.myprofile.ne.jp/blog/archive/acquire-mind/25
5. http://wwwc.fujitv.co.jp/wankei/index2.html

REFERENCES

Appadurai, A. (1996) *Modernity at Large: Cultural Dimensions of Globalization,* Minneapolis: University of Minnesota Press.

Carruthers, A. (2004) "Cute Logics of Multicultural and the Consumption of the Vietnamese Exotic in Japan," *positions,* 12 (2): 401–29.

Fabian, J. (1983) *Time and the Other: How Anthropology Makes its Object,* New York: Columbia University Press.

Hayashi, K. (2004) "Dorama Fuyu no Sonata no Seijiteki naru mono" (Political Aspects of *Winter Sonata*), *Journal of Information Studies,* University of Tokyo, 69: 56–81.

Hirata, Y. (2008) "Touring 'Dramatic Korea': Japanese Women as Viewers of Hanryu Dramas and Tourists on Hanryu Tours," B. H. Chua and K. Iwabuchi (eds) *East Asian Pop Culture: Analysing the Korean Wave,* Hong Kong: Hong Kong University Press.

Ivy, M. (1995) *Discourses of the Vanishing,* Chicago: Chicago University Press.

Iwabuchi, K. (2000) "Political Correctness, Postcoloniality and the Self-Represen-
tation of 'Koreanness' in Japan," in S. Ryang (ed) *Koreans in Japan: Critical
Voices from the Margin,* London: Routledge.

———. (2002) *Recentering Globalization: Popular Culture and Japanese Transnationalism,* Durham: Duke University Press.

———. (2004) *Feeling Asian Modernities: Transnational Consumption of Japanese TV Drama,* Hong Kong: University of Hong Kong Press.

———. (2005) "Multinationalizing the Multicultural: The Commodification of
'Ordinary Foreign Residents' in a Japanese TV Talk Show," *Japanese Studies,*
25(2): 103–18.

Lee, D-H. (2004) "Cultural Contact with Japanese TV Dramas: Modes of Reception and Narrative Transparency," in K. Iwabuchi (ed) *Feeling Asian Modernities: Transnational Consumption of Japanese TV Drama,* Hong Kong:
University of Hong Kong Press.

Mori, Y. (2008) "*Winter Sonata* and Cultural Practices of Active Fans in Japan:
Considering Middle-Aged Women as Cultural Agents," B. H. Chua and K. Iwa-
buchi (eds) *East Asian Pop Culture: Analysing the Korean Wave,* Hong Kong:
Hong Kong University Press.

Ogura, C. (2004) "The Spice of Love Story: From Disorder to Obstacle," *Weekly
Asahi,* 13–20 August.

Ryang, S. (2000) *Koreans in Japan: Critical Voices from the Margin,* London:
Routledge.

Tai, E. (2004) "Korean Japanese: A New Identity Option for Resident Koreans in
Japan," *Critical Asian Studies,* 36(3): 355–82.

Taylor, C. (1994) "The Politics of Recognition," C. Taylor and A. Gutmann (eds)
Multiculturalism and Examining the Politics of Recognition, Princeton: Princeton University Press.

9 Nonresident Consumption of Indian Cinema in Asia

Adrian M. Athique

INDIAN CINEMA AS NONRESIDENT MEDIA

The last decade has seen an increasing level of academic and commercial interest in Asian media. This new awareness of the media industries operating across the region has been fueled by the contemporary manifestation of global economic liberalization. It is in this context that Arjun Appadurai has emphasized the rapid spread of electronic media and their transformative effects upon the social imagination, particularly in the global south, as evdience of the "cultural dimensions of globalization" (1996). However, the contemporary focus of Appadurai's argument should not obscure the fact that photomechanical feature films have been inherently mobile cultural artifacts addressing globally dispersed audiences for almost a century prior to the current period of media proliferation. India has historically been an *exporter* of films and this is highly relevant to understanding the global nature of Indian cinema.

As early as the era of silent cinema, Indian films had been exhibited from Lahore to Rangoon and from Colombo to Singapore, serving a large territory in South Asia. By the 1930s Indian films were screening in the countries of the Eastern Mediterranean, the East Indies and in several parts of Africa. The reach of Indian cinema has continued to grow in the six decades after independence through a series of distinct phases that have extended the presence of Indian films within Asia and beyond. This widespread dispersal has consequently made Indian cinema a popular media format functioning across a broad range of social contexts found beyond India's borders. Accordingly, on a global scale, Indian films are patronized by a large number of what I describe here as "nonresident" audiences.

The term "resident" is, of course, a variable and often contested term, a signifier shaped by the social, cultural, geographic and bureaucratic territories where it is employed. Nonetheless, there continues to be a broad unifying context to the term that implies *belonging* in not only a spatial but also a symbolic sense. A media audience might therefore be considered "resident" under conditions where viewers perceive what is on screen as somehow coterminous with the society in which they live. The "nonresident" mode of media consumption, by contrast, is a term intended to identify audiences who fall outside the normative viewing position constructed by modern nationalisms. Thus nonresident audiences inhabit social conditions where the engagement of viewers with a media artifact operates in an environment where the artifact itself cannot reasonably be claimed to present a social imagination "about here and about us." In much of the world, where imports make up the bulk of films screened and where various television formats encompass a wide range of national territories, it is nonresident experiences of media consumption that are in fact the most common.

The suturing of the symbolic and spatial logics of the global and local is one of the most frequently noted aspects of the modern world. In this light, there is much to learn from the different relationships and scales of reference that are deployed in the consumption of nonresident cultural products. In the context of Indian cinema, it might be a perceived cultural proximity that makes Indian films appealing for some nonresident viewers, enacting discourses of affinity, cultural affirmation or "imagined community." For others, it is more likely the degree of cultural distance that serves to make Indian movies attractive, mobilizing the aesthetics of exoticism. For this reason, the popular Indian film provides a valuable insight into the relational spectrum that situates and contextualizes media consumption in an interconnected global environment.

Broadly speaking, we can categorize instances of the nonresident consumption of Indian films using a number of factors: the cultural geography of the territories to which Indian films are dispersed, the racial, cultural and political make-up of the audiences being served and the wider political, economic and social contexts within which those acts of consumption take place. In the context of the mediated exchange of symbolic capital, it becomes clear that the categories that arise from such measures are not uniform series, but should instead always be understood in terms of the relative distance between the point of consumption and the cultural presence of India (however notional, or indeed, misinformed). With this in mind I have elsewhere outlined three key groupings of audiences that are pertinent to the nonresident functions of Indian cinema at the present time: *crossover, diasporic* and *parallel* audiences (Athique 2006a). Given that I have discussed both crossover (2008) and diasporic (2005, 2006a/b) audiences in other works, I will focus here on the category of parallel audiences.

I take the term "parallel" from Brian Larkin's work on the interpretation of Indian films in Nigeria (1997, 2003). Among the Hausa people, Larkin describes the emergence of local cultural forms modeled on the themes of familial loyalty and romantic desire played out in the commercial Indian films that are widely patronized in certain parts of Nigeria. Larkin notes that the renunciation, negotiation and appropriation of modernity as found in Indian films, emanating as it does from another "non-Western" perspective, has proved highly resonant with the experiences of Nigerian audiences. In seeking to provide an explanation for this instance of nonresident consumption, Larkin proposes that the Hausa people understand Indian films as representing a "parallel modernity, a way of imaginatively engaging with the changing social basis of contemporary life that is an alternative to the pervasive influence of a secular West" (1997: 16).

Larkin's notion of parallel modernities thus provides a useful model for recognizing transnational relationships that exist between different parts of the "developing world." This is not a utopian proposition, however, since there is no reason to assume that the "parallel" nature of mediated exchange, and of modernity itself, existing amongst so many different locations should be understood as constituting any equitable exchange system between non-Western states. Similarly, the common popularity of Indian films amongst parallel audiences does not indicate any coherent third world public. In practice, there are indications of specific alignments and disjunctures of cultural relations to be found in each encounter of the kind that Larkin describes. Context, it would seem fair to say, matters a great deal within the dynamics of cross-cultural exchange. This indicates the diversity and relative positioning to be found amongst Indian cinema's parallel audiences. Not all parallel audiences for Indian films are equally foreign, perhaps, and such audiences are in any case unlikely to be foreign in the same way. As this chapter will demonstrate, this continues to be the case even when we restrict our discussion of parallel audiences to the consumption of Bollywood in Asia.

BOLLYWOOD ACROSS ASIA

The first example that I will employ here is the Indonesian case where Indian films first appeared in the last years of Dutch rule. Despite the Japanese interregnum, which closed the market from 1942 to 1945, Indian films had become popular with local audiences by the time of Indonesia's independence in 1949. Indeed, as the Indonesian film industry was attempting to establish itself in the 1950s a strike was staged against Indian film imports, due to their popularity with the mass audience and the fact that they were cheap for local distributors to import. This made them a direct form of competition for Indonesian producers, whereas American films mostly patronized by the upper classes were not (Said 1991: 44). These brief protests proved unsuccessful and the importation of Indian films into Indonesia has continued to the present day.

Pam Nilan has observed that in contemporary Indonesia, wider geopolitical events have "been reflected in the ratings decline for American programs and films while other exogenous content—South American soap operas, Bollywood films, and Hong Kong martial arts epics—remain hugely popular" (2003: 188). Nilan believes that: "A major reason 'Bollywood' has millions of non-Indian fans in the Middle East, Africa and Southeast Asia is because of the non-American quality of Indian films" (2003: 296). In the years following the Asian currency crisis of 1997 and

98, Indian films certainly became far more commercially viable for Indonesian distributors than the more expensive American product. The production of Indonesian films was also virtually halted by the increased cost of film stock and processing and it was Indian and Hong Kong films that filled the vacuum (see Sumarno and Achnas 2002: 160). However, the consumption in post-colonial Indonesia of films imported from other Asian nations has been too consistent to be only a phenomenon of current affairs. As an alternative explanation, a contributor to an Indonesian website, "Taman Bollywood," points out the historical influence of Indian narrative forms upon Indonesian culture:

> Most Indonesian people, especially who live in the island of Java (about 60% of Indonesian population lived here), have a Hindu background. Their culture, dances, language (based on Sanskrit), philosophy, and their traditional ceremonies, all reflect this Hindu influence in their lives which has come to be a mix between Hinduism and Islam (Sufism). We don't say that Hindi films are only loved by the Javanese, but also loved by so many Indonesians who live in other islands and also watched by many people who live in Islamic countries. (Khan 2003, accessed: 03/10/04)

It may be unwise to over-emphasize a direct link between two periods of cultural exchange between South and Southeast Asia that are separated by some five hundred years, but there is doubtless some sense of a contemporary inter-Asian dialogue in Indonesian discourse on Bollywood. India has historically been a major center of culture, and an exporter of culture, within Asia, and it is relatively unsurprising that it remains so today. Having said that, the same web site also offers other reasons for the popularity of Indian films in the archipelago, such as the physical and symbolic attraction to film stars, the cross-cultural appeal of pop music and the desire for entertainment "when many people are 'crazy and bored' with political issues and bad economic conditions" (Khan 2003).

Indonesia today has a diverse transnational mediascape that has been enriched by the diffusion of new media technologies and further complemented by the proliferation of new media outlets after the end of Suharto's New Order government in 1998. Therefore, Indian film culture in Indonesia is disseminated across a multi-media environment that includes cinema exhibition, various forms of TV broadcast, pirated digital playback formats, magazines, music recordings and web sites. Indian films are not merely objects of consumption but also represent a site of performance as fans attend star appearances and/or engage in imitations and appropriations of the Bollywood aesthetic. Lidia Oostepeev, a secondary educator based in Australia, was impressed during a visit to Indonesia by the broad range of media activities centered on Indian film culture:

Stuck on a housing estate in Semarang during the rainy season of '01, I found myself watching a lot of T.V. Via programs chosen by Maman and Taufik, my hostess's servants, I realized that "Bollywood" (or the Hindi-language film industry based in Mumbai,) was providing entertainment for many Indonesians. Every few minutes a shampoo ad would flash across the screen featuring a male celebrity with dandruff free, glossy hair. A popular Indonesian actor I thought but no, upon enquiry it turned out to be none other than Shah Rukh Khan—a Bollywood superstar. *Dangdut* singers clearly singing in Indonesian not Hindi but outfitted in saris and wearing bindis also made for some interesting viewing [see Lockard 1996]. Then of course there were the Bollywood films dubbed in Indonesian running for close to 3 hours and longer if commercial breaks were included ... The Hindi film "Kuch Kuch Hota Hai" (1998) was a bigger box office success than the "Titanic" when it was screened in Indonesia and when the same film was shown on T.V. (2002), ratings "shot through the roof." In 2002 three major Bollywood stars appeared in concert at Hall C Pekan Raya, in Jakarta, before an audience of approximately 2 thousand wealthy people. Tickets for the extravaganza ranged from 600 thousand to 3 million rupiah ($100–$500 AU) and there was live coverage by INDOSIAR across the archipelago. (Ostepeev 2004)

The longstanding popularity of Hindi cinema in Indonesia is paralleled by the continuing popularity of the genre in other smaller Asian nations, such as nearby Malaysia and Burma, the more distant Uzbekistan and Tajikstan, as well as the newest Asian nation of East Timor. Generally speaking, the trans-Asian spread of Indian cinema is found in southern rather than northern Asia, although Indian films have enjoyed occassional success in China and Japan. It is worth recognizing that the reception of Indian films in distant parts of Asia is of necessity qualitatively different from their reception by audiences in India's near neighbors. Naturally enough, given the size and diversity of the Asian region, there is still much to be learned about the universal registers invoked by watching Indian cinema as well as about the specific dynamics of each bilateral exchange.

BOLLYWOOD IN SOUTH ASIA

While Indian films might be seen as a nonthreatening alternative to US cultural production in Southeast Asia, they have frequently been regarded as a source of cultural imperialism acting upon other South Asian states (see Sonwalkar 2001). The continuing popularity of Indian cinema in the rest of South Asia has been seen as damaging competition for local film production in those states and has, at times, inflamed nationalist sentiments. In the first instance, the fact that the national divisions within South Asia do not have a linguistic logic means that Indian films remain intelligible for large audiences located across India's borders. Most of the other South Asian states share a language with their larger neighbor, for example, Bengali is spoken in Eastern India and in Bangladesh, Tamil in South India and Sri Lanka and Hindi/Urdu in North-West India and Pakistan.

The second point to note is that the South Asian region was a single multilingual market for a number of Indian film industries prior to the modern political map of Pakistan, India, Sri Lanka and, later, Bangladesh. One legacy of this period is a commonly shared and inter-referential cinematic tradition in terms of visual and narrative style as well as industrial practices. However, since independence, the relative presence of Indian films in other parts of South Asia has been affected by the political relationship between the governments of the post-colonial nation states, who have attempted to serve as both arbiters and guardians of their national publics. In the historical context of post-partition South Asia, this factor has proved restrictive (although not wholly so) to media exchange. For example, the government of Pakistan quickly moved to ban the importation of Indian films, first in West Pakistan in 1952 and subsequently in largely Bengali East Pakistan in 1962 (Willemen and Rajadhyaksha 1999: 23–24).

Despite such obstacles, the reach of Indian films in the region has been steadily bolstered by the deployment of new media technologies that have made state barriers against media exchange increasingly porous. In the late 1970s and early 1980s the introduction of feature films on playback media via VHS led to the widespread illegal reproduction and smuggling of Indian films throughout the region. More recently, the transnational reach of Indian films via the medium of television has greatly expanded with the proliferation of cable and satellite television operating in the region. A third point to note, then, might be that the physical, if not the political, geography of the subcontinent also appears to favor extensive overlaps within the regional media sphere. So, whilst watching Indian films is officially a transgressive act in Pakistan, it remains a widespread practice. As Rahimullah Yusufzai records:

> the popularity of Indian films like *Roja, Border, Mission Kashmir* and *Refugee* in the Pakistani home video market. These films, which depict the Indian view of the Kashmir Issue, are being secretly rented after a ban by the government, which of course clubs them all as Indian propaganda. Video stores in Islamabad report brisk demand for Bollywood films, including the "anti-Pakistan" ones. (Yusufzai 2001)

For their part, Pakistani audiences for Hindi films seem prepared to take the occasional jingoistic outburst with a pinch of salt. These acts of non-resident consumption on the part of Pakistani film fans are paralleled to a lesser extent by the market for Pakistani-produced Urdu dramas in India.

Thus, in the South Asian context the smuggling of media products across the border (compounded now by the emergence of cross-border non-state commercial broadcasters) is a major component for maintaining the cultural connections that have now been discouraged politically over a lengthy period. For this reason, it is far from insignificant that Hindi cinema retains a large following in Pakistan.

For Pakistan, the exclusion of Indian films has been far from beneficial for the national film industry in economic terms. In practice, given the prevalence of Indian films in Pakistani society via pirated DVDs and cable television, and the steady decline of Pakistan's own film industry in terms of both production and screen capacity, commentators in Pakistan have observed that the future of cinema in the country looks bleak without access to Indian films (Ghafoor 2005, 2006). In this light, despite tensions caused by anti-Pakistan rhetoric in some Indian films, Pakistan sent a delegation to the Indian film industries' FRAMES convention, hosted by the Federation of Indian Chambers of Commerce and Industry (FICCI), in 2004. As noted by Pakistan's *Daily Times:*

> Pakistani cinemas have spent a long time trying to convince the government that screening Indian films is the only solution to the low audiences at cinemas. They have threatened to close down cinemas over the unavailability of Pakistani films. Quite a few cinemas have already been closed and several have been converted into theatres. (Gill 2004)

It is not only Pakistani exhibitors that are seeking access to Hindi content. Cable TV operators in Pakistan went as far as striking in 2003 when the government of Pakistan attempted to restrict their broadcasting of Indian entertainment channels, an event recorded with some triumph by India's *The Hindu:*

> Every new attempt by Islamabad to deny its people access to Indian entertainment has had the opposite effect. Bollywood films, soap operas, filmi and non-filmi songs and Indian pop groups (mostly Hindi) have become the staple diet of a majority of the Pakistani society. (Reddy 2003)

For Indian film-makers, and for the Hindi cinema in particular, the population of Pakistan represents a large and loyal audience that it would like to access commercially. To compound their frustration, in the present situation, after four decades of official exclusion, Pakistan has emerged as a major piracy hub for distributing Indian films not only domestically but across the world (Khan 2005). As such, the prohibition of Indian films in Pakistan has had the paradoxical effect of making Indian films more available while also ensuring that the losses for the producers are felt on a global scale. Writing for the BBC, Sanjoy Majumder describes the ubiquitous presence of Indian films in Lahore:

> Large posters of Bollywood actresses share space with Pakistani independence leader Mohammad Ali Jinnah. Store-owner Nafeez grins as he shows off the latest film releases from across the border, illegally smuggled in via Dubai. "I sell about a couple of thousand cassettes a week. Everyone here loves Bollywood films. Last month, the Bollywood actress Urmila Matondkar was here. You should have seen the crowds—thousands and thousands gathered to catch a glimpse. There was almost a mini stampede." (Majumder 2004)

In an interview in 2003, Matondkar herself said: "Human suffering has no religion. We should work together for the betterment of our next generation. Let me tell you, Pakistanis love Indian films. Why not make them legal in Pakistan? This will help bridge the cultural gap between our two countries" (Ashraf 2003). Matondkar has not been alone in voicing this sentiment, with many other members of the Hindi industry lobbying for normalized trade links with Pakistan (2003). Nor is it only the film industry that sees Indian films as a resource for bridge-building between the two states (see Bharat and Kumar 2007). However, it is worth remembering that the current spirit of cultural fraternity follows a decade of unprecedented nationalist hostility on the big screen. As such, for the filmwallahs, the economic potential of audiences on the other side of the border has to be balanced by what constitutes a permissible articulation of India-Pakistan relations within India's political environment at any given time.

Nonetheless, it is clear at the level of consumption that despite the frequency of political tensions, Indian films have enjoyed consistent favour from non-Indians in South Asia. Working against the official strictures of reflexive otherness, and in marked contrast to the state-owned media of either nation, the role played by Hindi cinema in perpetuating cultural exchange between India and Pakistan is highly significant (perhaps even unique). In the east of the subcontinent, the exchange of Bengali media products and personnel between India and Bangladesh also serves to sustain cultural contact in the aftermath of political division. Indian films and film stars have also proved both popular and controversial in Nepal over the years (see BBC Online 27/12/2000; Burch 2002). The resumption of screenings for Indian films in Afghanistan was one of the first media developments following the invasion of 2001 (Srivastava 2001). It can be argued, therefore, that Indian media products are currently playing an important role in the further development of a South Asian media sphere that might, over time, contribute to better understanding between the South Asian nations. In any case, and it is fair to say that such optimism may be unwarranted, it seems likely that both sustained demand for, and sporadic resistance to, Indian films by culturally proximate audiences throughout South Asia will continue into the future and so, either legally or otherwise, will their distribution.

INDIAN FILMS AS INTER-ASIAN MEDIA

It has been my intention here to provide a general introduction to the scope of Indian cinema as a major media industry reaching audiences across Asia. I have emphasized that the consumption of Indian films in the region occurs across divergent social contexts, and thus across a differentiated, perhaps even contradictory, field of cultural practices. Despite the broad similarities between Pakistan and Indonesia as the largest nations in Asia with predominantly Muslim populations, their differing relational interfaces with the cultural presence of India provides for markedly different articulations around the Indian film as a cultural artifact. The two examples discussed here thus illustrate both the celebration of inter-Asian dialogues *and* the frictions of familiarity that can surround these exchanges, where "parallel" connections are subject to both positive and negative readings and where shared cultural practices can be sites of conflict as well as friendship. As such, nonresident viewers in Asia locate Indian films in a manner congruent with their different relative understandings of Indian cultures and their own local and national cultures.

We should also note that Asian audiences deploy global media knowledges by situating their engagement with Indian films relative to the other transnational media sources operating across the region that fill out the broader pattern of media consumption (such as American television and Korean or Hong Kong cinema). For this reason, the varied reception of Indian films at their different points of consumption is juxtaposed with the growing range of media products available to each of these audiences. It is fair to say, then, that in marked contrast with a recent past of state-regulated media for most Asian countries, what most characterizes the contemporary Asian media scene for its consumers is its multiple sources and its intertextuality. For all these reasons we need to understand media consumption in Asia today, not in discrete and singular but rather in comparative and relational terms.

REFERENCES

Appadurai, A. (1996) *Modernity At Large: Cultural Dimensions of Globalization,* Minneapolis: University of Minnesota Press.

Ashraf, S. F. (2003) "Why Bollywood Wants Peace," http://specials.rediff.com/movies/2003/dec/20bolly.htm.

Athique, A. (2005) "Watching Indian Movies in Australia: Media, Community and Consumption," *South Asian Popular Culture,* 3(2): 117–33.

——. (2006a) "The Global Dispersal of Media: Identifying Non-Resident Audiences For Indian Films" in T. Holden and T. Scrase (eds) *Medi@sia: Global Media/tion In and Out of Context,* London: Routledge.

———. (2006b) "The Diasporic Audience for Indian Films: Addressing and Consuming Non-Resident Subjects," paper presented at the University of Wollongong, New South Wales.

———. (2006c) "Bollywood and 'Grocery Store' Video Piracy in Australia," *Media International Australia,* 121: 41–51.

———. (2008) "The 'Crossover' Audience: Mediated Multiculturalism and the Indian Film," *Continuum,* 22(3): in press.

BBC Online. (27/12/2000) "Nepal Bans Bollywood Films," *BBC Online World Edition, http://news.bbc.co.uk/1/hi/world/south_asia/1088100.stm.*

Bharat, M. and Kumar, N. (2007) *Filming the Line of Control: The India-Pakistan Connection Through the Cinematic Lens,* London: Routledge.

Burch, E. (2002) "Media Literacy, Cultural Proximity and TV Aesthetics: Why Indian Soap Operas Work in Nepal and the Hindu Diaspora," *Media, Culture and Society,* 24: 571–79.

Ghafoor, U. (2005) "Pakistan's Dilemma—Bollywood or Bust?" *BBC Online World Edition,* http://news.bbc.co.uk/1/hi/world/south_asia/4617447.stm.

———. (2006) "Pakistan's Overtures to Bollywood," *BBC Online World Edition, http://news.bbc.co.uk/1/hi/world/south_asia/4952288.stm.*

Gill, A. (2004) "Cinemas to Get Bollywood Permission in Three Months," *Daily Times,* 7 July, 7–21, http://www.dailytimes.com.pk/default.asp?page=story.

Khan, A. A. (2005) "Pakistan—Copyright Piracy Hub," *BBC Online World Edition,* http://news.bbc.co.uk/2/hi/south_asia/4495679.stm.

Khan, N. S. (2003) "Popularity of Hindi Films in Indonesia," http://tamanbollywood .singcat.com/artikel/bollywood_in_indonesia.shtml.

Larkin, B. (1997) "Indian Films and Nigerian Lovers: Media and the Creation of Parallel Modernities," *Africa,* 67(3): 404–40.

———. (2003) "Itineraries of Indian Cinema: African Videos, Bollywood and Global Media," in E. Shohat and R. Stam (eds) *Multiculturalism, Postcoloniality and Transnational Media,* New Brunswick: Rutgers University Press.

Lockard, C. (1996) "From Folk to Computer Songs: The Evolution of Malaysian Popular Music, 1930–1990," *Journal of Popular Culture,* 30(3): 1–26.

Majumder, S. (2004) "Pakistanis Eager for Neighbourly Peace," *BBC Online World Edition,* http://news.bbc.co.uk/1/hi/world/south_asia/3366945.stm.

Nilan, P. (2003) "The Social Meanings of Media for Indonesian Youth," in T. Holden and S. Baum (eds) *Globalization, Culture and Equality in Asia,* Melbourne: Trans Pacific Press.

Ostepeev, Lidia (2004) "Discovering Bollywood in Indonesia," *The Indonesian Studies Newsletter of the Asian Studies Association of Australia (ASAA),* Iss. 41, August 2004, viewed 02/10/2004, http://intranet.usc.edu.au/wacana/isn/ bollywood_indo.html.

Reddy, B. M. (2003) "Bollywood Reels in Pakistan," *The Hindu Online Edition,* http:// www.hindu.com/thehindu/mag/2003/11/23/stories/ 2003112300220500.htm.

Said, Salim (1991 ed. Trans. Siagian, T.) *Shadows on the Silver Screen: A Social History of Indonesian Film,* Jakarta: Lontar Foundation.

Sonwalkar, P. (2001) "India: Makings of Little Media/Cultural Imperialism?" *Gazette,* 63(6): 505–19.

Srivastava, S. (2001) "Bollywood Eyes Afghan Market," *BBC Online World Edition, http://news.bbc.co.uk/2/hi/entertainment/1679115.stm.*

Sumarno, M. and Achnas, N. T. (2002) "In Two Worlds," in A. Vasudev et al. (eds) *Being and Becoming: The Cinemas of Asia,* New Delhi: Macmillan.

Willeman, Paul and Rajadhyaksha, Ashish (eds.)(1999 ed.) *Encyclopedia of Indian Cinema,* London: BFI.

Yusufzai, R. (2001), "In which Lollywood Gives Bollywood Those Ones," *Himal South Asian, http://www.himalmag.com/march2001/analysis.html.*

10 Bollywood in Bangladesh

Transcultural Consumption in Globalizing South Asia

Zakir Hossain Raju

Hindi movies . . . are like an overdose of chocolate that give us consti-
pation the next day. They cheapen us, debase us as human beings.

—A Bangladeshi blogger and viewer of Bollywood nicknamed
Ulysses (Ulysses, "The Curse of Bollywood" 2006)

South Asia in the 1990s and 2000s experienced the liberalization of the
economy, the proliferation of consumerist lifestyles and rapid changes in
its mediascape. The media in South Asia today may be seen as a key site
where the trade deregulation policies adopted since the 1990s had some
direct influence. There has also been acceleration in the dissemination of
South Asian media worldwide. The transnational media migrations into,
out of, and within contemporary South Asia prove that we can no longer
talk about one way traffic of media from the West to Asia, which some
scholars dubbed "invasion from the skies" (Chadha and Kavoori 2000).
Arjun Appadurai therefore emphasized the "cultural dimensions of globalization" and the effects of multi-directional media flows upon the social
imagination, particularly in the global south (1996). Within this context,
the increased inflow of Western screen media into South Asia and the rise
of Bollywood as a carrier of "Indian" culture and a transnational, globalizing agent since the early 1990s increased conversations about mediated
cultural exchange and globalization. In the face of globalization, scholars
started questioning the idea of nation and national culture as unified entities
(Anderson 1991; Bhabha 1990a, 1990b; Ashcroft 1989). Appadurai (1994),
Hall (1996) and Featherstone (1995) also argued that globalization of market and media transformed old categories of nation and culture and made
way for the intercourse of the local and the global. This essay is an attempt
to understand the circulation and consumption of Bollywood in South Asia
in such intercourse at a time when the transnational visual media are easily and quickly permeating the national borders in this region. By "Bollywood," I mean here not only the Hindi-language film industry of India, but
also the associated popular cultural paraphernalia of this industry, such as
songs of Hindi films, posters of the film stars, and so on.

This chapter looks at the workings of Bollywood as a major Asian transnational media industry in Asia's own backyard: how this global and regional cultural institution has been circulated, received and consumed in the South Asian region. Ironically, among the vast number of studies that have been conducted on Bollywood in the last decade or so, very few focus on its audience and consumption, especially in a South Asian context. Most of these studies look at the consumption of Bollywood by South Asian diaspora in non-Indian and non-South Asian locations such as Germany (Brosius 2005), South Africa (Hansen 2005), Guyanese East India (Halstead 2005), Nigeria (Larkin 2005), New York (Dudrah and Rai 2005) and the United Kingdom (Kaur 2005; Dudhrah 2006). The consumption of diasporic Indian or South Asian films that were produced in the United Kingdom also received attention from few scholars (Desai 2004; Hussain 2005). So the reception of Bollywood films in its home ground (that is, in the South Asian region) did not attract that many scholars. The few studies focusing on reception of various popular Indian cinemas (including Bollywood) in this region mainly look at the audiences in India and may be divided into two trends depending on the geographic parameters. The first trend of research looks at the Tamil or Telugu film stars and fan club activities in South India (Dickey 1993; Srinivas 2005). The other group of work that goes beyond South India is also a slim one. There are two studies I could identify; the first one looks at the reception of some selected Hindi films in northern India in the early 1980s (Pfleiderer and Lutze 1985) and the other focuses on the consumption of transnational media including Bollywood cinema in West Bengal in the early 2000s (Ganguly-Scrase and Scrase 2006). However, the circulation and consumption of Bollywood or Hindi cinema in other nation-states of South Asia (for example, Pakistan, Bangladesh, Sri Lanka and Nepal) have never been studied in a scholarly manner. Therefore this essay, which looks at consumption of Bollywood in Bangladesh, is an early effort towards understanding the reception of Bollywood in the South Asian region outside India.

I start my enquiry here with a simple question: How is Bollywood film culture circulated and consumed in one of India's neighboring nation-spaces like Bangladesh? I find that Bollywood cinema is in a longstanding love-hate relationship with the Bangladeshi nation-state and the middle-class Bengali Muslims. Here, the state is keen to keep Bollywood outside the national public sphere. This state-sponsored attitude has kept Bollywood films from Bangladeshi cinema theatres for the last four decades, as a ban was imposed by the Pakistani state leaders during the 1965 India-Pakistan war, when Bangladesh was the Eastern province of Pakistan. However, Bollywood as a popular culture is omnipresent in Bangladesh in many ways, especially through television and video and also through the print and audio media. In the private spheres of middle-class households Bollywood has a strong visual and aural presence. The visibility and popularity of Bollywood in Bangladesh somewhat hide the cultural politics around the consumption of Hindi films. In other words, consumption of Bollywood creates different threats and desires among various groups of Bangladeshis. The Bangladeshi middle class and the state locate the consumption of Bollywood from a cultural nationalist viewpoint and see it as a cultural-imperialist genie sent by India.

On the other hand, the ordinary viewership of Bollywood, crisscrossing the middle and lower middle class and consisting of the maid servants and housewives, university students, teachers and white-collar executives, are more interested in having some fun by watching these films and following the film stars. Therefore, an understanding of the cultural politics around the circulation and consumption of Bollywood in Bangladesh takes me to the next level of my investigation: What is the role of Bollywood within the sphere of everyday life of non-Indian South Asians (for example, Bangladeshis)? In order to contextualize and elaborate on this question, I looked at the Internet, conducted library research and carried out in-depth interviews with some avid viewers of Bollywood films in Dhaka, the capital city of Bangladesh. Based on these interactions, this essay provides insights into how the urban, middle-class men and women consuming Bollywood films in Bangladesh negotiate the sense of national (Bangladeshi), cultural/ethnic (Bengali) and religious (Muslim/Hindu) identities.

BOLLYWOOD CINEMA AS EVERYDAY CULTURE IN CONTEMPORARY BANGLADESH

The presence of Bollywood cinema as a form of popular culture is very visible and audible in contemporary Bangladesh. The stars of Bollywood cinema, gazing down from huge, glittering billboards and luring consumers to buy soaps and shampoos, can be found at major intersections of Dhaka city. Television regularly contributes to the presence of Bollywood in the everyday lives of ordinary people. Though city dwellers have been able to access satellite television channels only since the mid-1990s, most Bangladeshis living in small towns and even villages also watch Bollywood films, film trailers and film songs on various transnational television channels, ranging from B4U (Bollywood for You) to MTV India. Passengers in long-haul public transport vehicles (for example, inter-city coaches and steamers) are entertained by Bollywood films and film songs. Mobile companies offer Bollywood film songs as ringtones, and young people listen to the songs on their walkmans. Such songs also blare from horn speakers, radio sets and audio players in shopping complexes, at family gatherings such as weddings and puberty rites, as well as at religious and social festivals in the cities and villages.

The print medium is also busy popularizing Bollywood cinema. Numerous local film magazines, mostly in Bengali, carry the latest upheavals in the personal and professional lives of Bollywood stars. All the serious dailies and weeklies also devote one or more sections to the gossip and news of the Bollywood film industry. Posters, postcards, notebooks, writing pads (to be used by school students), calendars, albums—all bearing the pictures of Bollywood film stars—are also available on every street corner in contemporary Bangladesh. The walls in college and university dormitories are normally covered with posters of Bollywood stars like Shahrukh, Aiswaria, Hritik and Kajol (Hasan 2008a: 15). This glimpse of the contemporary mediascape of Bangladesh makes clear that Bollywood cinema has emerged as one of the most popular modes of entertainment in a globalizing Bangladesh. Though theatrical screening of any Indian film has been banned since 1965, Bollywood films are voraciously consumed by middle-class Bangladeshis by non-theatrical means, such as on videotapes, VCDs and DVDs and more recently, on cable and satellite television channels and via the Internet.

This trend of consuming Bollywood films at the household level started in the early 1980s with the advent of one of the first non-theatrical viewing options, that is, consumer VCRs. VCRs made household consumption of Hindi films among Bangladeshi audiences much easier. Small video-theatres started mushrooming in the cities and towns of Bangladesh, offering films like *Disco Dancer, Qurbani, Kabhi Kabhi, Silsila, Love Story, Sholay, Shan, Mukaddar Ka Sikandar* and *Lawarish* for an entry fee of only 10 Taka (20 cents US). Nightly renting of VCRs with four or five Hindi film videos also became very popular. Amitabh Bachchan, Mithun, Zeenat Aman and Hema Malini quickly became familiar names and popular icons among middle- and lower-middle-class viewers in the middle of the "culture war" between India and Bangladesh. In the words of a viewer of Hindi cinema in 1980s Bangladesh:

> The critics were incensed by the wanton sexuality in Indian films. Cultural commentators kept talking about how it was "corrupting our youth." . . . When Zeenat Aman's wet-dress look was copied by Mandakini, the poster became a Dhaka hot-seller. The morals squad were up in arms. "Indian films had to be stopped!" But how could you stop this free-floating market propelled by the VCR explosion? Ironically, as the debate over Sridevi's hips and Mandakini's chest set fire to local papers, I found myself more interested in Hindi films. (Mohaiemen 2003: 2)

In the 2000s Bollywood films are circulated in Bangladesh mostly illegally through pirated VCDs and DVDs. The new Bollywood films become available as pirated VCDs or DVDs during the same week (if not before) the film is released in cinemas in India or elsewhere. These VCDs cost less than one US dollar while a DVD may cost one dollar and a half. A recent newspaper article claims that each month more than seven million VCDs and DVDs are imported and/or produced in Bangladesh, most containing

Bollywood films (Hasan 2008b: 16). Most of the viewers I interviewed in Dhaka admitted that they buy the VCDs or DVDs of new Bollywood films. Interestingly, the people here who sell, copy, buy, rent, borrow and view these pirated VCDs and DVDs never consider their actions to be illegal. However, the "legal" manner through which Bollywood films are circulated in Bangladesh is the satellite television channels. Currently, there are more than eighty television channels available for viewing in Bangladeshi cities and towns, of which thirty-two channels offer Hindi-language films and programs mainly provided by two large companies: Z and Star groups (Hasan 2008c: 15). While some of these Hindi television channels broadcast Bollywood films on a twenty-four-hour basis, some channels offer film songs, news and gossip in quick intervals.

Since the vehicles of dissemination for Bollywood films in contemporary Bangladesh are VCDs, DVDs and satellite television, the viewing of these films essentially happens in middle-class households. Most respondents said they watch the films with friends and members of their family. The young males mostly watch with friends of similar age and gender while the married people said they often watch the films with their spouses and children. The domestic assistants are also welcome to watch Hindi films in middle-class households in Dhaka. One respondent, a housewife, said she watches the films with her maid servant at home, while another respondent, a male domestic assistant, made sure that he watched Bollywood films regularly with the family he works for.

CONSUMPTION OF BOLLYWOOD AS A THREAT AGAINST NATIONHOOD

It can be noted that the wide-ranging consumption of Bollywood films is not unique to Bangladesh; rather, its omnipresence in the popular culture sphere in non-Indian nation-spaces of South Asia is traceable for many years. Indian-produced films have seemingly enjoyed consistent favor from non-Indians in the subcontinent since the late colonial period. For example, India has been exporting films to its neighbors and beyond since the early twentieth century. Athique contends that Indian entrepreneurs built cinemas across South Asia in the 1920s (2006: 190).

So in contemporary South Asia, while Bollywood films are officially banned in Pakistan and in Bangladesh, they remain a hugely popular source of entertainment disseminated through widespread playback piracy and cable. Bollywood films have also proved both popular and controversial in Nepal, and the resumption of screenings of these films was one of the first media developments in post-Taliban Afghanistan. Such overwhelming presence of Indian films in South Asian popular culture has often been regarded as a source of cultural imperialism acting upon non-Indian nation-states in the subcontinent (Sonwalkar 2001). This is also a common complaint against Bollywood for cultural commentators in Bangladesh, mainly from a nationalist, and sometimes from a religious angle (see Hasan 2008a, 2008c and 2008e).

In the same vein, while Bollywood is hugely popular among urban and semi-urban Bangladeshis, the state has identified Bollywood as a "national enemy" since the Pakistan days. The state identifies this cinema as foreign culture that is not only useless but also dangerous and a damaging force in constructing a particular kind of state-nationalist discourse in postcolonial East Pakistan and Bangladesh. As a result of the state's attitude towards popular cinema, it exerts strong and conservative control over the institution. The Bangladeshi power elite's fear and anxiety over the popularity of Bollywood cinema is reflected in their continuous commitment to ban it from local film theatres. This is part of their attempt to assert and maintain, in the words of Annette Hamilton, "a curious repressive-modernist control over the political/social consciousness of a society plunged headlong into a postmodernist global economy" (1994: 142). Even in the globalizing mediascape of Bangladesh in the 1990s and 2000s, both the state and the nationalist elite kept the ban intact, though Bollywood films on DVDs and VCDs are available on every street corner in contemporary Bangladesh.

The ban on Indian films was first issued by the Ayub government of Pakistan during the 1965 India-Pakistan war. This timing clarifies that the Pakistan state utilized a peak moment of pan-Pakistani nationalism to order the historic ban, a step that ensured that only "Pakistani" films could be screened in both parts of Pakistan. The film capitalists of Lahore, Karachi and Dhaka demanded such a ban because Indian Hindi films were considered the main rival to local popular films produced in 1950s and 60s Pakistan. The war that broke out between Pakistan and India in September 1965 gave the Pakistan state a suitable time to perform the ban. The Pakistani leaders took the decision to ban on 10 September 1965, just four days after the war started ("Ban on Indian Films": 1). The Pakistan state and the local film producers used the discourse of pro-Islam (and anti-Hindu, anti-Indian) Pakistani identity successfully to make the ban work.

No South Asian film historian or cultural theorist interpreted the ban and its background with due emphasis. Then, we normally overlook the fact that in the early 1960s the two groups of Pakistani film capitalists, producers and exhibitors, fought each other on banning Indian films' theatrical release in Pakistan. In 1962, for the first time, the Pakistan government banned the showing of Indian films for five years, using the suggestion of the Film Investigation Committee. The exhibitors started a legal battle against the decision. Then, in 1963, the High Court of Pakistan, upon considering a petition lodged by the film exhibitors, declared that the ban was illegal (Quader 1993: 431). I find this legal battle between the Pakistani state wanting to ban Indian films and local film exhibitors and distributors wanting to screen Indian films an important instance of negotiation over cultural consumption between the nation-state and the cinema industry in a postcolonial nation-space. After the state lost the legal battle, it was waiting for a suitable time to implement the ban against Indian films. The war that broke out between Pakistan and India in September 1965 seemed a suitable nationalist moment for the state to order the ban. The ban was made effective through a notification made with powers conferred by an act passed two years earlier, that is, the Censorship of Films Act, 1963.[1] The relevant section of the act gave the government the power to decertify "a . . . class of certified films . . . in the interest of local film industry, or in any other national interest" (Hoque and Nasr 1992: 115).

I emphasize the 1965 ban because of its relevance to consumption of Bollywood cinema in Bangladesh from the 1970s to the 2000s. After the independence of Bangladesh in 1971, the Pakistani ban against Indian films was kept in action using the similar nationalist rhetoric by the Bengali-nationalist government led by Sheikh Mujib. In 1972, just after the liberation war, leading distributors and exhibitors of Bangladesh cinema expected that the newly established pro-Indian government would again approve the exhibition of Indian popular films in Bangladesh, as it was happening in pre-1965 East Pakistan. In the words of Alamgir Kabir:

> Veteran producers were reluctant to launch new films as they were not quite sure . . . about how much concession in the film sector would be made for the benefit of the film industry of India as a gesture of goodwill by the new Bangladesh Government to a country that, admittedly, played a vital role in the liberation of Bangladesh from Pakistani yoke . . . However, with active encouragement from higher level . . . , the fear subsided quickly enough. (1979: 52–3)

Khan Ataur Rahman, a veteran film director-producer of Bangladesh in the 1960s and 70s recalled that when Sheikh Mujib was approached about the exhibition of Indian films in 1972, he declined such a proposition, just saying "tell them, those [Indian] films will not be shown in Bangladesh" (Rahman 1990: 8). The ban on screening Bollywood films in theatres that is still in force in Bangladesh exemplifies how the nation-state and power elite in Bangladesh (and also in Pakistan) believed in the idea of a pure but vulnerable national identity that could be jeopardized through the showing of Indian films in cinemas. Similar to the timing of the 1965 war, Mujib and others used the nationalist discourse of the time at a peak moment of Bengali nationalism— that is, 1972, when Bangladesh had just been liberated—to order this ban.

Such state-nationalist will for a "national" audience who can/will watch only homegrown films and should have no access to popular transnational cinema such as Bollywood is linked to the notion of a "national" identity as envisaged by the Bangladeshi middle class in recent decades. The state leaders, afraid of Bollywood as an anti-Bangladeshi force, note that it can never serve the "national" public sphere, "the subject of evening news, the 'nation'"(Hansen 1993: 197). I find the words of Partha Chatterjee appropriate in this context: "The cultural identity of a nation is neither immemorial nor naturally given. It has to be fabricated, most deliberately so under the auspices of the nation-state" (1998: 18).

CONSUMPTION OF BOLLYWOOD AS
INDIVIDUAL DESIRES AND NEGOTIATIONS

Interestingly, the nationalist attitude that considers Bollywood a national enemy is hard to find in today's popular culture sphere of Bangladesh, as signified in the massive dispersion of Bollywood I outlined in the earlier section. In other words, while the state and the nationalist group of Bangladeshi middle class, relying on a discourse of political and/or cultural nationalism, see Bollywood cinema as an imperialist "curse" against "the gems of Bangla culture: . . . Baul songs; Tagore's veneation of nature; . . . the plays . . . staged in Dhaka" (The Curse of Bollywood 2006), there is another, possibly more powerful and pervasive discourse around the everyday consumption of Bollywood and identity construction in Bangladesh. It is not surprising then that when the ban on theatrical screening of Hindi films was lifted during the Third Bangladesh International Film Festival in 2006, thousands of viewers rushed to the Dhaka cinemas in a bid to watch Hindi films like *Hum Tum, Dhoom, Paheli, Black, No Entry* and *Hum Aapke Hain Kaun* on big screens (Indian Films 2006). An Indian film critic comments on the event:

> One was witness to hordes and hordes of people attending ticketed screenings of Bollywood blockbusters . . . , the main subsidy for the film festival one surmised. Living in India, I was astonished to see how starved people in neighbouring countries are to watch Bollywood fare. (Srinivasan 2007: 58)

So, despite the fact that Bollywood films cannot be shown on large cinema screens due to an "official" ban, unofficially they are part and parcel of the everyday life of the middle class in Bangladesh. Therefore, though Ravi Vasudevan, an influential scholar of Indian cinema, commented that the Bollywood films have been constructing "an overarching north Indian, majoritarian Hindu identity" and simultaneously defining all else as "other" (1995: 306), interestingly, when I conducted interviews with some of these "other" groups, such as Bangladeshi, Bengali-Muslim viewers, I found that they do not care much about this othering process of Hindi cinema.

Most Bangladeshi viewers enjoying the Bollywood films, though they are non-Indian and mostly non-Hindu, are not concerned about the "Indianization" and/or "Hinduization" role of Bollywood. A twenty-nine-year-old married female PhD student, Bengali-Muslim, explains:

> I see fantasy in Bollywood films. I like it. At least by the end everything turns out fine . . . I know these films show Indian, Hindu culture. I

don't care. Movies are not a guideline to follow. They simply reflect life, and its only natural they will show Hindu, Indian culture.

These viewers do not see Bollywood as a threat to Bengali culture. They do not feel that by watching these films they are jeopardizing Bangladeshi national culture. The same viewer, who watches a Bollywood film each week at home with her husband, comments: "I never follow Bollywood style/fashion at my home or in family functions. I don't think we've to follow them. Bangladesh has too much to offer on its own." Another respondent finds: "I don't think Bollywood films are threats for Bangla language and Bengali culture. We have to compete with Hindi movies and also with Hollywood movies." A twenty-year-old male engineering student in Dhaka echoes this view: "Our culture and language is ours. We will not forget about them." Interestingly, he even believes that some Bollywood films "carry good messages and these can also fit well in our culture and daily life." Similarly, a West-Bengali blogger says:

> Comparing rabindranath tagore and kaji najrul islam, against present day Hindi trend is absolute stupidity. . . . ha ha i don't think that bengali culture is such a cheap culture that it will get endengered by hindi movies. we here [in West Bengal] watch movies entertainment. we r not so unsecured. (Anonymous, The Curse of Bollywood 2006)

The Bangladeshi viewers define and accommodate Bollywood film watching as a fun activity in their everyday lives. One respondent, a thirty-one-year-old divorcee working for a private company in Dhaka comments:

> I like Bollywood movies because of dance, songs, music and for beautiful actors. The lifestyle in the films [are] based on fantasy, not the real life. I like to see [these films] just for entertainment, not to follow such lifestyle. My favourite stars are Aiswariya, Amisha, Bobby and Shahrukh. They are beautiful to look at. I like their getup, makeup, hairstyle and [physical] figure.

Almost the same view was expressed by a twenty-four-year-old female teacher of Dhaka: "I find Bollywood movies very entertaining—with songs and dances, latest trend in fashion and good looking people." When interviewing, I noted that the viewers of Bollywood films in Bangladesh are also interested in following the fashions as of their favorite stars. For example, this female teacher buys saris that Rani Mukherjee wears in various films. A twenty-year-old male domestic assistant wants the costumes used by John Abraham, while another nineteen-year-old single female student yearns for the costumes she saw in films like *Jab We Met* and *Om Shanti Om*. A twenty-eight-year-old housewife admits that she likes dresses like lehanga shown in Bollywood films very much; she wants to decorate her home with the furnishings shown in these films, but she cannot afford to for now.

Thus, the everyday consumption of Bollywood in Bangladesh opposes the cultural nationalist wish to bracket Bengaliness within a certain notion of national culture; rather, the perspective is to enlarge the meaning of Bengaliness in today's global world. Most of my respondents find no problem in appreciating provocative costumes and dances offered in Hindi films or in liking a Bollywood star whose religious affiliation is different. A thirty-year-old housewife says:

> Yes, sometimes Bollywood films offer some vulgarity, but I believe that Muslim and Bengali cultures have also moved ahead and are now quite progressive [read modern]. . . . My two favourite film stars are Hindu and me being a Muslim I have absolutely no problem with that. I admire them for who they are regardless of their religion.

This kind of globalist discourse on media consumption helps these viewers to successfully negotiate certain national, cultural identities and to construct a hybrid identity for themselves as a result of watching these "foreign" but entertaining films. A Bangladeshi blogger and viewer of Bollywood commented:

> The ["masses"] don't give a shit to the preservation of Bangla language, the political parties or the constant nagging of liberation war [ideals.] All they want is some fun time and the progress of their country. . . . While preserving Bangaleeness, they [cultural nationalists] have forgotten that times have changed and Bangalees don't want to be just Bangalee anymore, they want to be world citizens. A global citizen with a global view can only succeed in this modern and competitive world. (Rashedin, The Curse of Bollywood 2006)

The idea of a "global citizen" of Bangladeshi origin that Rashedin seeks here is obviously related to the transformations brought about through globalization of media and economy in South Asia. These changes have fostered the reformulation of individual and community identities, leading to transformations in and of public spheres, especially the "national" public sphere(s) in the subcontinent that has widened and segmented in the last two decades or so. In this context, I have reconsidered the consumption of Bollywood as a major transnational Asian media and its role in negotiating and constructing community and individual identities just outside Indian national borders. Deriving insights from middle-class Bangladeshi viewers of Bollywood films, I have attempted to locate how, through transcultural consumption of Hindi cinema, they construct and reconstruct a de-territorialized imagined community and a new identity in a rapidly globalizing South Asia.

NOTES

1. The notification number was C-40/65-Film. See Asian Mass Communication Research and Information Centre (AMIC), "Bangladesh: Cinema" in http://

sunsite.nus.edu.sg/amic/country/banglad/bangcine.html, accessed: December 11, 2007.

REFERENCES

Abecassis, D. (1990) *Identity, Islam and Human Development in Rural Bangladesh*, Dhaka: University Press.

Anderson, B. (1991) *Imagined Communities*, London: Verso.

Appadurai, A. (1994) "Disjuncture and Difference in the Global Cultural Economy," in P. Williams and L. Chrisman (eds) *Colonial Discourse and Postcolonial Theory*, New York: Columbia University Press.

———. (1996) *Modernity at Large: Cultural Dimensions of Globalization*, Minneapolis: University of Minnesota Press.

Ashcroft, B. et al. (1989) *The Empire Writes Back*, London: Routledge.

Athique, A. (2006) "The Global Dispersal of Media: Locating Non-Resident Audiences for Indian Films," in T. Holden and T. Scrase (eds) *Medi@sia: Global Media/tion In and Out of Context*, London: Routledge.

"Ban on Indian Films," (1965) *Weekly Chitrali* (10 September), p. 1.

Barnouw, E. and Krishnaswamy, S. (1980) *Indian Film*, New York: Oxford University Press.

Bhabha, H. (1990a) "Introduction: Narrating the Nation," in H. Bhabha (ed) *Nation and Narration*, London: Routledge.

Bhabha, H. (1990b) "DissemiNation: Time, Narrative, and the Margins of the Modern Nation," in H. Bhabha (ed) *Nation and Narration*, London: Routledge.

Brosius, C. (2005) "The Scattered Homelands of the Migrant: Bollyworld through the Diasporic Lens," in R. Kaur and A. Sinha (eds) *Bollyworld: Popular Indian Cinema through a Transnational Lens*, New Delhi: Sage.

Chadha, K. and Kavoori, A. (2000) "Media Imperialism Revisited: Some Findings from the Asian Case," *Media, Culture and Society*, (22): 415–32.

Chatterjee, P. (1998) "Introduction," in P. Chatterjee (ed) *Wages of Freedom: Fifty Years of Indian Nation-State*, Delhi: Oxford University Press.

"The Curse of Bollywood." (2006) Webblogs, 19 April, http://backtobangladesh. blogspot.com/2006/04/curse-of-bollywood.html, accessed on 1 January 2008.

Desai, J. (2004) *Beyond Bollywood: The Cultural Politics of South Asian Diasporic Film*, London: Routledge.

Dickey, S. (1993) *Cinema and the Urban Poor in South India*, Cambridge: Cambridge University Press.

Dudrah, R. (2006) *Bollywood: Sociology Goes to the Movies*, London: Sage.

Dudrah, R. and Rai, A. (2005) "The Haptic Codes of Bollywood Cinema in New York City," *New Cinemas: Journal of Contemporary Film*, 3(3): 143–58.

Featherstone, M. (1995) *Undoing Culture: Globalization, Postmodernism and Identity*, Thousand Oaks: Sage.

Ganguly-Scrase, R. and Scrase, T. (2006) "Constructing Middle Class Culture: Globalization, Modernity and Indian Media," in T. Holden and T. Scrase (eds) *Medi@sia: Global Media/tion In and Out of Context*, London: Routledge.

Hall, S., and du Gay, P. (eds.) (1996) *Questions of Cultural Identity*. London: Sage.

Hamilton, A. (1994) "Cinema and Nation: Dilemmas of Representation in Thailand," in W. Dissanayke (ed) *Colonialism and Nationalism in Asian Cinema*, Bloomington: Indiana University Press.

Halstead, N. (2005) "Belonging and Respect Notions vis-à-vis Modern East Indians: Hindi Movies in the Guanese East Indian Diaspora," in R. Kaur and A. Sinha (eds) *Bollyworld: Popular Indian Cinema through a Transnational Lens*, New Delhi: Sage.

Hansen, M. (1993) "Early Cinema, Late Cinema: Permutations of the Public Sphere," *Screen*, 34(3): 197–210.

Hansen, T. (2005) "In Search of the Diasporic Self: Bollywood in South Africa," in R. Kaur and A. Sinha (eds) *Bollyworld: Popular Indian Cinema through a Transnational Lens*, New Delhi: Sage.

Hasan, M. (2008a) "Influence of Hindi Culture in Bangladesh 1," *Daily Naya Digonto*, 12 January: 15–16.

——. (2008b) "Influence of Hindi Culture in Bangladesh 2," *Daily Naya Digonto*, 13 January: 15–16.

——. (2008c) "Influence of Hindi Culture in Bangladesh 3," *Daily Naya Digonto*, 14 Jaury: 15–16.

——. (2008d) "Influence of Hindi Culture in Bangladesh 4," *Daily Naya Digonto*, 15 January: 15–16.

——. (2008e) "Influence of Hindi Culture in Bangladesh 5," *Daily Naya Digonto*, 16 January: 15–16.

Hoque, A. and Nasr, M. (1992) *Mass Media Laws and Regulations in Bangladesh*, Singapore: AMIC.

Hussain, Y. (2005) *Writing Diaspora: South Asian Women, Culture and Ethnicity*, Hampshire: Ashgate.

"Indian Films Win Hearts in Bangledesh," (2006) Agency Report, 24 March. http://www.apunkachoice.com/scoop/bollywood/20060324-1.html, accessed 19 December 2007.

Kabir, A. (1979) *Film in Bangladesh*, Dhaka: Bangla Academy.

Kaur, R. (2005) "Cruising on the Vilayeti Bandwagon: Diasporic Representations and Reception of Popular Indian Movies," in R. Kaur and A. Sinha (eds) *Bollyworld: Popular Indian Cinema through a Transnational Lens*, New Delhi: Sage.

Larkin, B. (2005) "Bandiri Music, Globalisation and Urban Experience in Nigeria," in R. Kaur and A. Sinha (eds) *Bollyworld: Popular Indian Cinema through a Transnational Lens*, New Delhi: Sage.

Mohaiemen, N. (2003) "A Love Story Life Without Bollywood," *Daily Star Magazine*, http://www.thedailystar.net/magazine/2003/12/04/perceptions.html.

Pfleiderer, B. and Lutze, L. (1985) *The Hindi Film: Agent and Re-agent of Cultural Change*, New Delhi: Monohar.

Quader, M. (1993) *Bangladesh Film Industry*, Dhaka: Bangla Academy.

Rahman, K. (1990) "Tell Them . . . in Bangladesh," *Weekly Chitrali*, 13 April.

Rajadhyaksha, A. and Willemen, P. (1999) *Encyclopaedia of Indian Cinema*, London: BFI.

Sonwalkar, P. (2001) "India: Makings of Little Media/Cultural Imperialism?" *Gazette*, 63(6): 505–19.

Srinivas, S. (2005) "Kung Fu Hustle: A Note on the Local," *Inter-Asia Cultural Studies*, 6(2): 289–95.

Srinivasan, S. (2007) "Bangladesh International Film Festival," *Osian's Cinemaya*, 1(3): 58.

Vasudevan, R. (1995) "Addressing the Spectator of a 'Third World' National Cinema: The Bombay 'Social' Film of the 1940s and 1950s," *Screen*, 36(4): 305–24.

Part III

Everyday Life in Transition

Contesting Identity

11 Consuming and Producing (Post)modernity

Youth and Popular Culture in Thailand

Ubonrat Siriyuvasak

Popular culture consumption is central to the everyday life of youth in Thailand. It is more so when globalization speeds up the flow of local and transnational popular culture. For the industry the vast expansion of the market means achieving the goal of profit maximization. In this process the production of cultural product has been integrated and major emphasis has been placed on the distribution and marketing flow of these products. Hence, the energizing of capital's motor via informationalism (Castells 1996). The rapid flux of trans-cultural imageries on the electronic media of communication has elevated the lived society into an emerging society of signs. But in this transformative social arrangement cultural commodities such as Western popular music and Hollywood film, Japanese *manga*, and recently, Korean computer game, music and television drama, are competing with Thai cultural products in the everyday politics of youth. They become the pleasurable semiotic terrain of meaning construction and contestation that is closely connected to the socio-political context as well as the class position and gender of youth.

The power of signs constructed by the working-class and middle-class women in this study might be viewed in terms of the re-location of the modern centralized power of the male hierarchy in culture and knowledge production. Modernity from the start signifies the revolutionary break with tradition and social stability of the agrarian society. Its universalistic claims of instrumental rationality (represented by male intellectuals) have brought about massive social and cultural changes (Turner 1990). Interestingly, the consumption of popular culture by working-class and middle-class women in search of modernity and a new cultural identity is a vivid manifestation of pleasure over rationality. Popular culture itself professes to delegitimize the credibility of the grand narrative and scientific knowledge at the core of modernism (Lyotard 1984). This criticism valued local knowledge and lived experience as these are seen as horizontal knowledge and the presence of cultural diversity. But post-modernist theorists such as Baudrillard (1994), for instance, take post-modernism to another extreme. For him, where there is sign and an endless spiral of simulacra reality then ceases to exist. Signs become reality *in toto*. The cultural politics of popular culture consumption that will be elucidated in this chapter takes us neither here nor there. The juxtaposition of cultural consumption and production demonstrates that counter-modernity and modernity are, paradoxically, situated within the same process of symbolic construction and deconstruction of the post-modern. Significantly, the notion of class is brought into focus and problematized in the East-Asian transborder consumption and mediascapes.

This chapter looks at three cases of identity formation and transformation in the social transition in the 1980s, 1990s and 2000s. These exploratory studies investigate the cultural politics of working-class and middle-class youth in their everyday consumption of popular culture. The objectives of these three snapshots are; firstly, to bring class analysis back into the debate on media consumption in order to problematize the way in which class consciousness and identity formation are mediated through popular culture and discursive practice. Secondly, to look at the recent phenomenon of Asian popular culture and how it is Asianizing middle-class youth in Thailand and in East Asia. This is to see if a generation consciousness is forming among youth across the major metropolis of Southeast and Northeast Asia or, instead, a new class consciousness. In this chapter the actors we study are young women but the emphasis is on women as agency and as a class. Women are subordinated to men in the workplace, at home, in their leisure consumption and in their power relations in general. But, studying them as groups of social and class actors, I hope to discover how they can be subversive and relatively independent in their imaginary world and in the real world.

THE WORKING CLASS: FORMATION AND TRANSFORMATION OF IDENTITY

This section describes the identity formation process of the working-class and the middle-class youth in their cultural activities in everyday life. The framework is to look at *"audience reception"* in a different light. Here, the media audience is seen as a collective group, not as individual receivers of information and culture, and their cultural activities—consumption and production of cultural product and meaning—are approached from their material conditions of existence and the mode of the generating of practices. This is to shift away from the confines of reception study and take into serious account the situated condition of youth. As Silverstone (1994) argued, the concept of active audience becomes meaningless because it is now clear that most audiences are social agents actively engaging in their consumption in some ways. The problem is that although they are active social agents they may lack the power to transcend their material conditions without real organization. The more meaningful step is to look at how this process is circumscribed and connected to the conflicting and contradictory constraints of different forms of temporality in the lived condition of these audiences.

In his *Outline of a Theory of Practice,* Bourdieu (1977) defined *habitus* as "systems of durable, transposable dispositions, structured structures predisposed to function as structuring structures, that is, as principles of the generation and structuring of practices and representations" (72). Cultural identity is seen as a product of individual history and group history, and as the dialectic of the internalization of externality and the externalization of internality, or the incorporation and objectification of structures. Our exploratory studies look at how audiences or agents are objectively regulated by their *habitus.* By this structural constitution they cope with the unforeseen and act collectively, tending to reproduce the objective structures of which they are the product. Secondly, the analysis shows how the cultural resources or cultural capital in Bourdieu's (1984) conceptualization becomes the bedrock of an individual and of the collective group in changing their everyday life.

Working Conditions

This ethnographic study was grounded on the conceptualization that the public and domestic sphere, work and leisure, are inseparably interwoven. Audiences are not complete dupes who can be easily manipulated by the dominant ideology, as theorists of the Frankfurt School suggested (Adorno and Horkheimer 1973). Neither are they autonomous receivers of popular cultural product, as pioneering research in Cultural Studies of the Birmingham School would have us believe (Hall and Jefferson 1976). The research is based on the view that consumption and production of culture are dialectically connected to the discursive formation in the public sphere. The following investigation describes how women workers maximize pleasure within their *habitus* and how they turn their cultural capital around to struggle for their *modern* identity and change their welfare in the workplace or the economic sphere.

Aporn Textile, in Samutprakarn, fifteen kilometers south of Bangkok, is a large factory with thirteen hundred shift-workers (three shifts of eight working hours per day) and two hundred day-workers (male technical workers and administrative staff). Women between the ages of eighteen and forty-five make up 80 percent of the workforce. In 1986, the majority of workers are peasants from the Northeast and Central region of Thailand, with a primary school education. The everyday condition of the workers is positioned in a complex time and space coordinated by the regularity and rhythm of work, rest and leisure. Activities are organized into three rotating patterns to comply with the working of the machines, or the production motor of capitalism. The peasants, who are displaced from the peasant way of life, must readjust the rhythm of their bodies and minds to a new life pattern. But they struggle to retain their cultural identity by using the Northeastern language, eating Northeastern food, and traveling home on festive occasions with special donations for their local temples in the villages.

Popular Culture Consumption

Women workers' consumption of mainstream popular media is largely punctuated by the mass media and the women's circle of friends. Most of the television dramas they watch are romance and comedy. Channel 7 appeals to the mass audience around the country while Channel 3 is popular with urban and middle-class viewers. Apart from watching television women workers often go to the cinema and listen to *Luktoong* music or radio drama as they do their laundry. They spend about 8 percent of their 1,820–3,000 baht monthly income on leisure, for example, going to the cinema or buying cassette tapes. On rare occasions they go to a concert. They save a good part of their income for their family at their home village.[1]

In their leisure time groups of women workers go to the nearby cinema. Romance films, such as *Mia Tang* (*Wedded Wife*), are entirely pleasurable for the workers. These films reaffirm womanhood and allow them to gaze at the lives of the upper class. Films such as *Kamsing* (*Kamsing, the Boxer*) or *The Killing Field* are considered serious films by the workers. Watching *Kamsing*, they compare his life with their own, especially when Kamsing is taken advantage of by his employer. On the other hand, they feel that *The Killing Field* is educational and political. The workers sympathize deeply with the main characters, an American journalist in Cambodia and his Khmer interpreter, who fled to Thailand. They fear for the future of Thailand, seeing the tragedy the Khmer people have gone through.

For popular music, the women workers form two fan clubs, a Sayan Sanya and a Surachai Sombatcharoen fan club. Both are super stars of the popular *Luktoong* music genre. Sayan Sanya sings romantic and tragic love songs with perfect *Luktoong* sound and style. Young Surachai Sombatcharoen, who takes after his all-time super star father Surapol Sombatcharoen, sings romantic songs with a sexy persona. The two fan clubs often rival each other in showing off their cultural taste. *Luktoong* is the working-class music, whereas the middle classes listen to the pop tunes of the *Lukroong* and *String* genres. Most *Luktoong* singers come from peasant families and have minimal education. There is, obviously, a class connection between the workers and the singers. The cultural identity of the workers is formed around *Luktoong* music, which tells the story of rural young women and men who come to Bangkok to find employment and a new life.[2]

Cultural Practices and Discursive Formation

The new discursive practice is the unionization of the workers, which empowers them to negotiate with their employer in several disputes about work conditions (1981, 1985) and their living conditions (1980). The fifty-four-day strike in 1981 and the two-week slowdown in 1985 produced successful negotiations based on the mobilization technique of the core organizers of the union. These organizers rely heavily on the networks in the workplace and the cultural networks formed through common social and cultural activities. These groups become the real resource of power for the workers.

Although the women workers choose to reinforce the rural and peasant identity, their rituals of consumption are intervened by the educational program of the union and resistance discourse during union meetings and related activities. As this research shows, women workers experience identity transformation through their discursive practices at work and in their cultural activities. During a trip to a wedding ceremony the male workers try to sing "Kon Jon Pu Ying Yai" (The Great Poor Man), which is a *Pua Chiwit* song, but the women challenge them with a *Luktoong* hit song, "Krasae" (Come on, Boy!). At the wedding ceremony *Pua Chiwit* songs by the popular band *Carabao* are played, as well as other popular love songs of the *Luktoong* genre. In this cultural space, which combines leisure and tradition, the articulation of the peasant/worker identity becomes a contested terrain. But women workers are reluctant to show their working-class identity. Male workers, on the other hand, take the leading role in stating proudly their new class identity.[3] When the workers visit their home villages, however, most of the women workers present an urban worker persona. They dress in city attire, wear cosmetics and jewelry, and speak like people from Bangkok. In this way they easily differentiate themselves from their village kin and friends. This new identity represents the modern subject of the rural peasant.

The significance of the identity transformation becomes clear at the union annual meeting and at the fifty-four-day strike, when all the workers show their solidarity and fighting spirit. It is in this official public space that each individual is interpellated as a worker by his or her collective action against the employer. The workers sing "Saksri Kamakorn" (Dignity of the Working Class), "Sam Prasan" (The Three Coalition), and "Su Mai Toi" (No Retreat) in unison. Union members also convert an erotic song, "Jud Tien (Light the Candle)" into a protest song. The tune is the original tune, which is fun and playful, but the new lyrics are satirical and defiant. The song criticizes the employer's refusal to increase the daily wage. The dynamics of the workers' discursive practice enable a broader and changing *habitus* to emerge. Despite the incongruity between pleasure and ideology, the women workers slowly cross over to the oppositional discourse of politics and class.

The class identity of the workers is reaffirmed in the workplace and during union activities, creating solidarity among the workers and with other unions. One good example is the Thai Arrow Textile workers' strike in 1986. Aporn Textile workers made donations and joined the protest at the site near Thai Arrow Textile factory. The woman president of Aporn Textile Workers' Union organized a performance of *Likay,* a popular local play, based on the story of *Jantakorob*. She wrote the new plot by synthesizing pleasure with the popular rhetoric of their economic struggle. The original story was deconstructed and then reconstructed in the context of the industrial dispute and the negotiation process. To entertain the workers the narrative style juxtaposed satire with everyday humor and popular *Luktoong* music.

News reports about the strike appeared in the mainstream press for several days. The workers became visible in the public sphere as class actors demanding their economic rights. For a brief moment their obscurity was dispelled. In their politics of everyday life, work and leisure, the workers could connect their discursive practice in the public sphere with their popular culture consumption/production of music, drama and film. In this case, the woman union president was the driving force, strengthening the bond between women textile workers with her creative work. She and her colleagues used their passion and pleasure to fight against the economic structure and male hierarchical power. They showed that people could change the real world if they are able to put their imaginary world—the world of their ideals—to the test. Here we see the principle of the dialectic of the objective construction of structure. From an emerging class consciousness, however, the workers appeal to Thainess against the un-Thai/foreign capitalist. Modernity for the women workers is defined in terms of the hegemonic discourse of Thai nationalism rather than class identity despite their class confrontation. There is an ambivalence of class intertwined with citizen consciousness bounded by the logic of the nation state. This is contrary to the middle class, as our next illustrations show.

THE MIDDLE CLASS: RITUALS OF CONSUMPTION AND PRODUCTION OF CULTURE

The second and third snapshots investigate the rituals of popular culture consumption and the production of identity among middle-class youth. During the mid-1990s and 2000s J-pop and K-pop have been highly popular among middle-class youth in Thailand and many Southeast Asian countries (Rakprayoon 2002; Nissim 2006).[4] Both studies, in 2000 and 2005, look at the fans and their activities, and the music and television drama they consume. In the study on J-pop a small group of J-pop fans who read *manga,* listen to Japanese pop music, and watch Japanese television drama were interviewed. These fans are teenagers from eighteen to twenty-five years of age. In the study on K-pop fifty-two young middle-class respondents were interviewed. Most of them watch Korean television drama and listen to K-pop. These K-pop fans are fourteen to twenty-three years of age. The majority of the interviewees are secondary school and university students from middle-class families. Their parents are professional practitioners such as doctors, engineers, accountants, teachers, managers and entrepreneurs, and civil servants. The family income ranges from 100,000 to 500,000 baht/month. Some of them could be considered upper middle class. The information from both studies is based on interviews and observation of fan club meetings. In addition, two key participants were interviewed in September 2007 to update the analysis on the cultural practices of J-pop and K-pop fans.[5]

Living Conditions of Middle-Class Youth

As most of the interviewees are students, their everyday life is usually spent on schooling, rest and leisure. They live with their family in single-family units or in big compounds. The students receive a monthly allowance of 4,000 to 8,000 baht. Some students spend a large part of this amount on leisure, that is, media consumption, since their food, lodging and travel are provided for by the family. For a teenager school is roughly the equivalent of "work" for a grown up, only it does not bring any income. Thus, leisure activities such as popular culture consumption are a significant part of the youths' learning experience and their means of getting away from school work.

The students form their social network at their school or university and within the circle of kinship. As they get to know each other they discover that there are some classmates who share the same tastes in J-pop and K-pop. Their additional group of friends comes from the J-pop and K-pop fan networks outside school. They get acquainted through the fan web site and at frequent small group meetings in the city center where youth often mingle. For those who can afford to go to live concerts or club meetings, this is another opportunity to forge a broader network.

Because the cultural consumption of the textile workers is strictly circumscribed by their situated condition, such as their low income, limited media access, and lack of knowledge about (new) media technology, they must seek pleasure within this socio-economic boundary. Middle-class youth, on the contrary, circumvent the limitations of their consumption by creating new social networks through the Internet.[6] They are investing their time to accumulate the necessary cultural capital for their consumption and distinctive cultural taste (Bourdieu 1984). At some stage of the leisure and pleasure, consumption would be turned into "work" or real production.

Popular Culture Consumption

From the mid-1990s Japanese and Korean television dramas have been popular on free-to-air stations, but they are limited to certain time slots, such as on weekend mornings and at midday. They are not on the air during the evening prime-time slot, which is occupied by locally produced dramas. This limitation creates constraint for the compelling desire to consume a constant flow of the dramas. J and K-pop music are also unevenly played on FM radio in Bangkok. Young consumers must fulfill their quest by buying music and drama CDs or downloading from the Internet. They spend several hundred baht regularly or even thousands if they buy original music CDs or a VCD set of a drama series. Some of the interviewees spent more than 2,000 baht a month. This can go up to 4,000 to 6,000 baht if they attend a live concert, or up to 40,000 baht if they go abroad. But to save on costs they become members of the J-pop and K-pop fan clubs so they can share music and drama files and much more. The Internet becomes the most effective communication tool for finding and exchanging information and products. There are several dozen fan club sites and forums such as *http://fixxxboard.15.forumer. com/index.php?act=idx*, *http://www.angelicnews-thailand.com/board/*, *http://forums.popcornfor2.com/index.php?showforum=15* and *http:// www.soompi.com/forums/index.php?showforum=16*.

There is a clear economic rationale behind the infatuation with J-pop and K-pop. These products are of good quality and value compared with locally produced music and television drama. In a study in 2004 and 2005 on Japanese pop culture in six East Asian metropolises Nissim (2007) found that J-pop products are better produced in terms of sound, image and fashion, and there is sophistication in the content because they are artistically developed. Korean pop industry is following the example of Japanese pop in much of their music and drama production (Lee 2007). But the K-pop cultural industry does good marketing research and has a well-planned strategy that boost its profile in East Asia (Tada-amnuaychai 2007). Although the fans acknowledge the second-rate quality of K-pop compared to J-pop they are committed to their choice of cultural taste. They enjoy the lightness of the romantic story, R&B and hip hop music, and a dancing style that is one step ahead of the trend in the Thai mainstream pop scene.

These young fans obviously see themselves as more advanced in their consumption of style. Therefore, keeping up with the latest trend is highly fashionable and makes one feel cool and modern at all times. Consuming exotic cultural goods becomes a clear distinction of taste that demarcates these young consumers from their middle-class peers. J-pop fans, in particular, turn away from the majority of Thai mainstream pop. They feel more enlightened in their constant consumption of J-pop information and culture, some of which is rare and not readily available on the market. In their consumption practices they make serious attempts to beat time and space barriers to fulfill their passionate quest for what they perceive to be the "new" trend in Japan and Korea. The middle-class fans are drawn to pop modernism, for which often the old is destroyed and the new emerges from the ruins of yesterday's pop. In this kind of mediated transformation, where the restructuring of time and space and cultural deterritorialization and reterritorialization take shape, the lived experience and the social connections are differentiated from the traditional lived experience (Tomlinson 1999). These youth have crossed the cultural borders to be the "global modern" or "Asian modern" and at once loosen themselves from the confines of the "national" and locally produced culture.

J-pop Fans and Counter-culture

The J-pop fans in our study, in the latter part of 1990s, were expressive and displayed some degree of subversiveness. The popularity of X-Japan, a famous Japanese androgynous visual rock band, is a unique example. X-Japan, who played heavy metal rock music, stood out as a subversive icon because of the band's sexual imagery and the sound of speed rock. There was a sense of liberation in the ambiguous sexuality of X-Japan. Their good music technique, artistry and authenticity combined made the band instantly popular (Mudkong 2001). The music is mostly melodramatic lamentation on sexual desire, love and despair. There was an X-Mania Club and a monthly newsletter was produced for these X fans. In 1997, the band split up. And in 1998, Hide, the lead guitar player, committed suicide. Both incidents shocked the fans deeply. They organized a mock funeral for him but were criticized for their open adoration of a foreign band. The experience of the speed, the beat of the rock music, the sound and the long-haired glam costumes produced deep emotional involvement. The passion made the youth feel liberated even if this might have been illusory, as Frith (1997: 112) expounded: *"Music is the key to youth identity because it offers, so intensely, a sense of both self and others, of the subjective in the collective."*

Before the economic crisis in 1997 J-pop fans imitated the dress and hair styles of Japanese youth from the fashionable Harajuku area in Tokyo and displayed themselves at Center Point, an urban shopping and entertainment area for the young middle class. Thai teenagers came here to promenade in their constructed Japanese imageries. Their clothes and hair were strikingly different. They wore mini-mini skirts and displayed colorful hair, which made them look like they had popped out of Japanese fashion and youth magazines (Kiatwatiratana 2000). These youth gathered at Center Point to demonstrate their distinctive identity. Their intentional communication was clearly visible and constructed to be read (Hebdige 1979). It was a semiotic subversion of the official honing of a united and homogeneous Thainess in the culture. In their identity construction they claimed and transformed the cultural space at Center Point. They found a place to show their symbolic power and to communicate their style, which to them was cool and modern. In addition, they imaginatively transported the space of a distant metropolis to the urban center of Bangkok. The cultural practice of J-pop fans is a manifestation of the imagined cosmopolitanism of a (post)modern society based on the *"desirable other"* from a more developed society or culture (Tomlinson 1999). But their articulation was seen as decadent and a deviation from the Thai social norm. Most of all, there was the fear that Thai youth were being dominated by Japanese culture. Not surprisingly, their activity has been dispersed from Centre Point, after a short-lived celebration of youth freedom in their own public space.

K-pop Fans and Consumption Rituals

The research on K-pop explores how the production of consumption rituals is essential to the identity formation of youth. Two examples of highly popular K-pop stars, Rain (Jeong Ji Hoon) and Se7en (Choi Dong Wook) are selected. Rain started out as a dancer and singer under JYP (a major Korean music corporation) and also starred in the television drama series *Full House*. His music and dance project an image of a masculine, athletic person. But in the drama he is also shown as a gentle person who must hide his real feelings. By contrast, Se7en was designed by YG (another major Korean music label) as an effeminate prince, charming in his singing and dancing persona. He looks cheerful, warm and friendly. In the drama *Goong S* Se7en plays a comical and reluctant prince. Despite the fact that the mainstream culture industries in Thailand and Korea produce similar good looking, good humored, sturdy, cute, skillful dancers and actors to be their idols, there are well-drawn cultural divisions in these products. In the Thai society *Luktoong* music has been inscribed as popular working-class culture. In contrast, K-pop, as well as J-pop, are exotic and modern trends distinctively representing the life-styles of the young middle class.

Cultural consumption has its regular rituals of viewing, listening, going to live concerts, meeting and greeting the stars, joining in fan club activities, exchanging CDs, and so on. One of the fan club meetings, in June 2005, at a restaurant near Center Point, was attended by about forty members. In the introduction session the images of the idol pop star are (re)produced, as they show Se7en's hit MV, *Passion,* and their own video clips from the concert they attended together. The fans' imitation of Se7en—they sing and dance and dress in the style of Se7en—encourages them to internalize the identity of their imaginary pop star. In their newly formed cultural network *"individual imagination"* is turned into a *"collective imaginary"* of teenage girls (and a small number of boys). There are two important phenomena that should be noted. Firstly, while at play these youth are articulating cultural practices that show distinctions that differentiate them from other social classes. Secondly, they are contesting the rules that regulate their leisure time. These youth insisted on going out and joining the club ritual. The meeting was organized for a Sunday so that a large number of fans could participate. They also negotiated with their parents to take Korean language lessons or dancing lessons. For the middle-class youth a good part of their money, or their parents,' is spent on acquiring new cultural capital.

Network of Consumption and Production

For J-pop and K-pop fans the web site is the center of the organizing process where daily networking takes place. It is through this virtual space that their imageries of the J-pop and K-pop stars are consumed, produced and reproduced. Each web site forms a network of several hundred or thousand members actively organizing themselves and being organized by half dozen core organizers. Here, a kind of collective production is formulated. There is voluntary division of work according to each person's capability and dedication. The web mistress spends several hours a day updating the website and replying to the queries of members. There are translators who translate Japanese and Korean music lyrics and drama soundtracks into Thai subtitles. For the J-pop web sites a large number are knowledgeable in Japanese because the language is taught in the foreign language curriculum of most universities. But K-pop fans must learn Korean in special short courses, since the language is not part of the existing education structure. The six to eight week language course is about 2,000 baht. Sometimes, the group seeks help from Korean residents in Thailand. However, the translation process is not straightforward because the Korean volunteers do not know Thai and the Thais do not know Korean. They use English as their *lingua franca*. Korean lyrics must be translated into English first and then into Thai. The process involves, firstly, the transliteration of the sound and, secondly, the translation of the meaning of the lyrics. Finally, there is a Thai and an English transliteration and translation of each song from the hit album of Rain and Se7en up on the web sites. As a rule the cover songs are in great demand and they must be up as quickly as possible. The interviewees agree that this is a labor of love shared by all club members.

For television drama the work process is quite similar, except for the acquisition of a particular drama and the broad inter-Asia network of fan involved. The drama fans usually look out for the J-pop or K-pop series that are not broadcasted on local television stations. They identify the ones they like and search on the Internet for the web sites such as www.megaupload.com.4shared.com, http://www.d-addicts.com/forum/, http://clubbox.co.kr/thaibox. They use the BitTorrent and Clubbox programs to share, upload and download the pirated video files. The Thai translation is collectively worked out on http://poko.exteen.com/ or www.thaisubtitle.com. Normally, they download the Japanese and Korean drama files that already have English subtitles. The English versions are produced mostly by Korean, Hong Kong or Taiwanese, or sometimes Singaporean fans (Saengsri, interview, 3 September 2007; Vadhanapanich, interview, 6 September 2007). The virtual networks of J-pop and K-pop fans become the digitalized distribution nodes and simultaneously the points of consumption of the digital cultural product. The fans can consume products that are not available on the market at a speed synchronous with the original broadcasts, or with a little time lapse. The transnational on-line collective effort has been the prominent characteristic of the speedy consumption process. As Hu (2005) argued in her study of the on-line Chinese fans of Japanese television drama, the fans attempt to break down the time-space constraints and the hierarchy of industrial distribution. They are the guerrilla fighters in the politics of autonomy. Hu believed that the fans are working against the cultural industry by using low-cost digital technology and the on-line network. But there is a tension within this consumption and the production cycle. The fans may try to succeed in beating the system, yet they must internalize the various stages of the digital production of culture. Since their ultimate desire is the pleasure of consuming the selected drama they must labor to reach their goal. The young consumers eventually turn pleasure into work and find work in their pleasure. Along the way they have acquired the technical skills and the knowledge of the information processing line. As much as it is virtual guerrilla warfare, then, this is also incorporation into the modern mode of informational development of the Japanese and Korean information society. Would this be the cultural logic of late capitalism that Jameson (1991), the post-modernist theorist, ardently argued?

The Contradiction of Identity Transformation

Within the process of consumption guided by what Bourdieu (1977) called *habitus,* a set of ingrained experiences that limit the performance of an individual or a group, working class and middle class consumers have internalized their class distinctions. In Bourdieu's view education and culture are central to the formation and reproduction of social class. They work as if they are computer programs that provide the capability for agency to act, yet limit the parameter of the actual practices. I would argue that the social and cultural fields are not totally restrictive. They are dialectically positioned in the economic field and discursive practice in the social relations of class. The complexity of *habitus* and how it works is what our illustrations on popular culture consumption of the working class and middle class attempt to explain. The studies show that it neither closes the avenue for future changes nor does it stand wide open and readily welcome any kind of changes. In most cases active agents must struggle constantly to transform the material existence and the imaginative world around them. As a result, their class and gender identity is re-programmed and transformed through cultural consumption and production.

If the middle class and working class can, at some point, surmount the difficulty in their constricted *habitus* then what is the real problem of cultural consumption and identity production of today's youth? There are two theoretical assumptions that could be drawn from our studies, consciousness of class and of generation. We have observed how young women textile workers formed their class identity within the class structure of the Thai society. They were in search of an alternative social order in their discursive practice through their house union and the general union. The women workers are encouraged by their union to chart new political acts, seeking a new vision and a new world that is more equal, and less oppressive. A class consciousness emerges, although the power of the union is constantly weakened by the state and capitalist control (Piriyarangsan 1996). Thus, youth as a generation plays second to class in the workers' identity formation and transformation.[7]

The study of middle-class youth points in a different direction. Age acts as a mediation of class location. What we see is the formulation of youth identity, or generational identity, located within the middle class. They produce their sub-culture and distinctive styles based on the mainstream Asian pop in order to defy their parents or schools. Although they may be radical or subversive in their cultural practices they are soon contained by hierarchical rules at home and within the existing class norms. With the J-pop consumers, we could see the act of resistance in their counter-culture, but soon they had to comply with the hegemonic control forced upon them. With the K-pop consumers, their act of defiance is subsumed under the "conventional" media consumption (of dominant images sealed in the exotic product). The complexity of their cultural practice is in their alteration between consumer and producer roles, played out on the on-line network. Their frustration and subordination are articulated symbolically with class-based resonance that might be read as a coded expression of class consciousness transposed into the specific context of middle-class youth. But this may need further detailed investigation to explain how class and youth consciousness are related. At the heart of this identity (trans)formation process is a new tempo of economic change, globalization, that moves synchronously with the cycle of the rising East Asian cultural economy. In this milieu, a new temporal-spatial regulation emerges as Asianization deepens.

(POST)MODERNITY AND ASIAN POP IN CULTURAL CONSUMPTION AND PRODUCTION

There are significant points for future debate as the gap between the working class and the middle class widens in the spheres of economic and social change. The economic industrialization imposed by the Thai state for several decades has produced a shattered dream for the urban poor and displaced workers. With globalization and the shifting mode of development towards an informational economy based on new education and production skill in digital technology the working class is pushed further downward. The middle class, nonetheless, are able to adjust to the rapid pace of change, though not without tensions, and stay with the tide of modernization (Pongpaichit 1993).

The final discussion here is a critique of the consequence of modernity in the life-world of the young working class and the middle class. Could popular culture, communication and progressive/radical discursive practice forge an *"imaginary class alliance"*? Is Asianization a force to reckon with? Or is it a process by which new class consciousness of an Asian generation is in the making, thus pulling them further away from their local alliance? I will focus on some critical discrepancies in the analysis of the foregoing questions.

Modernity and its Political Economic Exclusivity

During the intensive period of economic modernization in Thailand from the 1960s onward income distribution has worsened and there have been no significant changes in the social and political power of rural and disadvantaged people. Between Thailand, Taiwan and Korea the bottom 20 percent of the Thai population received the least share of wealth and is getting poorer as the economy grows larger (Charoenlert 1991). Preecha Piampongsanti (1993) points out that the new middle classes have their own economic, socio-political and cultural identities. They are the intermediaries between the capitalist and the working class, who would politically ally with the capitalist class. Hewison (1996: 154) is also inclined to argue that "the middle class was virtually in a natural alliance with the capitalist class," although elements of the middle class might be proposing reforms after the 1997 economic crisis.

On the cultural aspect Nidhi Aewsriwong (1993) criticizes the middle class for sharing the same belief as the Thai ruling class. That is the notion of benevolent dictatorship. An ideal state is one in which a meritorious monarch rules and the polity are governed under moral righteousness rather than democratic political institutions based on popular votes. He asserts that the Thai middle classes are more concerned with their own class interests, not democracy or egalitarianism. The middle classes would not side with the majority of the peasantry and the working classes because they are alienated from the peasants and their culture. The peasantry is the real "other" for the Thai middle classes. In their professional role they would be the new priests of the ideological producer for the capitalist economy.

The analysis of popular culture consumption shows that the young middle-class consumers are actively networking in Thailand and in East Asia to form circles of fans crisscrossing national and cultural borders. This means that they are reformulating their class position in the new political economic condition of East Asia by looking outward. Secondly, they are not only consumers of trans-border cultural goods but are transformed into producers in this capitalist process of culture production/consumption. This is possible because their accumulated cultural capital is unaffordable by the working class. Whereas the middle-class pop fans could restructure their habitus within the hegemonic tensions of patriarchy, school and official political and cultural forces and transcend these borders to connect with Asian J-pop and K-pop fans in Thailand and abroad, the working-class consumers are confined by their economic condition. On the other hand, the middle-class youth are embedded in their urban "modern" setting, which differs fundamentally from the rural tempo, and are turned into new working-class agents. Both the middle-class and working-class consumers have formed their "modern" identities in their divisive social class milieus. But they are starkly different in their cultural taste and discursive practice. Modernity, as this analysis shows, deepens the existing class divide in the fragmented socio-cultural formations.

Asian Pop and Asianization of Cultural Consumption

Asian pop is a new category that combines the cultural products originally made in Northeast Asia, that is, Japan, Korea, Taiwan, Hong Kong, China, and to a lesser extent Southeast Asia, including Thailand, Malaysia, the Philippines, Singapore and Indonesia, into an all embracing classification. This phenomenon occurred at a time when the "trans-Asian cultural traffic" was making dramatic headway in Asia and was seemingly challenging the Western cultural flow coming into the region (Iwabuchi et al. 2004). In Chua's conceptualization it is a conjuncture whereby East Asian popular culture rises to compete with Western culture and Asianizes the cultural economy of Asia (Chua 2004). The shifting of economic development, from an industrial-based to an information-based economy, in Northeast Asia (excluding China) exemplifies the restructuring of capitalist production from an industrial mode of development to an informational mode (Castells 1996).[8] The question is whether this is a shift to sustain the economic growth of Northeast Asia by total commodification of culture and, in turn, to extend the market into Southeast Asia (Nakamura 2003; Lee 2007).

The assumption I want to put forth is that Asian pop and the Asianization process[9] are organizing young middle-class consumers of East Asia in some new ways. These developments are creating a kind of Asian taste in popular culture. But is this an extension of the capital logic of consumption or are there new values emerging? Chua was hypothesizing a pan–East Asian identity emerging from the dense flow of East Asian cultural products (2004). His vision rests on the assumption that Asian cultural production and consumption are located among nations populated with Confucianism and ethnic Chinese. However, my main concern is not so much with the "ideological effect" on the young audiences, as Chua was conceptualizing, although it might be quite true that a large majority of the middle classes, and capitalist class, in East Asia are ethnic Chinese. Nissim (2007), on the other hand, concludes in his analysis that the consumers in Southeast Asia are not being dispossessed of their sense of national identity and that consuming other cultures does not seem to conflict with their being loyal to their nation. Therefore, it would seem that this is not primarily a question of ethnicity or national identity. As the case in East Asia shows, consumer reception points strongly to apolitical consumers. They refuse to see any politics in their affection for popular culture. Their version of cultural politics is to fulfill their imaginary freedom in popular culture consumption. In addition, their semiotic subversiveness has brought them closer to the "global other," who are presumably middle-class youth, than to the "working-class other" from within. They are becoming cosmopolitan in their imaginary transformative act. But in reality it might be a different story.

Let me elaborate on the argument about how youth are turned into cultural producers. As Laing (1990) discusses in his "Making Popular Music: The Consumer as Producer," there are instances of the leap from consumer to producer being motivated by a desire to emulate admired sounds, such as in the rhythm and blues movement among young white British during the early 1960s. It can also be a revolt motivated by dissatisfaction with the music on offer. Consumers may turn to iconoclastic, avant-garde or radical production. The situation described by Laing is similar to the creation of the *Pua Chiwit* music genre by the student movement in the 1970s. Their admiration for American folk music and the peace movement turned them into music producers and social activists. They were also motivated by their resistance to the social upheavals of modernization, authoritarian rule, and the effect of the Cold War in Vietnam. Their localized counter-culture style was taken from the American counter-culture of the 1960s. Would the J-pop and K-pop fan express themselves beyond their cos(tume) play and cover music dancing? Would they produce their own version of (post)modern cultural products in the future? If so, what kind of cultural identity would they articulate? Would it be East Asianism? We certainly need more research into this area if we are to understand the coded expressions of class and youth in their pop culture consumption and production.

My last critique is on how Asianization organizes young consumers in East Asia into an "imaginary East Asian generation." Are these networks of popular culture consumers and producers connected because of their generational consciousness or class consciousness? Or are they connected because of their ethnicity, which is Chineseness? Are these products really classless cultural artifacts appealing to youth in general? Since cultural consumption in the age of Asianization has turned into a training milieu for future culture workers we need to explore critically this Asianization process and how it creates a new Asian generation of middle-class youth across the major metropolis of East Asia. If there is such a group, we need to research the worldview of this emerging "Asian pop generation." Do they share a pan–East Asian identity or a trans-Asian identity? Is this identity constituted in shared East Asian tradition, such as Confucianism and ethnicity, or is it a question of class and gender? In the longer term, would they form a new class consciousness within their generation?

* I would like to thank Shin Hyunjoon, Eva Tsai and Yang Fang-chih for their insightful comments on this chapter.

NOTES

1. Working-class income has always been under the poverty line (Tinakorn 2002). The minimum wage was 73 baht/day in 1986 in the Bangkok area (US $2.90). In 1999, the range of the working-class income is 1,560–6,500 baht/month (National Statistics Office 1999). In 2007, the daily minimum wage in Bangkok is 193 baht (US $5.80).
2. Thai popular music genres are divided into *Luktoong, Lukroong, String* and *Pua Chiwit.* The genre *Pua Chiwit,* which originated in the 1970s, is expressly political and critical of the social condition.
3. Women workers do not feel that they belong to the working class. But they admit that their everyday life is very different from that of their parents. It would be hard to go back to work in the field or to leave the urban lifestyle. Their subjectivity is mixed and divided between being a rural peasant and an urban worker.
4. J-pop and K-pop are used here to mean Japanese and Korean popular music and television drama. K-pop cultural products consumed in Thailand are mostly those made for export. They are also called Asian pop.
5. Natnicha Vadhanapanich interviewed nine J-pop fans, between the ages of twenty-three and twenty-eight, and Wasinee Sangsri interviewed and observed ten K-pop fans, between the ages of sixteen and twenty-two, in their home environments. All of them are girls.
6. There are 8.5 million Internet users or 12:100. Among these, 52 percent are ages fifteen to twenty-four (National Statistics Office 2005).
7. There are four levels of class consciousness defined by Michael Mann: *identity*—definition of oneself as sharing a particular class location; the perception of class structure as the *opposition* between capital and labour; *totality*—the acceptance of identity and class opposition in one's own social situation and the society; and the vision of an *alternative* social order (Murdock and McCron 1976).
8. Castells defines an informational society as one in which information generation, processing and transmission become the fundamental sources of productivity and power, because of new technological conditions emerging in this historical period. One of the key features of an informational society is the networking logic of its basic structure and spirit of informationalism, the ethical foundation of the network culture and capitalist competition.
9. The Asianization of popular culture and the Asian cultural economy is seen as national and regional processes combined, and these are trans-metropolitan, creating the cultural flow in a new mode of time-space compression (Siriyuvasak and Shin 2007).

REFERENCES

Adorno, T. and Horkheimer, M. (1973) *Dialectics of Enlightenment,* London: Allen Lane.

Aewsriwong, N. (1993) "The Cultural Dimension of the Thai Middle Class," in S. Piriyarangsan and P. Pongpaichit (eds) *The Middle Class and Thai Democracy* (in Thai), Bangkok: Political Economy Centre.

Baudrillard, J. (1994) *Simulacra and Simulation,* Michigan: University of Michigan Press.

Bourdieu, P. (1977) *Outline of a Theory of Practice,* Cambridge: Cambridge University Press.

———. (1984) *Distinction: A Social Critique of the Judgment of Taste,* London: Routledge.

Castells, M. (1996) *The Information Age: Economy, Society and Culture,* Oxford: Blackwell.

Charoenlert, V. (1991) "The Thai Economy in the Global Economy," in P. Pongpaichit and S. Piriyarangsan (eds) *Thai Dynamics: A Political Economy View* (in Thai), Bangkok: Political Economy Centre.

Chua, B. H. (2004) "Conceptualizing an East Asian Popular Culture," *Inter-Asia Cultural Studies,* 5(2): 200–21.

Frith, S. (1997) "Music and Identity," in S. Hall and P. du Gay (eds) *Questions of Cultural Identity,* London: Sage.

Hall, S. and Jefferson, T. (1976) *Resistance Through Rituals: Youth Subcultures in Post War Britain,* London: Hutchinson.

Hebdige, D. (1979) *Subculture: The Meaning of Style.* London: Methuen.

Hewison, K. (1996) "Emerging Social Forces in Thailand: New Political and Economic Roles," in R. Robison and D. Goodman (eds) *The New Rich in Asia: Mobile Phones, McDonald's and Middle-Class Revolution,* 137–160. London: Routledge.

Hu, K. (2005) "The Power of Circulation: Digital Technologies and the Online Chinese Fans of Japanese TV Drama," *Inter-Asia Cultural Studies,* 6(2): 109–36.

Iwabuchi, K., Muecke, S. and Thomas, M. (2004) *Rogue Flows: Trans-Asian Cultural Traffic,* Hong Kong: Hong Kong University Press.

Jameson, F. (1991) Postmodernism, or, the Cultural Logic of Late Capitalism, Durham: Duke University Press.

Kiatwatiratana, T. (2000) "Japanese style—Cultural domination on youth," *Chud Prakaai Krungthep Thurakit,* 13:4135, 18 January 2000.

Laing, D. (1990) "Making Popular Music: The Consumer as Producer," in A. Tomlinson (ed) *Consumption, Identity and Style: Marketing, Meanings, and the Packaging of Pleasure,* London: Routledge.

Lee, J. (2004) "Cultural Contact with Japanese TV Drama: Modes of Reception and Narrative Transparency" in K. Iwabuchi (ed.) *Feeling Asian Modernities: Consuming and Producing (Post)modernity Transnational Consumption of Japanese TV Dramas.* Hong Kong: Hong Kong University Press.

———. (2007) "When Development Meets Culture: Cultural Policy in South Korea Since 1990s," paper presented at Inter-Asian Cultural Studies Society (IACSS) Shanghai Conference.

Lyotard, J. (1984) *The Postmodern Condition: A Report on Knowledge,* Manchester: Manchester University Press.

Mudkong, N. (2001) Interview, 21 June 2001.

Murdock, G. and McCron, R. (1976) "Consciousness of Class and Consciousness of Generation," in S. Hall and T. Jefferson (eds) *Resistance Through Rituals: Youth Subcultures in Post-War Britain,* London: Harper Collins.

Nakamura, I. (2003) "Japanese Pop Industry," Standford Project on Regions of Innovation and Entrepreneurship (SPRIE) project, Stanford Japan Research Center.

National Statistics Office. (1999) *Monthly Wage/Salary Level* (4/1999), Bangkok.

———. (2005) *Internet Users in Thailand,* Bangkok.

Nissim, O. (2007) "Contesting Soft Power: Japanese Popular Culture in East and Southeast Asia," *International Relations of the Asia Pacific.*

Piampongsanti, P. (1993) "The Middle Class: Concepts and Theories," in S. Piriyarangsan and P. Pongpaichit (eds) *The Middle Class and Thai Democracy* (in Thai), Bangkok: Political Economy Centre.

Piriyarangsan, S. (1996) "Reforming Labor Relations in the Era of Globalization," in Thailand Research Fund (ed) *Restructuring Thailand: Forwarding Imagination to 2000* (in Thai), Bangkok.

Pongpaichit, P. (1993) "The Middle Class of Asia NICs and Thailand," in S. Piriyarangsan and P. Pongpaichit (eds) *The Middle Class and Thai Democracy* (in
Thai), Bangkok: Political Economy Centre.

Rakprayoon, T. (2002) *The Popularization of Japanese Youth Culture in the Media
in Thailand* (in Thai), MA thesis, Chulalongkorn University.

Silverstone, R. (1994) *Television and Everyday Life*, London: Routledge.

Siriyuvasak, U. (1989) *The Dynamics of Audience Media Activities: An Ethnography of Women Textile Workers*, Bangkok: Social Science Research Institute.

————. (2004) "Popular Culture and Youth Consumption: Modernity, Identity
and Social Transformation," in K. Iwabuchi (ed) *Feeling Asian Modernities:
Transnational Consumption of Japanese TV Dramas*, Hong Kong: Hong Kong
University Press.

Siriyuvasak, U. and Shin, H. (2007) "Asianizing K-pop: Production, Consumption
and Identification Patterns among Thai Youth," *Inter-Asia Cultural Studies*,
8(1): 109–36.

Tinakorn, P. (2002) "The Income Distribution Gap in Four Decades of Development, 1961–2001" (in Thai), paper presented at the 25th Annual Conference
2002, Faculty of Economics, Thammasat University, 12 June 2002.

Tomlinson, J. (1999) *Globalization and Culture*, Chicago: University of Chicago
Press.

Turner, B. (1990) *Theories of Modernity and Postmodernity*, London: Sage.

12 Consuming *Sex and the City*
Young Taiwanese Women Contesting Sexuality

Yachien Huang

In 2004, fans worldwide were saddened when the demise of the HBO-produced television series *Sex and the City* (hereafter *SATC*) made entertainment news headlines. Taking place in New York, *SATC* portrays the loves and lives of four white female professionals: Carrie Bradshaw (journalist/writer), Samantha Jones (PR executive and sexual libertine), Miranda Hobbs (corporate lawyer and relationship cynic), and Charlotte York (art gallery manager and romantic optimist). All are in their mid-thirties and earning considerable salaries that allow them to buy brand name clothing and lead an exuberant social life. Whenever they come together, they recount their romantic encounters and debate a wide range of personal topics from marriage, pregnancy, and commitment, to their partners' preferences in bed. Resembling an anthropological quest to discover the meaning of human relationships spiced up with unabashed fashion consumption and candid representations of contemporary female sexuality and friendship, *SATC* has often been held up as one of the two major successes—the other being *Friends*—that typify global popular television in the 1990s.

Since the inception of the series in 1998, *SATC* characters, in the Anglo-American West, have often been discussed with other media heroines, like Ally McBeal and Bridget Jones, as the post-feminist turn in blurring the boundary between the discourses of femininity and feminism (Akass and McCabe 2004; McRobbie 2004; Kim 2001; Moseley and Read 2001). With its focus on sexually independent childless career women and their unabashed quest for a fulfilling relationship, *SATC* has again raised issues of media's role in shaping the political agenda of feminism and of contesting perspective on the modern single woman and womanhood. In East Asia, however, the program has generated rather different responses, most of which pointed to a wider debate on the ramification of these alternative representations of foreign social lifestyle and values brought in by western television. The situation in Taiwan was no exception. Much of the discussion has been focused on how the program offers an interesting site for examining relations between local audiences and the global media in the context of emerging aspects of young women's lives in a rapidly modernizing Confucian society.

SATC was initially broadcast by HBO Taiwan, established in 1994, late on Saturday evenings in April 1999. The high household penetration of cable television (about 80 percent) offered an effective and convenient environment for distributing its programming. Each of the six seasons was repeated three times, together with an intensive review at the end of each season. The commercial success of the series prompted the other two cable channels, Super TV and Jet TV, to follow suit and broadcast *SATC* at various times between 2001 and 2005. The slow-moving local drama production, in grasping the changing social situation of women (Tsai 1999), gives the place to foreign drama, mostly from Japan and America, of providing arenas for testing values and gender representation. The series soon attracted many young Taiwanese women aged between twenty-four and thirty-five, spawning a chain of localized format adaptations aimed at the same age group (Huang 2008).

One way to interpret Taiwanese young women's enthusiasm for *SATC* is as closely related to a generational-specific experience marked by increasing contact with global capitalism and greater freedom for women. In this view, Taiwanese young women are often thought of as the generation that represents the process of "individualization" in late or reflexive modernity, outlined in the works of Giddens (1991) and Beck (1994, 2000). The theory holds that young people, and young women in particular, now live in a world where established identity markers (race, gender, family upbringing, class) are declining in importance and where they are now required to "make their own histories" and identities by learning to be independent and self-reliant.

However, much research on Taiwanese young women has also indicated that entrenched traditional values and strong family ties have proved more resilient than theories of de-traditionalization might suggest. Their "open process" of self-construction is often played out in part via the exercise of consumer choice in the global market, and in part shaped by the larger complex of social forces that constrain as well as enable agency. As Ang rightly pointed out:

> This does not mean that they are stripped of agency . . . but that that agency itself, or the "negotiations" subjects undertake in constructing their lives, is *overdetermined* (i.e., neither predetermined nor undetermined) by the concrete conditions of existence they find themselves in. (1997:183)

This revised concept of determinacy implies the setting of limits and the establishment of parameters, defining a space of operations as a process through which agency and meaning in consumption are continually reworked, confronted and negotiated (Ang 1997). This perspective also provides the starting point for this article's investigation of Taiwanese young women's *SATC* experience. It is argued that their consumption of this global text is related to their struggle for agency in a context where negotiation between the embedded and the emerging, the local and the global, intensified and where a variety of forms of power are exercised with different impacts and effects.

GENDER IDENTITY IN TRANSITION

One of the key contexts within which these young women's responses to *SATC* is embedded is the shifting gender relationship in contemporary Taiwanese society. Traditional gender identities in Taiwan have been securely rooted in Confucian teaching (Liu and Regehr 2006; Chien 1994). Confucius advocated three rules for women's lives: before marriage, a woman should be under the authority of her father; after marriage, she should obey her husband; and should the husband pass away, she must be subject to her eldest son (Tu 1998). Within this system a woman is always defined in relation to a male figure to whom she is subordinated. This ideology was reinforced by the traditional Taiwanese (Chinese) descent system, which only allowed the son to perpetuate family lines and to inherit family properties. The daughter was expected to marry out and devote her life to the husband's family. As a consequence, although women were declared equal to men in the constitution two generations ago, most ordinary Taiwanese families were reluctant to invest financially in the daughters' upbringing and sacrificed their development for the well-being of male members in the family. This gender-imbalanced development has gradually changed since 1958 when the government made junior high school education compulsory for all adolescents. The enforcement of this educational policy was closely linked to Taiwan's economic growth starting from the 1960s, when the country virtually became a labor-intensive manufactory for the West. Although it did not offer fulfilling careers, the manufacturing sector did provide opportunities for Taiwanese women, for the first time, to work outside the family and earn paid wages. In the following decades, women were encouraged or required to further their education to accommodate industrial upgrading. These changes laid the basis for a shift in women's self identity. By the late 1970s, economic prosperity had contributed to the growth of a new urban middle class and the emergence of both new forms of femininity and the beginnings of feminist movements. Middle-class women were increasingly attracted to a "variation on the feminine mystique" (Diamond 1975), while the first local women's organization, Awakening, emerged in 1982.

Consequently, Taiwanese women born after the late 1970s are the first generation to grow up enjoying both the material benefits of economic growth and the move towards greater gender equality. Trends in the taking up of higher education offer an index of both shifts. Not only has the number of women entering higher education increased with each successive age cohort, the gap between male and female attendance has also closed. The numbers of women entering higher education in the two most recent cohorts (408,000 in age group 20–24, and 272,000 in age group 25–29) has further outstripped males (356, 000 in age group 20–24, and 270,000 in age group 25–29) (Budget Accounting and Statistics Executive Yuan 2003). Improved education has contributed to better employment for women. The percentage of women in employment rose 19.8 percent from 1994 to 2004, with the sharpest increase from 19.7 percent to 35.0 percent among women with university qualification (Budget Accounting and Statistics Executive Yuan 2005).

Compared to previous generations, whose lack of educational and financial resources seriously limited their freedom in other areas, young women's improved material opportunities has provided a stepping stone towards greater independence. One symbolic event in this shift was the launching of the first women-oriented credit card, Tai-hsin Bank Rose card, in 1995. The television advertisements for Tai-hsin Bank Rose card linked control over one's finances with increased choice over lifestyle, intentionally portraying young women in various roles such as arty photographer, secretary and contented mother and suggesting how Taiwanese woman today can happily choose their profession, develop their potential, and enjoy their lives with new financial underpinnings. In public discourse the term "pink-collar" (fenling) or "pink-collar new aristocracy" (fenling xingui) emerged to describe a new "class" consisting of young women who have benefited from socio-economic change and who now possessed a cosmopolitan outlook and a fashionable profession (Huang 2008).

However, while women have become increasingly competitive participants in employment, higher education, and consumerism, changes to basic notions of gender roles and femininity, especially in relation to sexuality and the body, have come much slower. The local women's movement deliberately marginalized issues of sex and sexuality in the early stage of their development to avoid opposition to campaigns for changes in other areas of women's lives (Farris 2004; Ku 1998). The discrepancy in women's development caused by sidelining female sex and sexuality only started to change following the lift of Martial Law in 1987. In the early 1990s, a gender politics with the focus on women's sex and sexuality began to gather strength and challenge the historical silence on female sexuality. Events such as the first anti-sexual harassment public parade under the slogan "I want orgasm, not harassment" and the publication of the translation of Hite Report, an American project that used women's personal testimonies to discuss female sex experiences, were regarded as important steps in Taiwan's women's movement.

In the cheering mood for these "victories" however, it should also be noted that these events have generated polarized opinions and often became the focus for controversy. Although it is tempting to define these emerging changes as a sign of young women's liberated sexuality and to argue that this new sensibility is now commonplace among teenage girls in Taiwan (Ho 2003), the perception that old prejudices have now been blatantly overtaken ignores the extent to which female sexuality remains an area of both negotiation and struggle. Tensions are arguably more keenly felt among the middle class and the highly educated, as they, on the one hand, have easier access to material and cultural resources to contest existing structures while, on the other hand, are expected to pass on values and notions of decorum that are rooted in traditional conceptions.

The event of "National Taiwan University Female Students Watching Adult Film," which took place in 1995, was an anecdote to epitomize tensions of such kind. The event was prompted by the decision of a group of female university students in the Women Studies student club to organize a film night on campus showing an adult film. The aim was to provide an intimate space for women to freely discuss their sexuality. However, this event soon became a major news story of the year. The perception of female students as future intellectuals and professionals who should set a positive example for the society, prompted widespread criticism that the event was immoral and would send out the wrong message to the public (Luo 1997). In response, the film night was redefined by its organizers as an academic exercise and advertised itself as an event that critically examined gender representation in adult films.

YOUNG UNIVERSITY-EDUCATED
FEMALES WATCHING *SATC*

It was against these general shifts and tensions that *SATC* appeared in Taiwan and offered a fertile case study of young women's negotiations of gender identity in a contemporary Confucian society. Moreover, the program's reception among university-educated young women—who are more likely to be subjected to the forces of social and familiar expectations, as pointed out in the last section—is particularly revealing of the ways meanings and personal pleasures brought in by global cultural texts and their clashes with traditional (Confucian) gender codes are negotiated. Therefore, the analysis that follows is based on the experiences of university-educated females gathered from postings on the local university-based bulletin board system (BBS), PTT, coupled with in-depth interviews. PTT, starting out in 1995, is one of the biggest and most influential BBS sites in northern Taiwan. At the time of this writing (1 November 2005), the total postings on the discussion forum for *SATC* stood at 3,563, with the first posting dating back to 10 July 2001. Both qualitative and quantitative criteria were used to select a group of sub-samples for further analysis. Only postings in a discussion thread that generated more than ten responses were included, and the content had to, in some ways, reflect or comment on issues of either gender or culture, rather than simple descriptions of the plot or the actors (see Appendix 1). In addition, nineteen young women were interviewed in Taipei during June and July 2004. The interviews were semi-structured and recorded for later transcription (except from one respondent who refused to be recorded).

Viewing Strategies

Before intending to account for young women's viewing experience of *SATC* as a process of negotiating over gender identity, it is important to highlight the limitations of present research data, which precludes attempts to construct either an overall account of social change or a comprehensive analysis of the pleasures generated for Taiwanese women by the series. Rather, the intention is to pinpoint issues raised in the present data that potentially lead to fruitful future research into a set of relationships between young women's media consumption, contest for greater independence, and contradictions involved in the prevailing matrix of structures and relationships.

To begin with, I would like to draw attention to the first-hand accounts of viewing strategies, as they not only confirm television consumption as a valued activity in everyday life but also expose the power relationships that surround it. *SATC* has posed a particularly interesting case study as its manufacturing of materials of women's sex and sexuality into a mass-oriented entertainment has clearly defied a traditional Confucian gender politics that operates with a strict dichotomy between private and public space. The rule of thumb in the Confucian ethics holds that displays of sex, while perfectly acceptable in one's private bedroom, are entirely inappropriate in the public domain, including television. Consequently, although *SATC* bypassed government regulation and censorship in the newly deregulated television market, its consumption by young women remained at odds with the residual of patriarchal control exercised within networks of family and friends. This led to a culturally specific viewing experience constructed around conflict and compromise and commonly addressed in the BBS postings and interviews.

Some women were "nagged," "warned off" or socially deterred from watching *SATC*, and others had their viewing experiences "sabotaged" by parents and boyfriends. In seventeen BBS postings relating to viewing experience, only four regarded it as disturbance-free, including one from a male author. Instances of interference included verbal denunciation (criticizing the program) and/or physical deterrence (changing the channel).

> When my father sees me and my mother watching *SATC*, he would complain "again, you are watching this no-class third-rate programme." And my boyfriend says "*SATC* is just grumpy women after having sex, and having sex after being grumpy." I do not have time to explain to them. I just ask them not to talk to me. I need to concentrate. (sby, 11 February 2003)

> Sometimes I want to watch television at the same time as my dad. He would let me watch *SATC* for a while, and whenever the series started to get sensual, he would immediately change the channel. Usually there is not much left in an episode. It is really annoying!! (jullypit, 26 August 2004)

These male efforts to devalue and trivialize women's viewing experience point to the persistence of embedded gender codes and asymmetrical power relationships within the household. In both the above instances, fathers emerge as dominant domestic figures, exercising judgement and scrutiny over (young) women's private leisure choices. One way to interpret these paternal sanctions is to see them as reactions to feelings that their traditional right to "manage" and "safeguard" women's sexuality and bodies is being challenged or threatened (Chou 1995). Young women's viewing of *SATC* in a domestic setting therefore surfaced as a locus of tension resulting from frictions between an established patriarchal tradition and new, western-styled conceptions of an emancipatory gender politics. Similar accounts of tension also emerged in the interviews. One interviewee, for instance, described how she began watching *SATC*:

> I started watching when I was in high school. I felt lonely because I was the only one in class who watched it. When I discussed it with my friends, they said I shouldn't watch the program as such, for the girls need to have a pure mind. I also had to watch it in secret at home. If my mum found out, I would have been nagged. At the time I envied the characters in *SATC,* because they can choose the way they like to live. (Interview with R7)

This respondent, R7, had been to New York as a one-year exchange student and has since run a web site selling tampons. Confident and liberal as she might appear from the outside, she nonetheless felt the need to conceal her viewing from her family to avoid unwanted embarrassment and tension. For the same reason, other interviewees devised strategies to avoid possible confrontation. Some resorted to watching the program on DVD or as an internet download; some voluntarily changed channels back and forth depending on what was being shown or who was around; some watched it on another television in a separate room, and others only watched when they were alone in the house. This tendency towards "discrete viewing" appeared to be more common for young women who lived at home, and pointed to the way that the traditional dichotomy in addressing sex behaviour and discourses was sustained by the institution of family. The negotiations engaged in by these young women, although seemingly voluntary, have effectively transformed the practice of watching *SATC* from a public, communal, activity to a privatized individual experience, demonstrating how an individual's media consumption was embedded in and over-determined by dynamics in play within a broader socio-cultural context. One indication of how powerfully these dynamics frame viewing is provided by the subtitle "not suitable for family viewing," carried in the opening scene when *SATC* was broadcast on HBO Taiwan. Replacing a more typical screen announcement like "not suitable for children under 15 or 18," the wording implied that the basis of exclusion evoked here was the social context rather than simply age.

However, women's interrupted viewing practices should not merely be taken as signs of dominated subjects. On the contrary, although their viewing experiences were often shaped by their positioning within a set of power relationships, the fact that they continued watching was, in itself, an act of contestation. Moreover, their accounts of using DVD, internet downloads, personal computers and sometimes a second television in the household indicate that the spread of new communication technologies has extended their repertoire of strategies for evading male surveillance and exercising personal viewing choice in ways that had rarely been available to previous generations.

Constructing Pleasure

These young university females' viewing strategies not only staged an intensified struggle for greater autonomy within often circumscribed and policed personal spheres but also offered an entry point into a further exploration of the ways they constructed interpretation of *SATC*. A pertinent point of the following analysis on their interpretations corresponds with Fiske's postulation that "the activation of the meaning potential of a text can occur only in the social and cultural relationship into which it enters. The social relationship of a text occurs at the moment of reading as they are inserted into the everyday lives of the readers" (1989: 4). Therefore, by situating responses of these young women in relation to the context of their struggle to (re)invent and adapt a sense of self against shifting grounds in a rapidly modernizing Taiwan, it emerged that women's autonomy coupled with western-style individualism inscribed in *SATC* has been the main melody along which meanings and viewing pleasure were composed. I now elaborate on this.

Although appearing through different themes, women's autonomy coupled with western-style individualism has been consistently identified as the central message and the most gripping element of *SATC*. The fact that the parents of the main characters were conveniently omitted in the script and other authoritative figures also largely disappeared from the scene made it possible for the characters to freely exercise personal choice. This tendency was accentuated on various occasions recounted by my interviewees. For instance, some pointed out that when Carrie decided to relocate from New York to Paris following a boyfriend she had only been in a relationship with for less than a year (presumably less than one year as he only appeared in one season), she did not discuss her plan with anyone apart from the other three women at their usual brunch gathering. Despite the fact that the other three women were apprehensive about her decision, Carrie stood tenaciously behind her plan and eventually moved to Paris. In a similar fashion, when Charlotte suddenly decided to convert to Judaism for her second husband, Harry, who was a Jew, all she did was "just do it." On these occasions, major life decisions, such as moving and settling abroad and commitment to a different religion, were made primarily based on individual lifestyle preference with the slightest hint of consultation with parents or other senior figures. Although drastically different from the daily experience of the young women, these scenes effectively played a central role in structuring some responses to the series. As one interviewee put it:

> [SATC] is about how women should love themselves. Choose what you want, and don't make yourself miserable. Don't make yourself miserable for men, family members, or your friends. Do what you want to do ... after watching SATC, I have learnt that the characters choose what they want and live well, even if they made wrong choices sometimes ... I think this series has accompanied me to mature. I didn't think about my life seriously before. I just tried hard to pass exams after exams and to get good grades. Only when I started watching in my third year in senior high school did I start to think about making choices for my own life. (Interview with R7)

Interpretation of this kind points to young women's desires to take control of their own lives within a social and psychological space where traditional gender roles, familial responsibilities, academic achievements, western feminism and global consumerism are continually jostling for attention and supremacy. Similar dynamics were replayed in other responses, such as the interpretation of women's single status from an angle of independence and freedom:

> SATC is about four single women with different personalities, all in thirties, earn well, and all unmarried. The story is about their relentless search for true love after reaching their thirties ... but because of living in a different culture, they are luckier than us. Their family does not push them to get married although they are single in their mid-thirties. Imagine the treatment we will receive in Chinese New Year if we were in the same shoes! (Interview with R9)

For the young women who identified the constant search for true love as the central narrative, their accounts were often coupled with fears of spinsterhood, stemming primarily from worries about external reproach and less from their own preferences or needs. As they repeatedly returned to the tension between the social pressures towards marriage in Taiwanese society and the satisfactions of the single-by-choice lifestyle portrayed in SATC, they tended to construct interpretations celebrating female single women and one's freedom to stay in control of the pursuit of Mr. Right on one's own terms, rather than seeing *SATC* as a series about "the modern female angst syndrome," centering on the ticking of the biological clock and the fear of aging out of the marriage market, as described by some western feminist critics (Orenstein 2003). It arguably took the pressures from the society and family at the background to romanticize the searching process in *SATC* as a quest for a woman's *right* to lead a contented and carefree single life without suffering a backlash of censure. At times, some interviewees, like R2, while not rejecting marriage, had become increasingly sceptical of its conventional construction and rationale.

> *SATC* is about are women destined to look for "true love." I started to think is there such thing as "true love." Also I questioned if remaining single is a sin? What if we don't find true love before the age of thirty? I am already 25 and I have been thinking what does age means to me? (Interview with R12)

These shifts in perception, however small they might be, provide important clues to the processes in which challenges to existing values and thinking were generated through the interactions between social contexts and media texts, geographical places and imaginative spaces.

Following this thread of reception, it was probably not surprising to learn that almost unanimously among interviewees marriage-obsessed Charlotte was considered the least interesting character. To a large extent, Charlotte's belief and behavior were perceived by interviewees as "familiar"—but ridiculously old-fashioned. By advocating feminine gender roles closest to the good mother and virtuous wife, her character offered little novelty but capitulation to traditional expectations for the young Taiwanese women. In contrast, it was the "choice politics" represented by the other three characters—particularly in the almost caricatured portrayal of Miranda and Samantha—that set the tone for constructing meanings in their reception.

An interesting point emerged that Miranda, who in the series played a professional lawyer, was admired by my interviewees less for her succinct cynical opinions on modern relationships than for her successful career. Compared to the other three women whose work sphere collapsed into the private sphere and became another form of self-expression (Arthurs 2003), Miranda demonstrated professionalism based on ability rather than heterosexual charm. She was therefore read by the young women as having a greater degree of emotional and financial security, which paved her way to freedom and independence. Even in the situation where she accidentally became pregnant because of a one-night-stand with her ex-boyfriend, Steve, the ensuing single parenthood was not only dealt with with little backlash but also with a reduced degree of difficulties—Miranda got by hiring helpers and negotiating terms with the newborn's father.

Consequently, Miranda was seen as a potent source of mediating the positive image of the prototypical career women living in a cosmopolitan modern city. Her role tapped into the aspiration of many university-educated young women, who are the first generation to enjoy equal opportunities in education and employment and have come to regard the pursuit of a fulfilling career and financial resources as a major mission in life. As one interviewee responded:

> I like Miranda the most. I think she is very independent and has a successful career. She is the type I desire to become the most. She is so successful at her job while at the same time bringing up her son single-handedly. She does not depend on men. She only depends on men when she needs a sperm for producing a child. She can do everything else on her own. She is my role model, although I don't think I am so competent like her . . . The message *SATC* threw at me was the importance to be economically independent, so that one can live on without depending on the parents or husband. I have never felt so strongly about that before. (Interview with R4)

Similarly, another interviewee, who initiated a *SATC* discussion forum hosted by Ptt's sister BBS site, Ptt2, informed me that a large percentage of participants in her discussion forum identified themselves with Miranda or modeled themselves on her.

Compared to Miranda, who offered a typical career woman role model, Samantha, a sophisticated woman who pursued everything without strings attached, was enjoyed by many Taiwanese young women as a source for a virtually unattainable autonomy powered by an uncompromising individuality. A BBS discussion thread titled "We all love Samantha" generated a high volume of responses, including some that were unashamedly admiring: "Does anyone like Samantha like me? I think she is very true, so I like her. I envy her because I think she lives her life true to herself" (Icecherry, 30 March 2003). Others, though, were more ambivalent: "I like her too. The most important thing is to be brave in pursuing what one wants regardless of other's opinion. This is really a difficult thing to do, especially in an environment like Taiwan" (Xchair, 3 April 2003). As the second comment suggests, the social and psychological distance between Samantha and themselves became a prism that refracted participants' real life dilemmas in breaking free from embedded social constraints despite their advantaged economic and cultural backgrounds. In this ambivalent admiration towards Samantha's character, however, was a negotiation process in action. The increasing contact with representations of alternative, more individualized, lifestyles, on the one hand, inspired the young women to resist identity constructions around traditional identity markers, while on the other hand, making it more difficult for them to form stable, manageable and satisfying lives (Miles 2000).

Other more specific admiration towards Samantha was inspired by her repudiating the shame of being single and sexually active in defiance of the bourgeois codes that used to be imposed on middle-class women. In a special case where the interviewee declined to be recorded, she recounted *SATC* as an emotional crutch that had helped her to pursue a lifestyle that those in her social circle—drawing on traditional Taiwanese standards—labeled as promiscuous. She only agreed to participate in my interview because she wanted to talk to someone who would not judge her. According to her, on occasions when she could not find such a person in time, she resorted to watching *SATC*. She insisted that watching the program, especially the character of Samantha, gave her a sense of confirmation, and sometimes comfort, in her conviction that women are entitled to own their sexuality and to act upon it. As noted earlier, although local women's movements have started to address female sex and sexuality since the mid-1990s, the reach and the impact of these efforts has been asymmetrical. Her case again pointed to a situation where, for many young university-educated females— typecast as "good girls"—development surrounding the issue of sexuality has often been overlooked, marginalized, or even lambasted, compared to issues of intellectual acquisition and future career ambition.

For the rest of the interviewees, this negligence contributed to an ambivalence about Samantha's sexual freedom and a culturally specific reception that saw consuming *SATC* as a chance to negotiate and explore desire and sexuality imaginatively.

> In Taiwan people tend to suppress their sexuality. But it [*SATC*] can inspire your fantasy . . . I have the feeling of having a conversation with the television . . . I might look like Charlotte from the outside, but I am more like Samantha or Carrie deep down. Yet I dare not express the real me. Maybe it has something to do with the clash between outer morality and my inner self. They [*SATC* characters] did the things I dare not to do. It is cathartic. (Interview with R3)

By dramatizing choices that had not featured widely in mainstream public culture before, *SATC* provided symbolic resources through which young women could redraw their understanding of existing sex-related boundaries and their personal desires. Although not necessarily prompting drastic behavior changes, the time these young women spent alone with *SATC* created a field of possibilities in which they can work through the contradictions between their conventional cultural upbringing and the more liberal and individualistic values inscribed in transnational television.

CONCLUSION

Contemporary Taiwan has seen embedded and emerging forces confronting each other in a battle to define gender relationships and gender identities. As a result, the society is best described as a modified rather than a traditional patriarchy (Xu and Lai 2004). It is upon these shifting grounds that we have to situate the consumption space of the young women in this study and the culturally specific responses that *SATC* generates. The popularity of *SATC* among young women in Taiwan offers an instructive example of the different ways in which a transnational media text can be adopted and allow viewers in different localities to imagine and re-imagine their own social biographies in ways that diverge from western feminist politics and history (Vidmar-Horvat 2005). By subverting social conventions and casting them in a comic light, *SATC* has provided a cultural resource that young Taiwanese women can deploy in their efforts to negotiate the tensions between the obligation to be the "good girl" and the attractions of more individualistic lifestyles and open sexuality.

However, while many of the young women in this study are attracted to the financial independence and politics of personal choice portrayed in the program, they have not chosen to completely abandon the importance of family, community, and social harmony. Instead, what we see is a complicated mix of ambivalence coupled with an intensified self-awareness of their own social positioning and life condition. Seen from this perspective, their engagements with *SATC* are best conceived of as part of a broader repertoire of negotiating strategies through which these young women search for a middle ground on which they can construct a gender identity that continues to draw on the cultural heritage whilst also embracing new thinking and aspiration. For many, their encounter with *SATC* has been an important staging post in their journey towards a sense of self that is

Appendix 1   Data from BBS Postings

Category	Topic thread Thread (themeTheme)	Frequency	Posting Dates
Viewers' Gender	What do men see in *SATC?*	24	18/06/03–22/06/03
	Who is watching?	10	05/03/05–09/03/05
Storyline	Is *SATC* real?	13	19/05/03–10/06/03
	About the ending?	10	25/02/04–27/02/04
	Conflicts between the four characters	19	04/12/04–09/12/04
	Does Party Queen need to die?	19	16/12/04–21/12/04
Characters	Selfishness in Carrie	17	14/11/03–19/11/03
	We all love Samantha	25	30/03/03–14/04/03
Format Adaptations	About Mature Women's Diary	13	24/08/03–28/08/03
	Anyone watching *Desperate Housewives?*	13	08/07/05~–15/09/05

Source: Ptt/Entertainment/TV/TV Series/*Sex in the City*, complied by author.

constantly being (re)shaped by the intensified clash between new and old, global and local, in a rapidly modernizing Taiwan.
* This work has previously been published in *Asian Women*, 23(2), 2007, and appears here with the permission of the publisher, with a slight revision.

REFERENCES

Akass, K. and McCabe, J. (2004) *Reading Sex and the City*, London: IB Tauris.
Ang, I. (1996) *Living Room Wars: Rethinking Media Audiences for A Postmodern World*, London: Routeledge.
——. (1997) "On the Politics of Empirical Audience Research," in M. Durham and D. Kellner (eds) *Media and Cultural Studies: Keyworks*, London: Blackwell.
Arthurs, J. (2003) *"Sex and the City* and Consumer Culture: Remediating Post-feminist Drama," *Feminist Media Studies*, 3(1): 83–97.
Beck, U. (1994) "The Reinvention of Politics: Towards a Theory of Reflexive Modernization," in U. Beck et al. (eds) *Reflexive Modernization: Politics, Tradition and Aesthetics in the Modern Social Order*, Cambridge: Polity.
——. (2000) *What Is Globalization?* Cambridge: Polity.
Budget Accounting and Statistics Executive Yuan. (2003) *Report on Education*, http://www.stat.gov.tw/public/Attachment/592016204171.xls.
——. (2005) *Report on R.O.C. Female Employment and Marriage* (in Chinese), http://www.stat.gov.tw/ct.asp?xIltem=835&c+Node=531.
Chien, M. (1994) "The Characteristics of Chinese Culture," *Asian Culture Quarterly*, 22(1): 1–36.
Chou, Y. (1995) "The Prayer of Sluts: Unpacking Meanings of Being a Female in Newspaper Coverage," *Media's Women, Women's Media*, 79–147 (in Chinese).
Diamond, N. (1975) "Women Under Kuomingtang Rule: Variations on the Feminine Mystique," *Modern China*, 1(1): 3–45.
Farris, C. (2004) "Women's Liberation Under 'East Asian Modernity' in China and Taiwan," L. Farris et al. (eds) *Women in the New Taiwan: Gender Roles and Gender Consciousness in a Changing Society*, New York: M. E. Sharpe.
Fiske, J. (1989) *Reading the Popular*, London: Routledge.
Giddens, A. (1991) *Modernity and Self-Identity: Self and Society in the Late Modern Age*, Cambridge: Polity.
Ho, J. (2003) "From Spice Girls to Enjo Kosai: Formations of Teenage Girls' Sexualities in Taiwan," *Inter-Asia Cultural Studies*, (4)2: 325–35.
Huang, Y. (2008) "Pink Drama: Reconciling Consumer Identity and Confucian Womanhood," in Y. Zhu et al. (eds) *TV Drama in China: Unfolding Narratives of Tradition, Political Transformation and Cosmopolitan Identity*, Hong Kong: Hong Kong University Press.
Iwabuchi, K. (2003) *Recentering Globalization: Popular Culture and Japanese Transnationalism*, Durham: Duke University Press.
Kim, L. (2001) "Sex and the Single Girl in Postfeminism: The F Word on Television," *Television and New Media*, 2(4): 319–34.
Ku, Y. (1998) *Selling A Feminist Agenda on A Conservative Market—The Awakening Experience in Taiwan*, http://taiwan.yam.org.tw/womenweb/sell.htm.
Liu, C. and Regehr, C. (2006) "Cross-cultural Application of Self-in-Relation Theory: The Cases of Taiwanese Young Women," *International Social Work*, 49(4): 459–70.

Luo, C. (1997) "Competing Discourses on Gender Model—Discourse Analysis on Reports of 'NTU Adult Film Event' in the Newspapers," *Taiwan Social Studies Quarterly*, 25: 169–208 (in Chinese).

McRobbie, A. (2004) "Post-feminism and Popular Culture," *Feminist Media Studies*, 4(3): 255–64.

Miles, S. (2000) *Youth Lifestyles in a Changing World*, Buckingham: Open University Press.

Moseley, R. and Read, J. (2001) "Having it Ally: Popular Television (Post) Feminism," *Feminist Media Studies*, 2(2): 231–49.

Orenstein, C. (2003) "What Carrie Could Learn from Mary," *The New York Times*, http://www.nytimes.com.

Tsai, Y. (1999) "University Students' Television Drama Aesthetic Experience," *Broadcasting and Television*, 14: 111–38.

Tu, W. (1998) "Probing the 'Three Bonds' and 'Five Relationships' in Confucian Humanism," in W. Slote and G. DeVos (eds) *Confucianism and the Family*, Albany: State University of New York Press.

Vidmar-Horvat, K. (2005) "The Globalisation of Gender: Ally McBeal in Post-socialist Slovenia," *European Journal of Cultural Studies*, 8(2): 239–55.

Xu, X. and Lai, S. (2004) "Gender Ideologies, Marital Roles and Marital Quality in Taiwan," *Journal of Family Issues*, 25(3): 318–55.

13 Cybercute Politics

The Internet Cyworld and Gender Performativity in Korea

Larissa Hjorth

One of the central tenors of contemporary everyday life in Asia is the increasing role of global Information and Communication Technologies (ICTs) and negotiation between online and offline spaces. In the region, divergent uptake and characteristics can be noted, with each location demonstrating that the global media is far from homogenous. The cultural significance of such mediated spaces as the Internet makes it an apt symbol for discussion of the issues of globalization, democracy, capitalism, individualism and redefinitions of place.

The various nodes of consumption and production of media cultures in the region have notably changed since the 1997 financial crisis, as noted eloquently by Chua Beng Huat (2000). In particular, as this anthology addresses, media cultures in the region have seen emerging forms of modernization and individualism that do not fit a Eurocentric or Anglo-American model. Through the vehicle of technological spaces such as the Internet we are seeing new contestations of what it means to experience and represent place and community that disrupt Western precepts.

Far from the homogeneous "global village" Marshall McLuhan (1964) detailed, the global space of the Internet is giving rise to multiple and divergent formations of what it means to be co-present (virtual and actual, here and there) and how this reflects offline notions of community, mobility and locality. One of the enduring modes of customizing technological spaces in the region is through the role of the cute. Unlike Western models, where cute culture is simplistically defined as child's play, in the region cute capital is used by both young and old to help humanize the often-cold associations with new technologies (Ariés 1962; White 1993).

In each location in the region, cute culture takes on different forms and associations. Once symbolized by Japan's Hello Kitty or *Pokémon*, and thus conflated with the consumption of Japan, the cute has grown into various localized forms that are not just an example of Japanization in the region. In South Korea (henceforth Korea), the dominant virtual community (Cyworld mini-hompy), accessed by over one third of Korea's population, is structured by the aesthetics and attitudes of cute culture. This leads us to ask: What is the relationship between the consumption of cute culture in virtual spaces and how does this reflect the mores of individual lives and a sense of community in Korea? In particular, what role does the stereotype of cute culture—girl's culture—play in the gendering of technologies in Korea?

In this chapter I will explore the role of cute capital in Korea and its particular habitation of the Korean Social Networking Site (SNS), Cyworld mini-hompy. A hybridization of blog, simulation game, and virtual space, mini-hompy's nine-year experience demonstrates its success in the global center for broadband penetration rates (OECD 2006; Cashmore 2006; Cameron 2006), Korea. As the most popular SNS, mini-hompy houses various daily visitations from over one third (18 million) of Korea's population of 48 million (Moon 2005; Jacobs 2006). One of the key representational modes is the role of cute capital—that is, cute characters and customization—that palpably inhabits the visual architecture of mini-hompy.

Through case studies with mini-hompy users, I will investigate the currency of cute capital in negotiating online and offline relations and how it reflects a sense of locality. I argue that the sense of play imbued in cute capital infuses technological spaces with sociality. This role of cute capital is interwoven with the gendered usage of technology in the region; the symbolic dimensions of technology in the region's rise to being a key site for twenty-first-century modernity cannot be underestimated. In Korea, the instrumental role of technology has ensured a shift from Korea as a global site for economic prowess and technological savvy to an ideologically powerful conveyer of soft capital (Yoon 2003; Borland and Kanellos 2004). Technology, and particularly the socio-technological space of Web 2.0 and the emergence of SNS, has increasingly become a space in which offline power struggles and transformations can be played out upon various levels; particularly prevalent in the role of gender struggles around technological spaces.

L. H. M. Ling (1999), in "Sex Machine: Global Hypermasculinity and Images of the Asian Woman in Modernity," argues that this hypermasculinity is not just the product of East Asia but rather of the global economy. Through the conduits of modernization and post-industrialization, hypermasculinity is both disseminated and camouflaged. Hypermasculinity is accompanied by hyperfemininity; the later takes on traditional roles of reproductive, unpaid, care labor in order to compensate for the growing economic imperative of hypermasculinity in which welfare systems and the divide between the haves and have-nots continues to flourish. For Ling, globalization carries with it an association of "capital-intensive, upwardly mobile hypermasculinity," as opposed to a localized and "socially regressive hyperfemininity" (1999: 278).

Cute capital is unquestionably an example of the "hyperfeminine," not just in its aesthetics and emotive visual economy, but also in the way it is used to humanize and socialize technological spaces into sites nurturing social capital. Despite the fact that the role of technology—as a site for both production and consumption—has been associated with hypermasculinity, the rise of highly social and emotional spaces such as SNS demonstrate that pervasiveness of hyperfeminine customization is being deployed by both male and female users in different ways. Through the practice of negotiating online and offline identities and social capital in the case of mini-hompy, we can see various forms of contestation from gendered modes of consumption and production.

Drawing on revised notions of Pierre Bourdieu's (1984) "capital" as knowledge and Judith Butler's (1991) de-essentialization of gender through the precept of "gender performativity," this paper will consider the role of cute capital in the gendered politics of online and offline performativity in Korea. Significantly reconfiguring Brian McVeigh's (2000) notion of Japanese "techno-cute" within the context of Korean techno-nationalism, this paper will consider how gender relations are shifting. We will see that global mediascapes such as the Internet are being used in everyday Korean practices to center, de-center and re-center localized notions of community, place and co-presence.

HOME PAGE: LOCATING CYWORLD IN KOREA

> Money pours in when the Cyworld population goes on a decorating, gift buying or music-downloading spree to adorn their "room." The more attractive and interesting the room, the more visitors it gets. And in Cyworld, popularity equates to fame and success. The site even measures sexiness and friendliness, which it gauges by the number of gifts a person gives or receives. (Cameron 2006)

Owned by Korea's super-giant, SK communications, Cyworld popularity—symbolised by the ubiquity of mini-hompy—seems all-pervasive in Korea. Cyworld's 2006 launch in the Asia-Pacific region and United States has put it on the global radar in the rise of Web 2.0 (Borland and Kanellos 2004; Cameron 2006; Cashmore 2006). Featuring a photo gallery, music section, message board, guest book, and personal bulletin board, what differentiates mini-hompy from blogs is its "mini room" in which the users' avatars can be housed. This mini-room often reflects the users' own lounge room (or ideal one) and users can invite friends—in the form of an avatar—to visit. In this way, mini-hompy tries to replicate the offline lives in a location where high broadband speeds make the seamless and instantaneous connection a reality. In another way, the significance of Korean notions of space as intrinsically social—as entailed by the various *bang* (rooms) such as PC, *jimjil* (hot), *norae* (music)—is highlighted in the function of the mini-room as a type of third "inbetween" space of the *bang* (Chee 2005).

Cute capital is intrinsically linked to play cultures and the deployment and contextualization of new technologies. As Brian Sutton-Smith (1997) observes, play cultures are *social spaces,* informed by the local. As I will discuss in the context of mini-hompy, the role of the cute allows for different forms of performativity—most notably, gender—that, in turn, reflect the particular definitions of community and social capital in Korea. However, before doing so, I sketch out the particular role of technology—and the now "global" Cyworld—in the rise of what we have come to understand as Korea today.

Korea has been lauded as the country with the greatest broadband access by the Organization for Economic Co-operation and Development (OECD 2006) and is easily one of the dominant examples of twenty-first-century modernity, but it is easy to forget that Korea's rise has been relatively recent. The experience of a tumultuous twentieth century of Japanese rule (1910–1945), in which much Korean culture was subjugated—such as the Korean language—is not lost on a contemporary Korea that boasts one of the ninth largest economies globally in terms of gross domestic product (GDP). Two events in the twentieth century have left an indelible mark on Koreans in general: the colonial experience, which destroyed a five-hundred-year dynasty, the *Chosôn* (1392–1910), and the subsequent division of the country into North and South. The resulting Korean War (1950–1953) was one of the bloodiest conflicts, undoubtedly shaping the national identity of South Korean postmodernity.

Since the Korean War, South Korea's government and major companies (*chaebôl*) have worked hard to regain a sense of national pride and global strength. This effort was weakened in the Asian economic crash of 1997 in which the South Korean reserve bank had to be rescued by the International Monetary Fund (IMF). Part of Korea's rapid rise has been thanks to the governmental and industry focus on technologies. The IT policies of Korea have been noted as the best in the world (West 2006), and the IT industry in Korea represents over 15 percent of GDP (MIC 2006). On average, Koreans are on line at least thirteen hours per week (National Internet Development Agency of Korea) using email and information searching and connecting online through Cyworld mini-hompy, and, to a lesser degree, online massive multiplayer games.

In Korea, the intertwining of net and mobile telephonic spaces has helped facilitate Korean forms of democracy (Kim 2003: 325). For Korean sociologists Shin Dong Kim (2003) and Haejoang Cho (2004), the rise of a specific type of democracy in Korea was facilitated by, in part, new technologies such as mobile phones and the ubiquity of broadband. In the case of online communities such as Cyworld, the success has been, in part, attributed to the dominant lifestyle trends in Korea, the high-rise identical blocks of flats and an easy accessibility of broadband coverage. The importance of Cyworld ("Cy" meaning "between" worlds or "relationship" world) is demonstrated by the fact that over one third of Korea's population continue to access theirs and friends' mini-hompys after many years.

In Cyworld friends are called *ilchon*, a concept once used to denote one degree of distance (for example, one's mother is one *chon*) from family members in a traditional Korean kinship. This phenomenon of virtuality goes hand in hand with Korea's rise as one of the most broadbanded countries in the world (OECD 2006). Once used to denote degrees of distance between family members (that is, your mother would be one *chon* from yourself), Cyworld has re-branded its cyber-rooms with the notion of *ilchon* (*il* meaning one) and non-*chon* to infer "friends" and "non-friends." *Ilchon* can gain more access to their fellow *ilchon* information and be invited to visit their cyber-room. *Non-chon* can only gain cursory access.

The fact that users deploy their "real" offline names (users must log in with their citizen ID number) and fill the pages with offline activities—camera phone images, music, right down to their mini-room reflecting their offline lounge room—attests to the importance given to weaving the online with the offline. As I shall discuss here, the constant blurring of offline/online identities in Cyworld allows the participants to build up and maintain social capital in the world of their real relationships with family and friends.

However, in this complementing between online and offline identity and social capital there is also contestation. In particular, the role of cute culture so prevalent in mini-hompy's architecture and avatars operates to harness online/offline gender perfomativity that is both subversive and conventional. Far from uniform in its associations and meanings, cute culture has grown to become a dominant socio-emotive currency in Asia-Pacific socio-technologies. In Korea, cute culture, just like gender perfomativity, is a localized and contested practice (Ko 2003; Kinsella 1995; Kusahara 2001). Although the avatars can be customized according to users' moods, one thing remains prevalent: all avatars are "cute." And this cute capital has an agenda: gender.

WWW.CUTEINKOREA.KR: THE ROLE OF
CUTE CAPITAL BEYOND CHILD'S PLAY

One of the defining features in the practice of customizing technologies in the region is the role of cute aesthetics; in the Asia–Pacific region the cute is all-pervasive and yet disjunctive in its meanings. The use of cute capital (that is, cute characters) has long been viewed as a popular mode for both young and old to domesticate new technologies[1]: a phenomenon that does not translate into other contexts such as the United States (Hjorth 2005, 2006). I argue that by investigating customization techniques as indicative of the socio-cultural context, we can gain insight into the relationship between online and offline and attendant localized notions of individualism, community and social capital.

In Korea, cute avatars provide a vehicle for negotiating co-presence between online and offline spaces. Avatars, as Cyworld's mini-hompy attests, are quintessential in the investment—both financially and emotionally—of users and their maintenance of co-present communities. The role of the cute is pivotal in the aesthetics of the avatars, playing into what Anne Allison (in the context of the *Pokémon* global phenomenon) characterized as the "postmodern" qualities of the cute that allows it to be open to polysemic readings, contexts and re-appropriations (2003).

However, while the cute may allude to polysemic readings, this does not mean a loss of local specificity. Behind the "cuteness" is a struggle to humanize social technological spaces, to highlight the mediated role of intimacy regardless of technological interference (Kinsella 1995; Kusahara 2001). Although the use of the cute in the West has been associated with child's play (Ariés 1962; White 1993), in the Asia–Pacific region the cute is an integral part of the adaptation of new technologies into sociocultural artifacts.

Much has been written about the role of cute culture (*kawaii*) in Japan, often resulting in the cute being seen as a symbol of Japanization both in the region and globally (Kinsella 1995; Iwabuchi 2003; Whittier Treat 1996). And yet, despite the forms of cute emerging from locations outside of Japan, little research has been conducted into the ways in which the production and consumption of cute is tied to specific forms of locality. In particular, the deployment of cute culture outside of Japan is marked by differing cultural and gendered inflections. In the case of Korea, with its history of Japanese occupation, it is not only deeply problematic to define Korea's own cute cultural as derivative of Japanese *kawaii* culture, but indeed wrong. In the Asia–Pacific region, one continuity can be noted about cute culture, that is, it is about emerging modes of gender performativity that run concurrently to the rise of domestic technologies. The cute localizes and remediates new technologies such as the Internet.

Just as constructions of female performativity and femininity in the region are different in each cultural context, so too is the "feminized" element of cute culture. Cute culture is not necessarily about female consumers, but, rather, about a type of feminizing and socialising of new technologies—a phenomenon that has risen concurrently to the expansion of convergent ICTs. In the rise of convergent ICTs we can see a particular phenomenon, the ubiquity of social labor, or what Misa Matsuda called "full time intimacy" (2005). Once the predicament of women, as were all unpaid-for "domestic" forms of labor, now both men and women are fallen prey to the insidious forms of social labor—epitomized by customization—found in today's global media.

In a sample study of mini-hompy users in 2004, Heewon Kim and I investigated the role of cute avatars in negotiating online and offline identity (Hjorth and Kim 2005). Most notably there was a vast difference between the identification with cute capital between male and female respondents. Many female respondents enjoyed the "playful" nature of cute avatars in representing online performativity. Respondents stated that they liked to change and modify their cute avatar—"mini-me"—according to mood and feelings. In this way, cute customization afforded respondents a way to inject offline emotions and personality into online spaces. Many of the respondents noted little disjuncture between online and offline identity even though the cute avatar was often not a realistic depiction of themselves online. In a way, the cute avatars and re-presentation of offline activities and sense of community were re-enacted and developed through mini-hompys.

Cute culture operates to suture online and offline worlds at the same time that it complicates conventional notions of gendered identification. On the one hand, the cute culture of Cyworld ensures a playful tie between online and offline identity. On the other hand, that collation is also bound to revising the "gendered" nature of cute culture by the fact that equal amounts of male and female users partake in the unavoidable cute politics of Cyworld. The dominance of cute culture in Cyworld suggests not only that the cute is no longer synonymous with girl culture (and, specifically, stereotypes about Asian femininity) but, also, that it contests gendered and youth conflations around practices of co-presence (on line and off line).

Through the cultural intermediary of cute culture we see a localized form of what it means to be virtual—exemplified by Cyworld. We can see that cute culture mediates gendered performativity within and between online/offline identity and sociality. The contestation of identity politics (specifically in relation to the construction of gender) is also apparent in the role of convergent media—epitomized by mobile media—in maintaining a presence and co-presence. In the increasing role of mobile media in the customizing of online presence and the negotiation of co-presence, the divisions blur even further. As Dong-Hoo Lee's (2005) seminal ethnographic research into camera phone practices in Korea has observed, these emerging mobile technologies (often coordinated with online/offline co-presence) have given rise to new contingencies for female empowerment and new ways of seeing and presenting gender.

With females becoming more active in their adoption of new technologies, one wonders about the effect this "produser" (Bruns and Jacobs 2006) agency will have on the industry. Will this lead to more female producers in the very male dominated area? As Lee and Sohn (2004) observe, the rise of convergent mobile media is leading to new modes of accessibility and distribution for female users. In their study, Lee and Sohn find that women are more "active in adopting new multi-media functions of the mobile phone" and that "their willingness to adopt such functions is significantly stronger than men's." Moreover, the types of gendered images we are seeing is changing, in a sense reflecting new modes of gender performativity in Korea. I cautiously deploy a reworked notion of Judith Butler's performativity here. As Butler notes, gender is a construct that is naturalized through a set of regulations informed by the cultural context.

In the case of the ways in which cute avatars and user-created content (UCC), such as the products of camera phone practices, are used to denote gendered practices, we can see many examples of Lee's observations. Lee's discussion of female camera phone users shifting from the role of consumers to producers provides significant evidence in support of rethinking gender performativity and the attendant modes of agency or empowerment. These forms of media are allowing female users to take a "prosumer" role, and this will undoubtedly have effects on not only the content of new media in Korea but also the gender divisions between producers and consumers of media. With the rise in female consumers of new technological spaces such as mini-hompy and mobile media such as camera phones, one wonders when the industry itself will begin to be constituted of more female producers.

Interrelated with the role of cute customization and hand phone UCC such as the camera phone, users are able to humanize and socialize the new technology. Central to this customization practice is the role of gift giving and its contextualization by the local. It is not by accident that both cute customization and mobile technology re-enact gift giving traditions. This is particularly prevalent in Cyworld, which operates on a myriad of gift giving levels. The rise of Internet and mobile communication has often been discussed in terms of gift giving rituals (Taylor and Harper 2002). Integral to gift giving practices is the performativity of localized modes of gender. By exploring mini-hompy's cute customization we can gain insight into the remediated and emerging modes of gender performativity. In order to expand on these notions, I will discuss the role of cute customization and gender in a sample case study conducted in 2005.

FEMOCUTE: EMERGING SHIFTS IN GENDER ONLINE PERFORMATIVITY

In a sample study of thirty university students (between the ages of twenty and twenty-nine, equal males and females) I interviewed in Korea from September to December 2005, many of the respondents observed the pivotal role of the mini-hompy in providing a sense of community and continuity (Hjorth and Kim 2005). This sample study does not claim to represent all Korean online and offline relations but, rather, aims to provide an initial study of a dominant phenomenon demanding more research. By discussing the respondents' thoughts and feelings towards their mini-hompy, this study hopes to impart some of the contested identity politics at play.

In this case study, the role of cute customization served to make this process playful and, most notably, to reinforce already existing offline relationships, social capital and sense of community. Some mini-hompy's—through perpetual customization that translated into particular forms of social and cultural capital—did acquire a cult-like status in the world of mini-hompy. These mini-hompys were often highly customized and continuously updated to reflect the individual users high cultural capital. The maintenance and upkeep of mini-hompys was seen as a gendered activity, with male respondents noting that young females tended to have the best mini-hompys.

In discussions about the "celebrity" mini-hompy there seemed to be a conflation between cute and cultural capital; in particular, the successful mini-hompys were those that exploited a type of socio-emotive logic best understood as a feminization (or "hyperfemininity") of the virtual space. This feminization was a practice that was bound to the logic of cute culture and was apparent in both male and female mini-hompys; hence suggesting that gender perfomativity was becoming more progressive, especially in the case of male users adopting feminized customisation modes. For one male respondent, age twenty-five, mini-hompys are about identity, and, more specifically, gendered identity. He states:

A lot of girls use the mini-hompy in a more obsessive manner. I think it can be a competition sometimes. I know a lot of girls who spend a lot of time on their mini-hompys. Some mini-hompys are amazing. In Korea, accessing the Internet all the time anywhere is part of everyday life.

As the respondent notes, the Internet is very much "part of everyday life" and thus the offline/online distinction can seem artificial. Thus, the dominance of females producing "amazing" mini-hompys begs the question: At what point does this practice shift from nebulous consumerism and unpaid social labor to creative production? Can the dominance of female prosumers on the Internet in Korea be read as a sign of future shifts in the gendered employment in the industry?

With the rise of UCC and Web 2.0 creative industries, in which Korea features dominantly, we could argue that this female "prosumerism" provides a model for thinking through future scenarios regarding new digital industries and, notably, shifts in gender divisions between consumption and production. In the study, it was undeniable that female users were feeling degrees of empowerment and also an increasingly familiarity with technological spaces. However, it will be some time before we can access whether these gender balances are reflected in the industry employment demographics.

For Koreans, for whom the average working day is often from 8 a.m. to 10 p.m., vehicles such as the Internet and particular SNS like the mini-hompy afford users the ability to perform their offline identities on line. The mini-hompy is, as respondents indefatigably noted, not about replacing offline relationships and community, but, rather, a vehicle for co-presence. Just as choices in clothes, music and fashion are often influenced by ones' social capital, the mini-hompy allows users to make social, cultural and economic distinctions, in a Pierre Bourdieu sense, through mini-hompy customization. The choice as to who is a non-*chon* or *ilchon* reflects offline social differentiation. This differentiation, in turn, illustrates that the Internet is far from horizontal in its architecture; rather, like offline sociality, it is deeply imbued with vertical hierarchies of knowledge—whether cultural, economic or social. As modes of reciprocity become key players in determining one's image to others, such sites as Cyworld infuse gift giving practices with social capital, feeding to and from online and offline identifications. Cute avatars allow users to reflexively engage with the constructions of identity. As one female, age twenty-one, noted:

> I update my character once a month. I like to change it to match the way I'm feeling, or the way I would like to be seen as feeling. I tend to change my mini-room more. This is because friends often buy me objects (*cyber-gifts*) for it. Often they buy objects that they know I would like to have in my (*offline*) lounge but can't afford. I like my mini-room to represent my ideal lounge room.

As this female respondent noted, the role of customization operates on two levels simultaneously. On the one hand, she wanted her avatar and mini-room to reflect her offline identity and yet, on the other hand, she utilized the online space to represent an ideal. This seems to be a familiar scenario for users as they negotiate the online and offline co-presence. The choices around customization play out both in ideal and actual worlds, with users mindful of not displaying too much differentiation between their online and offline identities. The fact that friends bought other friends cyber-gifts to reflect desires in the offline world further reflects this online/offline reflexive correlation, which maintains both individual and social mores.

Here we see that the cute culture provides a space for identity translation, a contested space full of ambivalences that revolve around identity politics both on line and off line. Cute customization is, on the one hand, a source for liberation; it is, on the other hand, a leash tying users down to a compulsion to customize in order to maintain a constant co-presence. The leash/freedom paradox associated with forms of Internet and mobile media has been noted by many critics (Qiu 2007; Arnold 2003). In this case, the negative components of a seamlessness between online and offline could be felt, where co-presence becomes about maintaining a set of compulsory practices and images. Thus the freedom to contest identity and gender normativity through customization also, paradoxically, becomes to leash in terms of upkeep. As one female respondent, age twenty-eight, noted:

At one stage I felt like all I was doing was taking pictures, editing and uploading them. Whilst this was initially fun because my friends enjoyed seeing them—especially when they were in them! However, I found the novelty wore off and then my friends came to expect me to be the photographer that meant that I couldn't enjoy the event as much because I had to concentrate on getting "good" pictures of everyone. One time I pretended the camera wasn't sending pictures properly so someone else would take the responsibility.

And although the highly engaged mini-hompy users may soak up the funds (in the form of *dotori*) by perpetual customization, one could argue that their input is not about exploitation or being duped, but rather about a creative and "performative" space. As noted earlier in a revising of Butler's gender performativity, we can see that the various customizing modes enhance not only a sense of performing gender, but also power, emotion and sociality. The customization of cute avatars dependent upon mood allowed users to give emotion a "face," helping to forge a continuity between online and offline identity. The use and choice of features for the avatar, mini-room and also the camera phone images and music affords users the ability to preform their offline identity in their online community spaces.

LOGGING OFF: CONCLUSION

Although cute customization of new technologies dominates the region, it is far from homogenous in its production, consumption and representation in different localities. Rather, like the concept of media globalization, cute customization demonstrates distinctive modes of fragmentation—echoing the multitude of what Youna Kim (2008) defines as the "regionalization, nationalization, localization" of the region. If the region can be reconceived as clusters of trans-Asian "communities of consumers," as Chua (2006) suggests, then it is indeed the various UCC and customization practices that are highlighting new emerging "imaging communities" that operate to resist and adapt so-called global media. Through customization practices—such as the cute—we can see the negotiation of technologies by the dynamics of the local.

This chapter, through its discussion of the case study of Cyworld mini-hompy, has attempted to give one example in many that demonstrate the local practices at play in negotiating the contested and "globalized media spaces" such as the Internet. One of the central visual and social tenors of mini-hompy, cute customization, is significant to understanding the localized nature of gender performativity.

In the case of Korea, with its techno-nationalist agenda, which has seen it become the most broadband country in the world, the use of technology and the attendant modes of co-presence are very much part of everyday life. The use of mini-hompys affords people the chance to be connected and to reinforce already existing offline social capital. The role of cute capital, as I have suggested, is linked to the specific role of play and gender performativity in Korea. It will be interesting to see the impact of these innovative socio-technological practices and the shifts in gender agency.

As I have identified in this case study, we can gain much insight into contested modes of identity—particularly gender—through exploring the role of identity and its collation between online and offline spaces. Through the cultural intermediary of cute culture in the case of Cyworld we can see that conventional forms of gender performativity are being contested. Not only is cute culture no longer subsumed under "girl" or youth culture, but, also, the role of co-present customization is becoming increasingly marked by techniques once defined as feminine: socio-emotive customization. This practice is feminized: whether practiced by men or women. The fact that the mini-hompy demographic is half male and half female, with both genders actively participating in domesticating the virtual space to reflect offline relationships, is significant. No longer are technological spaces such as the Internet dominated by males; rather, increasingly female users are becoming more proactive in their presentation and upkeep of their online identities, so much so that the Internet is becoming more and more governed by feminized social labor. How cute?

* I would like to thank the respondents interviewed in both 2004 and 2005 as well as Heewon Kim for our initial collaborative research in 2004. I would also like to thank the Yonsei CCIC BK project (Yonsei University, Seoul), Professors Yoon Youngchul and Yoon Tae-jin, and, of course, Youna Kim.

REFERENCES

Allison, A. (2003) "Portable Monsters and Commodity Cuteness; Pokémon as Japan's New Global Power," *Postcolonial Studies,* 6(3): 381–98.

Ariés, P. (1962) *Centuries of Childhood: A Social History of Family Life,* New York: Knopf.

Arnold, M. (2003) "On the Phenomenology of Technology: The 'Janus-Faces' of Mobile Phones," *Information and Organization,* 13: 231–56.

Borland, J. and Kanellos, M. (2004) "South Korea Leads the Way," *CNET News.com, http://news.com.com/South+Korea+leads+the+way/2009–1034_3–5261393. html.*

Bourdieu, P. (1984) *Distinction: A Social Critique of the Judgment of Taste,* Cambridge: Harvard University Press.

Bruns, A. and Jacobs, J. (2006) *Uses of Blogs,* New York: Peter Lang.

Butler, J. (1991) *Gender Trouble,* London: Routledge.

Cameron, D. (2006) "Koreans Cybertrip to a Tailor-made World," *The Age,* 9 May.

Cashmore, P. (2006) "Cyworld US Launches—Will It Topple MySpace?" *Mashable* blog, *http://mashable.com/2006/03/30/cyworld-us-will-it-topple-myspace/.*

Chee, F. (2005) "Understanding Korean Experiences of Online Game Hype, Identity, and the Menace of the 'Wang-tta," paper presented at the Digital Games Research Association (DIGRA) Conference: Changing Views—Worlds in Play, Vancouver.

Cho, H-J. (2004) "Youth, Internet, and Alternative Public Space," paper presented at the Urban Imaginaries: An Asia-Pacific Research Symposium, Lingnan University.

Chua, B. H. (2000) *Consumption in Asia,* Routledge: London.

———. (2006) "East Asian Pop Culture: Consumer Communities and Politics of the National," paper presented at the Cultural Space and Public Sphere in Asia Conference, Seoul.

Hjorth, L. (2005) "Odours of Mobility: Japanese Cute Customization in the Asia-Pacific Region," *Journal of Intercultural Studies,* 26: 39–55.

———. (2006) "Playing at Being Mobile: Gaming, Cute Culture and Mobile Devices in South Korea," *Fibreculture Journal* 8, *http://journal.fibreculture. org/issue8/index.html.*

Hjorth, L. and Kim, H. (2005) "Being There and Being Here: Gendered Customizing of Mobile 3G Practices through a Case Study in Seoul," *Convergence,* 11: 49–55.

Ito, M. (2002) "Mobiles and the Appropriation of Place," *Receiver Magazine 8,* www.receiver.vodafone.com.

———. (2005) "Introduction: Personal, Portable, Pedestrian," in M. Ito et al. (eds) *Personal, Portable, Pedestrian: Mobile Phones in Japanese Life,* Cambridge: MIT Press.

Iwabuchi, K. (2003) *Recentring Globalization: Popular Culture and Japanese Transnationalism,* Durham: Duke University Press.

Jacobs, D. (2006) "Cyworld Lands on MySpace," *International Business Times,* 31 July, *http://ibtimes.com/articles/20060731/cyworld-myspace-sktelecom-newscorp.htm.*

Kim, S. D. (2003) "The Shaping of New Politics in the Era of Mobile and Cyber Communication," in K. Nyiri (ed) *Mobile Democracy,* Vienna: Passagen Verlag.

Kim, Y. (2008) "The Media and Asian Transformations," in Y. Kim (ed) *Media Consumption and Everyday Life in Asia,* New York: Routledge.

Kinsella, S. (1995) "Cuties in Japan," in L. Skov and B. Moeran (eds) *Women, Media and Consumption in Japan,* Surrey: Curzon Press.

Ko, Y-F. (2003) "Consuming Differences: 'Hello Kitty' and the Identity Crisis in Taiwan," *Postcolonial Studies,* 6(2): 175–89.

Kusahara, M. (2001) "The Art of Creating Subjective Reality: An Analysis of Japanese Digital Pets," *Leonardo,* 34(4): 299–302.

Lee, D. H. (2005) "Women's Making of Camera Phone Culture," *Fibreculture Journal* 6, http://journal.fibreculture.org.

Lee, D. H. and Sohn, S. H. (2004) "Is There a Gender Difference in Mobile Phone Usage?" paper presented at the Mobile Communication and Social Change Conference, Seoul.

Ling, L. H. M. (1999) "Sex Machine: Global Hypermasculinity and Images of the Asian Woman in Modernity," *positions,* 7(2): 277–306.

Matsuda, M. (2005) "Discourses of *Keitai* in Japan," in M. Ito et al. (eds) *Personal, Portable, Pedestrian: Mobile Phones in Japanese Life,* Cambridge: MIT Press.

McLuhan, M. (1964) *Understanding Media,* New York: Mentor.

McVeigh, B. (2000) "How Hello Kitty Commodifies the Cute, Cool and Calm: 'Consumutopia' versus 'Control' in Japan," *Journal of Material Culture,* 5(2): 291–312.

MIC, Ministry of Information and Communication (2006) *IT Statistics,* Seoul.

Moon, I. (2005) "E-Society: My World is Cyworld," *BusinessWeek Online,* 26 September, *http://www.businessweek.com/magazine/content/05_39/b3952405.htm.*

OECD, Organization for Economic Co-operation and Development. (2006) *OECD Broadband Statistics, http://www.oecd.org/sti/ict/broadband.*

Qiu, J. (2007) "The Wireless Leash: Mobile Messaging Service as a Means of Control," *International Journal of Communication,* 1: 74–91.

Sutton-Smith, B. (1997) *The Ambiguity of Play,* London: Routledge.

Taylor, A. and Harper, R. (2002) "Age-old Practices in the 'New World': A Study of Gift-giving between Teenage Mobile Phone Users," paper presented at the Changing Our World, Changing Ourselves Conference, Minneapolis.

West, D. M. (2006) *Global e-government 2006,* Rhode Island: Brown University Center for Public Policy.

White, M. (1993) *The Material Child: Coming of Age in Japan and America,* New York: Free Press.

Whittier Treat, J. (1996) "Introduction," in J. Whittier Treat (ed.) *Contemporary Japanese Popular Culture,* Honolulu: University of Hawaii Press, pp. 1–16.

Yoon, K. (2003) "Retraditionalizing the Mobile: Young People's Sociality and Mobile Phone Use in Seoul, South Korea," *European Journal of Cultural Studies,* 6(3): 327–43.

14 Cultural Migrants and the Construction of the Imagined West

The Japanese Youth

Yuiko Fujita

This chapter explores how media consumption in everyday life impacts upon the changing lives and identities of youths in Japan today. In recent years, a large number of young Japanese have been migrating to New York City, London, and other Western cities for the purpose of engaging in the production of art and popular culture, in areas such as dance, fashion design, film, fine arts, hairstyling, photography, popular music, and so on. Some follow a conventional way of *ryūgaku* (studying abroad), by attending college or vocational school. But many others find a new way of participating in cultural production overseas—they acquire student visas through English language schools, as a means of legally remaining at their destination. Actually, many of them rarely attend school, but instead practice dance or play music in studios, make drawings in their rooms, or work in clothing shops or beauty salons. These young Japanese tend to attempt to stay at their destination as long as possible, changing their visa status between different categories (for example, tourist, vocational or language student, and academic student).

Previous studies point out the cultural aspect of international migration, such as American artists moving to Paris or Japanese elites sojourning in the West to learn Western culture. Even so, what is significant is that while a relatively small number of artists or elites migrated for cultural reasons in the past, it has expanded to a large number of young people in the middle class in Japan today. How can we explain young Japanese migration, whose channels, motives, and movements are different from the previous cases? The central objective of this paper is to explore the factors of young Japanese migration, particularly looking at the critical role of the media. It investigates how the everyday experience of the media impacts upon their conception of "the West" and decision to migrate there. The rest of this chapter will first examine theoretical discussions on transnational flows of people and media, then explain research methods and examine the results of the case study.

TRANSNATIONAL FLOWS OF PEOPLE AND THE MEDIA

Over the past several decades, international migration has rapidly grown in volume, and the composition of migrant-sending countries has considerably diversified. As recent international migration is a complex, multifaceted phenomenon, there has been no dominant theory that can explain all phases of migration. Rather, a variety of theoretical models coexist across academic disciplines. Particularly, "neoclassical economics theory" (or "push and pull" theory), "world systems theory," and "migration systems theory" are often considered among the most influential approaches (Castles and Miller 2003; Massey et al. 1993). These theories have developed mostly from cases studies of "immigrants" (for example, labors, "family reunions," refugees), as well as those of "non-immigrants" (for example, guest workers, highly skilled workers), and tend to focus on economic and political factors. However, these approaches cannot fully explain the case of young Japanese migration. Young Japanese, generally, do not migrate for economic or political motives. Instead, they usually migrate with their accumulated savings or parental support and do not have a full-time job at their destination. If their funds run out, most will take up low-wage jobs at Japanese restaurants, night clubs, and so on, in order to continue their cultural activities in the host country. Indeed, these young Japanese tend to have a better economic standard of living at home, as they can have a better job or family support in Japan. If so, how can we account for this migration?

Following Arjun Appadurai's theory of the relation between media and migration, I would propose that the media have greatly influenced the transnational mobility of Japanese youth. According to his theory, electronic media and mass migration have their joint effect on "the work of the imagination" (1996). Cinema, television, video, and computers have transformed the ways in which people imagine themselves and everyday life, because of the sheer multiplicity of the forms in which media appear and because of the rapid way in which media move through daily life routines. People tend to construct "imagined selves" and "imagined worlds" or to make scripts for possible lives, as a result of being exposed to the media—whether in the form of fantastic film plots, news shows, or documentaries (Appadurai 1996: 9). Appadurai remarks that of course the role of imagination is not a new feature in human history. Imagination, however, has begun to play a newly significant role. For one reason, as electronic media have come into wide use throughout the world in the past decade or two, imagination has broken out of the special expressive space of art, myth, and ritual. That is, electronic media have allowed ordinary people to be exposed to a variety of images of foreign countries and have enabled them to deploy their imaginations in the practice of everyday lives. As a result, more people than ever before imagine routinely the possibility that they will live and work in places other than where they were born (5–6). As Appadurai puts it:

Those who wish to move, those who have moved, those who wish to return, and those who choose to stay rarely formulate their plans outside the sphere of radio and television, cassettes and videos, newsprint and telephone. For migrants, both the politics of adaptation to new environments and the stimulus to move or return are deeply affected by a mass-mediated imaginary that frequently transcends national space. (6)

In the case of young Japanese migration, probably, the media have diffused information and visual images of the United States and European countries in Japan, constructing particular images of "the West" over a long period. Moreover, young Japanese have grown up being exposed to American and European architecture, dance, drawings, fashion, films, and music, as well as the landscapes of cities and tourist attractions. Subsequently, they have begun to imagine themselves living there.

Here it is important to carefully look at how they imagine their lives at their destination. It is reported that a considerable number of young Albanians were exposed to Italian satellite television and actually migrated to Italy in search of a "modern" lifestyle (Mai 2001); in a similar way, the long-term consumption of Western popular culture influenced both the "physical" and "mental" emigration of young Moroccans to Western countries (Sabry 2003). These studies show that young migrants moved from non-Western countries to the West in search of Western modernity (Mai 2001; Sabry 2003). However, in the case of young Japanese migration, Japan has long since developed its own sense of a "modern" lifestyle. Is it possible that young Japanese migrate to Western cities in search of Western modernity? If not, what are they looking for through their migratory projects? This chapter examines how the media lead young Japanese to imagine their destination and to actually migrate there.

The data were gathered by qualitative interviews with twenty-two young Japanese who planned to migrate to New York City or London. These cities are two of the most popular destinations among young Japanese migrants. Respondents were recruited mainly at the British Council in Tokyo and the US Embassy in Tokyo, as well as through bulletin boards on several Internet web sites. The age of respondents ranged from nineteen to thirty at the time of their departure and the average age was twenty-five. Ten planned to go to New York City, while twelve planned to go to London. Fifteen were female and seven were male. This is part of my "multi-sited ethnography" (Marcus 1995), in which I followed the same respondents from Tokyo to New York City or London and continued interviews with them at their destinations over four years from 2003. I would like to call these young Japanese "cultural migrants" as they move in order to satisfy their cultural aspirations. All names used in this paper are pseudonymous.

YOUNG JAPANESE MIGRATION AND
THE ROLE OF THE MEDIA

Before exploring the role of the media, I shall briefly explain other migration factors in this case. Firstly, the most important "push" factor is the high youth unemployment rate and the increasing number of part-time employees in Japan. Partly because of an economic recession and partly because of changes in the industrial structure in Japan in the 1990s (Genda and Kurosawa 2001), the unemployment rate reached 10.1 percent among youths in the fifteen to twenty-four age bracket in 2003, and the number of part-time employees increased from 9,860,000 in 1993 to 15,040,000 in 2003 (MHLW 2004). Under these conditions, a large number of young people have few options but to live on a series of part-time jobs, and they are called "freeter" (a Japanese vernacular term combining "free" and "arbeiter," German for "worker"). Moreover, these working conditions and low salary have emerged as contributing to the increasing number of single people in the twenty-five to thirty-five age group (Yamada 2004). Indeed, about half of the respondents have only worked as part-time employees, and they tend to think that they have reached "a dead end" in Japanese society. They are dissatisfied with their lifestyles, in which they find it difficult to take on interesting full-time jobs or start an independent life with a partner. Thus, a considerable number of young Japanese have begun to search for a way to escape their environment, and emigration often emerges as an option. Significantly, both in the sample of this case study and in governmental statistics, about 70 percent of young Japanese who go to live in the United States or Britain are female.

Secondly, one "pull" factor is the cultural opportunities. All respondents consider New York City or London the most attractive place to engage in cultural production because these cities are the birthplaces of a variety of arts and popular culture and possess many educational institutions for the arts. In addition, they expect that there might be working opportunities in the cultural industries. Another "pull" factor is the English language. Most respondents have decided to go to the city, partly because they seek opportunities for attaining fluency in English. Thirdly, in recent years, travel agencies and governmental organizations have established "migration systems," by providing individuals with a variety of channels to migrate to Western cities for cultural activities. These "push" and "pull" factors and the "migration systems" all contribute to young Japanese migration.

The Two Notions of "the West"

Now let us look at the role of the media. Because these young Japanese hope to migrate to Western cities, first of all, their image of "the West" should be investigated. According to Naoki Sakai, "the West" is associated with those regions, communities, and peoples that appear politically or economically superior to other regions, communities, and peoples (1988:

476). In the Japanese language, there are two words closest to the English phrase "the West." One is *ōbei,* whose Chinese character, *ō* represents "Europe" and *bei* represents "America." The other is *seiyō,* whose Chinese character *sei* represents "west" and *yō* represents "ocean." Both words are usually translated into "the West." Most respondents consider that *ōbei* (Europe-America) means the United States, and to a lesser extent, Europe; *seiyō* (west-ocean) corresponds to Europe, which is particularly symbolized by France. In addition, some respondents say that *ōbei* or *seiyō* is the place where white people live:

> Actually, I've never thought about what the West means. *Seiyō* is opposite to the East, isn't it? Well, it's white people. Where is *ōbei?* My impression of *ōbei* is not so white. *Seiyō* is medieval. *Ōbei* is contemporary (Yoko, female freeter migrating to New York City, age twenty-seven)

> From *seiyō,* I recall Michelangelo's oil paintings. It's Western Europe, inland, from Belgium to Austria. When it comes to *ōbei,* I think of America . . . News media usually use the word *oh-bei.* In that case, it is usually about America. *Seiyō* is related to Western art history or Western cuisine. (Kumiko, female magazine designer migrating to London, age twenty-five)

These young people tend to think *ōbei* (America and, to a lesser extent, Europe) is "now," "contemporary," and "popular." In contrast, they tend to think of *seiyō,* (Europe, and most especially France) as "cultural" and "classical." Thus, for them, at least two ideas of "the West" exist. As each respondent has a slightly different idea about where the West is, it is difficult to define the borders of the West in their mental geographies.

When asked, "Do you think Japan is part of the West?" no one answered "Yes." Instead, most respondents said that Japan was part of Asia because Japan and Asia were similar in terms of "appearances," "culture," "race," "mentality," and "geography." This is probably because they have been influenced by Japan's new Asian identity widely diffused in the 1990s. According to Koichi Iwabuchi, the rise of global Asian economic power has pushed Japan to once again stress its "Asian" identity, as Japan could not neglect Asia as a vital market for its products (Iwabuchi 2002: 12–3).

Nonetheless, many respondents have a great sense of affinity to "America" and assume that their everyday life in "America" will be almost the same as their everyday life in Japan. This is partly because American military bases and American popular culture have greatly influenced Japan since the US occupation. According to Shunya Yoshimi, in the early post war period, "America" was an object of admiration among young people. By the late the 1970s, however, it had become part of the quotidian life of Japanese people, partly because the media had been conveying a great quantity of mediated images of "America" to them over a long period

(Yoshimi 2003). For my respondents, American popular culture is not an exotic but distant object of admiration; rather, it has become part of everyday life. Some even emphasize that they do not long for "America" but they long for "*living in* America":

> I think life in America is the same as life in Japan. I don't admire America. But I long to live abroad. My image of America is that people lead lively, fulfilling lives, so I think it's better for me to live in such a place. (Nana, female part-time salesperson migrating to New York City, age twenty)

> I think few [Japanese] people admire America or Britain. Rather, they admire a person like me who can go abroad. I mean, they admire people who actually carry out living abroad but don't admire America itself. Many people don't have the courage to live abroad. (Toru, male freeter migrating to New York City, age twenty-five)

By contrast, respondents migrating to London tend to consider *sei-yo* to be supreme in terms of art and culture. However, when it comes to their lives in Europe:

> In London, I want to lead a "normal" life that is similar to my life in Tokyo, meeting a lot of people, going out to have fun, or working as a graphic designer. (Wakana, female graphic designer migrating to London, age twenty-six)

As their accounts reflect, respondents tend to expect that their everyday life in the West will be almost the same as their everyday life in Japan. In fact, these young people, who come from the middle class in Japan, can enjoy the same economic standard of living at home as middle-class young people do in New York City or London. Therefore, they seldom talk about ambitions for a "modern" lifestyle or emphasize the West as the place of "progress." By contrast, in Tarik Sabry's research, young middle-class Moroccans associated the West with "superiority," "progress," and "development" (2003: 163–74). Clearly, these young Japanese do not migrate in search of a "modern" lifestyle or "progress" in a general term, which is the most important migration-inducing factor in the cases of young Albanians and Moroccans. In order to understand what leads respondents to move to New York City or London, their image of each destination city should be examined.

The Image of New York City

Most of the young people migrating to New York City have long had a great interest in American popular culture and have had much access to images of the city conveyed by American television programs and movies, as well as by Japanese television programs, magazines, and websites. Subsequently, many of them actually traveled to New York City. Significantly, those who have visited the city have quite a positive image of it:

> I often watched American television programs. *Beverly Hills 90210, Full House, Ally McBeal.* I've watched American programs since I was in junior high school. I've been interested in America for a long time. As for movies, I only watch American ones. I like *Soul Food.* I love black culture . . . I spent two weeks in New York City . . . My friends told me I shouldn't expect so much because I would be disappointed. But New York City was exactly what I had expected! (Haruka, female dance school student, age twenty-two)

A few respondents have never been to New York City. Yet they also have come to hold a particular image of the city, mainly through the media:

> I imagine people wear long coats [in New York City]. They are eating Macdonald's hamburgers. There are many galleries. There is the Empire State Building . . . I sometimes read travel books. I've read art books in the library. I have seen *Basquiat* and *Taxi Driver.* They are so impressive. (Toru, male freeter, age twenty-five)

Furthermore, it is significant that many respondents can imagine their lives in New York City with remarkable concreteness, although they have never lived there:

> I imagine my life in New York City, by watching movies, which were shot in the city, or reading travel books. Like, I eat here, shop there, in such a place . . . But, to be honest, I'm not very sure about it. I'm anxious that reality might be different from what I am expecting . . . My ideal life is, I concentrate on classes during weekdays and I go to museums and galleries and have parties with friends on weekends. (Fumiko, female office worker, age twenty-six)

Thus, these young people tend to believe that New York City is "urban," "stylish," "beautiful," "fun," "lively," and "exciting." Because they have been exposed to American television programs, movies, and music, it can be inferred that media have affected their images of New York City and their interests in cultural production and learning English there. Hence we might assume that "America" is still an object of admiration positively charging their desires to migrate. However, according to their accounts, it turned out that "admiration" is not a reason for migration. Most importantly, all of them take an interest in the so-called American dream and emphasize that New York City is the place where everyone can have a chance at *success:*

I want to know the limits of my ability in New York City . . . This time, I will go to New York City to learn what I can do . . . I have led an easy life in Japan without making any efforts. When I was in my early 20s, I worked as an *OL* [Office Lady] and spent all my money on having fun. Then I realized I had nothing. (Mayumi, female part-time office worker, age twenty-five)

I am going to New York City to fight. As a means, I'll bring my drawings . . . I want to change myself . . . I will go to the gallery that found Basquiat. I will first fight there. Since I was working as a salesperson, I can sell my drawings . . . I want to be a well-known figure. (Toru, male freeter, age twenty-five)

As discussed earlier, most of the respondents migrating to New York City have recognized that they have few prospects in their careers in Japan. In the meantime, they have been much exposed to American popular culture, as well as to images of New York City conveyed by the media. This has led them to perceive that there are many stories of success in New York City, and to start planning to migrate there. These young people expect to start their lives over and to create a more fulfilling life in a new place.

It should be noted that their idea of making a success is not the same as the old American dream, or the desire to enjoy an economically better life held by the past Japanese migrants to New York City at the turn of the nineteenth century. As Japan has achieved economic development, Japanese people's basic values and goals have shifted from giving top priority to economic growth to placing increasing emphasis on the quality of life. According to Takatoshi Imada, statistics show that, since the 1980s, many people in Japan indeed have begun to attach importance not only to occupation, income, and education, but also to identities and lifestyles (2000: 7–9).

In the case of the young Japanese interviewed, because of the boom of the Japanese economy after the Second World War, the generation of their fathers enjoyed increasing salaries as well as the stable corporate seniority system and gathered considerable savings (Miyamoto et al. 1997). The young Japanese grew up in the 1980s and 1990s when many Japanese began to attach much importance to their identities and lifestyles. One result is that these young people came to hope to become artists, creators, or performers, have a sophisticated lifestyle (for example, wearing European, Japanese or American designer brands clothes, going to posh restaurants or night clubs, and socializing with people in the culture industry), and identify themselves as "cool" people. However, partly because the youth unemployment rate and the number of part-time employees began to increase rapidly in the mid-1990s, most respondents cannot even find a full-time job that matches their interests. So they tend to continue to work part time and pursue their dreams, rather than attempting to find a full-time job as *sarariman* (company employees) or *OL* (office ladies). Parents allow their grown-up sons and daughters to live rent-free in their houses or apartments and to do "*honto ni yaritai koto*" (what they really want to do). When they recognize that there are few opportunities to create a fulfilling life in Tokyo, they begin to plan to migrate to New York City, which appears to provide them with more opportunities. Probably, this is the reason why some respondents emphasized that they do not long for "America" but they long for "*living in* America."

The Image of London

Respondents migrating to London show different patterns of media exposure and attitudes towards their destination, compared to those migrating to New York City. Some have been interested in British popular culture, and have had access to images and information about London conveyed by British and Japanese media. However, other people have had little interest and access to these. As for travel experience, more than half of this group had visited the city before. And many of them commonly have a mixture of positive, neutral, and negative images of their destination, such as "cool," "sophisticated," "new," "historical," "dark," "cold," "lazy" and "dangerous." For example, Kumiko, who has been much interested in British culture, says:

> I had often read [a Japanese magazine] *Street Fashion* and I had expected there should be many stylish people in London. But I didn't see many stylish people. It was the most surprising thing . . . I had watched [a Japanese television program] *Beat UK*. I think recently we are getting more information about Britain than before in Japan. But it might be because I'm more interested in Britain than before. I have watched Jamie Oliver's show on CATV. (Kumiko, female magazine designer, age twenty-five)

Jun, who had not been interested in London until he decided to live there, notes:

> My image of London is that it's cool. When I traveled to London, I took pictures every night. Lighting in the city was very sophisticated . . . As I had not had much information about London, I just felt London was like this. I hadn't heard much about London before. I became interested in London after my parents encouraged me to study abroad. I have visited websites and read magazines to get some information. But I'm still not so eager to gather information about London. (Jun, male art college student, age twenty-two)

In this way, while some have an interest in British popular culture and have access to information about London, others do not. If so, what has commonly led them to desire to migrate specifically to London for the purpose of cultural production? It turned out that most respondents expect to acquire "cultural capital" in Pierre Bourdieu's sense, such as English proficiency and an art degree or certificate; and thus, they could "distinguish" themselves from other people in Tokyo's art worlds, as Bourdieu notes, "social subjects, classified by their classifications, distinguish themselves by the distinctions they make" (Bourdieu 1984: 6). For instance, Yayoi and Nozomu say:

> I will go to study performing arts. I want to be an actress . . . I have wanted to study abroad and have heard that Britain is famous for performing arts . . . I didn't want to go to America because it's *too ordinary*. Everyone goes to study in America. It doesn't make any difference. (Yayoi, female freeter, age nineteen)

> I want to have my own design office in the future, so I need to distinguish myself from others [in Japan]. Most people in the apparel industry are domestic and are making very similar products within Japan. I should have some strong points in order to start my own business. I want to find good manufacturers in Britain. "Made-in-Britain" makes a difference. If I find some, I will place orders for my future business. (Nozomu, male fashion designer, age twenty-five)

As with respondents migrating to New York City, those migrating to London also hope to become artists, creators, and performers. However, it is characteristic of the London group that many respondents are from middle-class families whose householder's occupation is relatively culture-oriented (for example, designer, journalist, teacher). Because of their social backgrounds, many of them graduated from or attend an art college or have some work experience in the cultural industry in Japan. So they attempt to acquire cultural capital in order to retain affinity with the class in which they were born.

Because American culture is part of everyday life and popular among the young people at large in Japan, these respondents tend to consider that migrating to "America" is "too ordinary." Many of them say that they have learned or heard in school and/or through the media that European art and culture is the most eminent. Among European countries, they have chosen to go to Britain because they can also learn the English language, which they regard as a means towards having more opportunities in their art careers. They consider that if they acquire such cultural capital in Europe, they can have an advantage over other Japanese who have obtained an art degree or work experience only in Japan.

In the Meiji period (1868–1912), travel to Western countries became a rite of passage for the Meiji elite. This tradition of going, for a period, to live in the West, to acquire cultural capital seems to continue to this day.

In the past, however, it was available only to elites, whereas now it extends to young people of the middle class. While "America" is part of everyday life in Japan, foreign travel is popular, information channels regarding foreign countries have increased, and people's interests, needs, and tastes are diversified. To the extent that some young people conceive of the cultural, classical West as connoting Europe (including Britain), they hope to migrate to London in order to achieve "distinction."

An Illusory Image of "the West"

Overall, these young Japanese emphasized more positive images of New York City or London than negative ones. However, it is significant that some note that they have heard about negative aspects of their destination by word of mouth:

> Americans seem friendly and we have good impressions. But surprisingly, my dance teacher told me that they are very cold when you need help. (Rie, female office worker, age twenty-seven)

> When my friend was walking on a street in London, a black man told him, "You stink, Chink!" (Ryo, male freeter, age twenty-five)

Television programs, films, magazines, and books, as well as travel experience, tend to lead them to have positive images of their destination, but interpersonal communication with their friends who have lived in their destination tends to let them know negative aspects of it. While their image of New York City or London is mostly centered on popular culture and tourist attractions, what they have heard by word of mouth is mostly problems in relationships between their peers and local people. In fact, only a few people voluntarily referred to races and ethnicities in their destination. When asked, "What kind of people are in the city?" most of the young Japanese described misleading images:

> I heard New York was like Tokyo, as many people in the country go up to the city. But I didn't know there are so many Chinese in the city. I thought only white and black people, I mean, *real Americans* lived there. There were swarms of people who I couldn't tell if they were Chinese or Koreans or Japanese. (Haruka, female dance school student, age twenty-three)

"White people" seem to be at the center of their image of people in London:

> Many white people live in London, right? I don't think there are many black people in the city. (Nozomu, male fashion designer, age twenty-six)

I was surprised to see there were many races in London. I had imagined British people were Monty Python people. (Kumiko, female magazine designer, age twenty-five)

Almost all of these young Japanese interviewed seldom imagine that they might become involved in race and ethnic relations in the host country. This is partly because the majority of Japanese believe that Japan is a "homogeneous" nation, which consists of the only one race, one ethnic group, and one nation, although there are ethnic minority groups, such as Ainu, Koreans, Okinawans, and so on (Oguma 2002). Therefore, while living in Japan, most respondents have never consciously experienced race and ethnic relations.

Even the influx of foreign popular culture and foreign workers in the past decades has not changed their awareness. According to Marilyn Ivy (1995), in Japan, the foreign can only operate as a commodified sign of reassurance. The foreign must be transformed into a manageable sign of order, a transformation indicated most clearly by what, in Japan, is perhaps the dominant political concept of the past decade or two: internationalization (*kokusaika*). While internationalization elsewhere implies a cosmopolitan expansiveness, the Japanese state-sponsored version tends towards the domestication of the foreign. Therefore, instead of opening up Japan to a conflict among different nationalities and ethnicities, the policy of internationalization implies the opposites: the thorough domestication of the foreign and the dissemination of Japanese culture throughout the world (Ivy 1995: 2–3). Accordingly, the young Japanese tend to associate commodified signs, such as art, popular culture, landscapes of cities and tourist attractions, with the West, rather than people or race and ethnic relations, whether they go abroad to sightsee or they are exposed to the media in their homeland.

After migration, however, their image of the West becomes a problem. This is partly because the young Japanese have a strong belief in the "natural" status of a "homogenous" nation, and partly because the media provide them with images and information about the desirability of life in the West without telling them much about social discrimination and racism. Their friends attempt to tell them more realistic information about life in the city, but they are full of optimistic images that lead them to have prospects of creating a more fulfilling life. After arriving in a city where Anglo-Saxons or the English are the dominant ethnic group, however, most respondents gradually come to realize the gap between their previous images of the West and what they actually experience. Nearly all of them encounter (consciously) race and ethnic relations for the first time in their lives, experience subtle or blatant racism, and face various obstacles, not only due to their elementary-level English skills but also due to their "marked" race. For instance, Mayumi says:

Before coming to New York, I imagined that I would hang out with *gaijin* [foreigners or Westerners], speak a lot of English, and learn dancing. But I have achieved none of these . . . I hoped to make it. But I can't. (Mayumi, female, age twenty-six, after ten months in New York City)

These young Japanese had come all the way to New York City or London in the hope of participating in Western culture, of making friends with American or British people, and of developing social networks in art worlds in the city. Contrary to their expectations, many of them found it difficult to enter American or British society; instead, they had to hang out mostly with Japanese peers or live in local Japanese communities.

CONCLUSION

The media play an important role as one of the migration-inducing factors for young Japanese. Through media consumption in everyday life, on the one hand, respondents conceive of the popular, contemporary West, which is represented by "America." Some of them come to believe that New York City is a very familiar place where they can continue to lead "a normal life" with better prospects. On the other hand, respondents also conceive of the cultural, classical West, which connotes Europe, including Britain. Some begin to hope to migrate to London, in order to achieve "distinction."

Thus, the media, especially the electronic media, such as television, film, video and the Internet, have contributed to the construction of the "imagined West" among the young Japanese. This leads them to imagine their new lives and identities in Western cities and to actually migrate there. Without the above symbolic meanings of "the West," they would not dare to carry out migration to these cities only for the purpose of cultural production and learning English. Overall, the results indicate that because of the advanced means of communication, nowadays the transnational flows of mass-mediated images have begun to mobilize the large flows of young people from non-Western countries to Western countries, although a longing for Western modernity does not necessarily explain their motivations. It is also important to note that such mass-mediated images often construct an illusory image of "the West," which is different from what young migrants actually experience at their destination.

NOTES

1. This chapter is an expanded and revised version of an article originally published in Fujita, Y. (2004) "Young Japanese Cultural Migrants and the Construction of Their Imagined West," *Westminster Papers in Communication and Culture*, 1:23-37.

REFERENCES

Appadurai, A. (1996) *Modernity at Large,* Minneapolis: University of Minnesota Press.
Bourdieu, P. (1984) *Distinction: A Social Critique of the Judgment of Taste,* Cambridge: Harvard University Press.
Castles, S. and Miller, M. (2003) *The Age of Migration,* London: Macmillan.
Genda, Y. and Kurosawa, M. (2001) "Transition from School to Work in Japan," *Journal of the Japanese and International Economies,* 15: 465–88.
Imada, T. (2000) Posutomodan jidai no shakaikaisō, in *Nihon no Kaisō sisutemu,* University of Tokyo Press.
Ivy, M. (1995) *Discourses of the Vanishing,* Chicago: University of Chicago Press.
Iwabuchi, K. (2002) *Recentering Globalization: Popular Culture and Japanese Transnationalism,* Durham: Duke University Press.
Mai, N. (2001) "Italy is Beautiful," in R. King and N. Wood (eds) *Media and Migration,* London: Routledge.
Marcus, G. (1995) "Ethnography in/of the World System," *Annual Review of Anthropology,* 24: 95–117.
Massey, D. et al. (1993) "Theories of International Migration," *Population and Development Review,* 19: 431–66.
Miyamoto, M. et al. (1997) *Mikonka Syakai no Oyako Kankei,* Tokyo: Yuhikaku.
Oguma, E. (2002) *A Genealogy of "Japanese" Self-Images,* Melbourne: Trans Pacific Press.
Sabry, T. (2003) *Exploring Symbolic Dimensions of Emigrations,* part of PhD thesis, University of Westminster.
Sakai, N. (1988) "Modernity and its Critique," *South Atlantic Quarterly,* 87: 475–504.
Yamada, M. (2004) *Kibo Kakusa Shakai,* Tokyo: Chikuma Shobo.
Yoshimi, S. (2003) "America as Desire and Violence: Americanization in Postwar Japan and Asia during the Cold War," *Inter-Asia Cultural Studies,* 4: 433–50.

Contributors

Adrian M. Athique teaches Media and Communications in the Department of Sociology, University of Essex in the UK. His research interests include the social practice (and malpractice) of film exhibition in South Asia, unofficial networks of media distribution and the transnational reception of Indian and Australian media. He is currently producing a book (with Douglas Hill) on the phenomenon of the multiplex cinema in India for Routledge.

Chua Beng Huat leads the Cultural Studies in Asia Research Cluster at the Asia Research Institute, National University of Singapore, where he is also Professor of Sociology. He is a founding co-executive editor of *Inter-Asia Cultural Studies* journal. His most recent books are (co-edited with Chen Kuan-Hsing) *Inter-Asia Cultural Studies Reader* (2007) and (co-edited with Koichi Iwabuchi) *East Asian Pop Culture: Analysing the Korean Wave* (2008).

Yuiko Fujita is Associate Professor at the Institute for Media and Communications Research, Keio University in Japan. She holds a PhD from Goldsmiths College, University of London. Her current research project focuses on the new second generation of Japanese migrants in the USA and the UK, their identity formation and use of transnational media.

Anthony Y. H. Fung is Associate Professor in the School of Journalism and Communication at the Chinese University of Hong Kong. His research interests include political economy of popular culture, gender and youth identity, cultural studies, and new media technologies. His recent books (co-authored with Michael Keane and Albert Moran) include *New Television, Globalisation, and the East Asia Cultural Imagination* and *Global Capital, Local Culture: Transnational Media in China* (forthcoming).

Larissa Hjorth is researcher, artist and lecturer in the Games and Digital Art programs at RMIT University, Melbourne, Australia. She has been researching and publishing widely on gendered customizing of mobile communication, gaming and virtual communities in the Asia–Pacific. Recently she is editing a special issue of *Games and Culture Journal* on gaming in the Asia-Pacific region and has a forthcoming book on gendered mobile media in the Asia-Pacific region entitled, *The Art of Being Mobile* (Routledge).

Kelly Hu is Associate Professor at the Department of Communication and Institute of Telecommunications, National Chung Cheng University, Taiwan. Her most recent publications include "Made in China: The Cultural Logic of OEMs and the Manufacture of Low-Cost Technology" (*Inter-Asia Cultural Studies,* 2008) and "The Power of Circulation: Digital Technologies and the Online Chinese Fans of Japanese TV Drama" (*Inter-Asia Cultural Studies,* 2005).

Yachien Huang is a PHD candidate at Loughborough University in the UK. Her thesis focuses on the impact of imported dramas on the television industry and local audiences in Taiwan. Her research is concerned with the processes of cultural globalization and regionalization in East Asian popular culture. Her recent articles include "TV Drama in China: Unfolding Narratives of Tradition, Political Transformation and Cosmopolitan Identity" (2008).

Koichi Iwabuchi is Professor of Media and Cultural Studies at the School of International Liberal Studies of Waseda University in Tokyo. He (with Chris Berry) is an editor of a Hong Kong University Press book series, *TransAsia: Screen Cultures.* His publications include *Recentering Globalization: Popular Culture and Japanese Transnationalism* (Duke University Press, 2002), *Feeling Asian Modernities: Transnational Consumption of Japanese TV Dramas* (editor, Hong Kong University Press, 2004) and *East Asian Pop Culture: Analysing the Korean Wave* (co-editor with Chua Beng Huat, Hong Kong University Press, 2008).

Vamsee Juluri is Associate Professor of Media Studies at the University of San Francisco. His research interests are media audiences, globalization, Gandhian philosophy and media violence, Indian cinema, and religion and mythology in the media. He is the author of *Becoming a Global Audience: Longing and Belonging in Indian Music Television* (Peter Lang, 2003/Orient Longman, 2005). He has also written numerous opinion pieces for the *San Francisco Chronicle, Times of India,* and *India-West.*

Youna Kim is Associate Professor of Global Communications at the American University of Paris, joined from the London School of Economics and Political Science where she had taught since 2004, after completing a PhD at Goldsmiths College, University of London. She is the author of *Women, Television and Everyday Life in Korea: Journeys of Hope* (Routledge, 2005). Her book has been reviewed in various academic journals including *Media, Culture and Society, Feminist Media Studies,* and *Political Studies Review.* Her current project, *Diasporic Daughters,* explores transnational mobility, media and identity of young Asian women in the West.

Joanne B. Y. Lim is a PhD candidate at the School of Social Sciences, Media and Cultural Studies, University of East London. Her research focuses on discourses of media globalization and the implications of cultural politics affecting postcolonial nations, especially within Asia. She is a former journalist for Malaysia's leading newspaper, *The Star Publications Sdn Bhd,* and also teaches part time in Broadcast Journalism.

Pamela Nilan is Associate Professor of Sociology in the School of Humanities and Social Science at the University of Newcastle, Australia. She is a member of the Centre for Asia Pacific Social Transformation Studies (CAPSTRANS) and a vice president of the Asia Pacific Sociological Association (APSA). Her recent books include *Australian Youth: Social and Cultural Issues* (with R. Julian and J. Germov, Pearson Education, 2007), *Global Youth? Hybrid Identities, Plural Worlds* (co-editor with C. Feixa, Routledge, 2006) and *Indonesian Masculinities* (co-editor with M. Donaldson and R. Howson, Southeast Asian Studies Press, forthcoming).

Zakir Hossain Raju is Senior Lecturer of Communication and Culutral Studies at Monash University, Sunway campus, Malaysia. He is the author of *Bangladesh Cinema and National Identity* (Routledge, 2008). He has published many articles in journals including *Screening the Past, Journal of Chinese Cinemas, Cinemaya,* and in anthologies including *Being and Becoming: The Cinemas of Asia* (Macmillan, 2002) and *Contemporary Asian Cinema* (Berg, 2006).

Ubonrat Siriyuvasak is Associate Professor at the Faculty of Communication Arts, Chulalongkorn University, Thailand. She is the author of *The Political Economy of Thai Radio and Television System and Its Impact on the Rights and Freedom of Expressions* (1999, in Thai). Her recent articles include "Asianizing K-pop: Production, Consumption and Identification Patterns among Thai Youth" (*Inter-Asia Cultural Studies,* 2007, with Shin Hyunjoon) and "People's Media and Communication Rights in Indonesia and the Philippines" (*Inter-Asia Cultural Studies,* 2005).

Index

For Product Safety Concerns and Information please contact our EU
representative GPSR@taylorandfrancis.com
Taylor & Francis Verlag GmbH, Kaufingerstraße 24, 80331 München, Germany

www.ingramcontent.com/pod-product-compliance
Lightning Source LLC
Chambersburg PA
CBHW070400270326
41926CB00014B/2635

9 780415 878388